# Arthur Conan Doyle

## Sherlock Holmes
# The SIGN of FOUR
# 四签名

**An English-Chinese Novel**
英汉对照

[英] 阿瑟·柯南·道尔-著 ＊ 听泉-译注 ＊ 王琴文-插图

东华大学出版社

图书在版编目（CIP）数据

四签名：英汉对照 /［英］阿瑟·柯南·道尔（Conan Doyle,A.）著；听泉译注. -- 上海：东华大学出版社，2012.5
（福尔摩斯探案集）
ISBN 978-7-5669-0041-8

Ⅰ.①四… Ⅱ.①阿…②听… Ⅲ.①英语—汉语—对照读物②侦探小说—英国—现代 Ⅳ.① H319.4：I

中国版本图书馆 CIP 数据核字（2012）第 072630 号

## 四签名

［英］阿瑟·柯南·道尔 著
听 泉 译注
东华大学出版社出版
上海市延安西路 1882 号
邮政编码：200051 电话：021-62193056
联系邮箱：dandes.shen@gmail.com
微博：http://weibo.com/editeur
本社网址：http://www.dhupress.net
淘宝店：http://dhupress.taobao.com
营销中心：021-62193056 62373056 62379558
新华书店上海发行所发行 苏州望电印刷有限公司印刷
2012 年 5 月第 1 版 2012 年 5 月第 1 次印刷
印数：0001-5000 册
开本：890×1240 1/32 印张：9 字数：343 千字
ISBN 978-7-5669-0041-8/H·381
定价：25.00 元

# 前言

《四签名》是阿瑟·柯南·道尔继《血字的研究》之后创作的第二部长篇推理小说,仍以夏洛克·福尔摩斯为主角,是开辟侦探小说黄金时代的不朽经典。故事发生在1887至1888年之间,四个参与过印度战争的军官偶然获得了一批宝藏。多年后,这批宝藏成为使他们的后人遭遇不幸的根源。小说一经问世,就获得巨大成功。作者也因而一举成名。

本书在翻译和注解过程中,得到了廉凤仙、崔芙蓉、王莹阁、张连亮、刘建东、王超、闫丽萍、王琦薇、王红、乔滢、魏艳萍、宋春艳等同志的热忱帮助,在此深表谢意。

听泉

# CONTENTS

02     Chapter 1   THE SCIENCE OF DEDUCTION

22     Chapter 2   THE STATEMENT OF THE CASE

38     Chapter 3   IN QUEST OF A SOLUTION

52     Chapter 4   THE STORY OF THE BALD-HEADED MAN

76     Chapter 5   THE TRAGEDY OF PONDICHERRY LODGE

94     Chapter 6   SHERLOCK HOLMES GIVES A DEMONSTARTION

116    Chapter 7   THE EPISODE OF THE BARREL

142    Chapter 8   THE BAKER STREET IRREGULARS

166    Chapter 9   A BREAK IN THE CHAIN

190    Chapter 10   THE END OF THE ISLANDER

212    Chapter 11   THE GREAT AGRA TREASURE

228    Chapter 12   THE STRANGE STORY OF JONATHAN SMALL

# 目录

03　第一章　演绎学

23　第二章　案情陈述

39　第三章　寻求解决方案

53　第四章　秃头人的故事

77　第五章　樱塘别墅惨案

95　第六章　夏洛克·福尔摩斯论证

117　第七章　木桶的插曲

143　第八章　贝克街的非正规军

167　第九章　线索中断

191　第十章　岛民的结局

213　第十一章　大笔阿格拉财宝

229　第十二章　乔纳森·斯莫尔的奇异故事

《四签名》是阿瑟·柯南·道尔继《血字的研究》之后创作的第二部长篇推理小说,仍以夏洛克·福尔摩斯为主角,是开辟侦探小说黄金时代的不朽经典。故事发生在1887至1888年之间,四个参与过印度战争的军官偶然获得了一批宝藏。多年后,这批宝藏成为使他们的后人遭遇不幸的根源。小说一经问世,就获得巨大成功。作者也因而一举成名。

# Chapter 1

**THE SCIENCE OF DEDUCTION**

# 第一章

## 演绎学

Sherlock Holmes took his bottle from the corner of the mantelpiece, and his **hypodermic syringe**[1] from its neat morocco case. With his long, white, nervous fingers he adjusted the delicate needle and rolled back his left shirtcuff. For some little time his eyes rested thoughtfully upon the sinewy forearm and wrist, all dotted and scarred with innumerable puncture-marks. Finally, he thrust the sharp point home, pressed down the tiny piston, and sank back into the velvet-lined armchair with a long sigh of satisfaction.

Three times a day for many months I had witnessed this performance, but custom had not **reconciled**[2] my mind to it. On the contrary, from day to day I had become more irritable at the sight, and my conscience swelled nightly within me at the thought that I had lacked the courage to protest. Again and again I had registered a vow that I should deliver my soul upon the subject; but there was that in the cool, **nonchalant**[3] air of my companion which made him the last man with whom one would care to take anything approaching to a liberty. His great powers, his masterly manner, and the experience which I had had of his many extraordinary qualities, all made me **diffident**[4] and backward in crossing him.

Yet upon that afternoon, whether it was the Beaune which I had taken with my lunch or the additional **exasperation**[5] produced by the extreme deliberation of his manner, I suddenly felt that I could hold out no longer.

"Which is it to-day," I asked, "morphine or cocaine?"

He raised his eyes **languidly**[6] from the old black-letter volume which he had opened.

"It is cocaine," he said, "a seven-per-cent solution. Would you care to try it?"

"No, indeed," I answered brusquely. "My **constitution**[7] has not got over the Afghan campaign yet. I cannot afford to throw any extra strain upon it."

He smiled at my **vehemence**[8]. "Perhaps you are right, Watson," he said. "I suppose that its influence is physically a bad one. I find it, however, so **transcendently**[9] stimulating and clarifying to the mind that its secondary action is a matter of small moment."

"But consider!" I said earnestly. "Count the cost! Your brain may, as you say, be roused and excited, but it is a **pathological**[10] and **morbid**[11] process which involves increased tissue-change and may at least leave a

夏洛克·福尔摩斯从壁炉架的角上取下瓶子，从整洁的摩洛哥山羊皮盒里取出皮下注射器，用修长白皙、神经质的手指调整好精细的注射针，然后卷起衬衣左袖口，目光若有所思地在肌肉发达、布满无数刺痕的前臂和手腕上停了一小会儿。最后，他把针尖刺进肉里，按下小小的针心，满意地长叹一声，躺回了天鹅绒面的扶手椅。

我目睹他这样一天注射三次已经好多个月了，但我还是不习惯从内心去接受。正好相反，日复一日，我对此情景越来越恼火。我没有勇气抗议，每到夜里想起这件事，良心就越来越不安。我一次又一次发誓自己应该对这件事说说心里话，但我的同伴不动感情、若无其事的样子，使他成为谁都不爱贸然靠近的人。他的卓越才能、巧妙态度和我体验到的他的许多非凡品质，都使我胆怯退缩，不敢反对他。

然而，那天下午，无论是我在午饭时喝的波恩红葡萄酒，还是他极端从容的态度，都让我更加恼怒，我突然觉得再也不能忍耐了。

"今天是哪一种？"我问，"吗啡还是可卡因？"

他从刚打开的一本黑花体字旧书上无精打采地抬起眼睛。

"是可卡因，"他说，"7% 溶液。你想试试吗？"

"不想，真的不想，"我粗暴地回答说，"我的身体还没有从阿富汗战役中恢复过来。我不能给它任何额外损伤了。"

他对我的激烈情绪微微一笑。"华生，也许你是对的，"他说，"我想它对身体有不良影响。然而，我发现它有如此非凡的提神和醒脑作用，所以它的副作用也就无足轻重了。"

"可是要考虑一下！"我认真地说，"考虑一切后果！你的大脑也许像你说的那样能被激起和兴奋，但这是一种病理和病态的过程。这种过程意味着组织变化

四签名

permanent weakness. You know, too, what a black reaction comes upon you. Surely the game is hardly worth the candle. Why should you, for a mere passing pleasure, risk the loss of those great powers with which you have been **endowed**[12]? Remember that I speak not only as one comrade to another but as a medical man to one for whose constitution he is to some extent answerable."

He did not seem offended. On the contrary, he put his finger-tips together, and leaned his elbows on the arms of his chair, like one who has a relish for conversation.

"My mind," he said, "rebels at **stagnation**[13]. Give me problems, give me work, give me the most abstruse **cryptogram**[14], or the most intricate analysis, and I am in my own proper atmosphere. I can dispense then with artificial stimulants. But I abhor the dull routine of existence. I crave for mental **exaltation**[15]. That is why I have chosen my own particular profession, or rather created it, for I am the only one in the world."

"The only unofficial detective?" I said, raising my eyebrows.

"The only unofficial consulting detective," he answered. "I am the last and highest court of appeal in detection. When Gregson, or Lestrade, or Athelney Jones are out of their depths—which, by the way, is their normal state—the matter is laid before me. I examine the data, as an expert, and pronounce a specialist's opinion. I claim no credit in such cases. My name figures in no newspaper. The work itself, the pleasure of finding a field for my peculiar powers, is my highest reward. But you have yourself had some experience of my methods of work in the Jefferson Hope case."

"Yes, indeed," said I cordially. "I was never so struck by anything in my life. I even embodied it in a small brochure, with the somewhat fantastic title of 'A Study in Scarlet.'"

He shook his head sadly.

"I glanced over it," said he. "Honestly, I cannot congratulate you upon it. Detection is, or ought to be, an exact science and should be treated in the same cold and unemotional manner. You have attempted to tinge it with romanticism, which produces much the same effect as if you worked a love-story or an

增加,至少会留下永久性的虚弱。你也知道它对你产生多么糟糕的反应。这种游戏的确是得不偿失。你为什么要只图一时之快,冒着损失上天赋予你的卓越才能呢?记住,我这样说不仅是作为朋友,而且是作为对你的体质负责的医生。"

他好像并没有生气。正好相反,他把手指并在一起,然后两肘倚靠在椅子的扶手上,就像对谈话感兴趣的人那样。

"我的思想,"他说,"厌恶停滞。给我难题,给我工作,给我最难解的密码,或者给我最复杂的分析,这样我才如鱼得水。那样,我才能不用人工刺激物。但是,我痛恨死气沉沉的生活常规。我渴望精神提升。这就是我选择自己特殊职业——或者更准确地说,创造这个职业——的原因,因为我是世界上唯一从事这种职业的人。"

"唯一的私人侦探?"我扬了扬眉问道。

"唯一私人咨询侦探,"他回答说,"我是侦探最后和最高的上诉法庭。当格雷格森、雷斯特雷德或阿塞尔尼·琼斯超出自己的能力时——顺便说一下,这是他们的正常状态——就会把问题摆到我面前。我以专家身份审查材料,发表专家意见。我在这种案例上从不要求荣誉。我的名字也不出现在任何报纸上。工作本身,为我的特殊才能找到用武之地的快乐,就是我最高的报酬。但是,在杰斐逊·霍普一案中,你已经亲自体验过我的工作方法。"

"是的,的确是,"我诚恳地说,"我一生从来没有如此感动过。我甚至写成了一本小册子,用的是稍微奇异的标题:《血字的研究》。"

他伤心地摇了摇头。

"我扫过一眼,"他说,"说实话,我不能向你祝贺。侦查是——或者应该是——一种精密科学,应该用同样冷静客观,而不是感情用事的方法对待。你企图让它染上浪漫色彩,这产生的效果完全像是你把爱情故事或情人私奔

elopement[16] into the fifth proposition of **Euclid**[17]."

"But the romance was there," I **remonstrated**[18]. "I could not **tamper with**[19] the facts."

"Some facts should be suppressed, or, at least, a just sense of proportion should be observed in treating them. The only point in the case which deserved mention was the curious analytical reasoning from effects to causes, by which I succeeded in **unravelling**[20] it."

I was annoyed at this criticism of a work which had been specially designed to please him. I confess, too, that I was irritated by the egotism which seemed to demand that every line of my **pamphlet**[21] should be devoted to his own special doings. More than once during the years that I had lived with him in Baker Street I had observed that a small vanity underlay my companion's quiet and **didactic**[22] manner. I made no remark, however, but sat nursing my wounded leg. I had had a **Jezail**[23] bullet through it some time before, and though it did not prevent me from walking it ached wearily at every change of the weather.

"My practice has extended recently to the Continent," said Holmes after a while, filling up his old **brier**[24]-root pipe. "I was consulted last week by Francois le Villard, who, as you probably know, has come rather to the front lately in the French detective service. He has all the Celtic power of quick intuition, but he is deficient in the wide range of exact knowledge which is essential to the higher developments of his art. The case was concerned with a will and possessed some features of interest. I was able to refer him to two parallel cases, the one at Riga in 1857, and the other at St. Louis in 1871, which have suggested to him the true solution. Here is the letter which I had this morning acknowledging my assistance."

He tossed over, as he spoke, a crumpled sheet of foreign notepaper. I glanced my eyes down it, catching a **profusion**[25] of notes of admiration, with stray *magnifiques*, *coup-de-maîtres* and *tours-de-force*, all testifying to the ardent admiration of the Frenchman.

"He speaks as a pupil to his master," said I.

"Oh, he rates my assistance too highly," said Sherlock Holmes lightly.

插进欧几里得第五定理。"

"但是，那里有浪漫情节，"我抗辩道，"我不能篡改那些事实。"

"有些事实不应该让人知道，或者至少在处理它们时，应该有一种合理的均衡感。这个案子唯一值得一提的是，我从结果进行奇特分析推出原因，由此成功破案。"

我对自己特意构思想取悦他的一篇作品受到批评感到不快。我也承认，我被他的自负激怒了。他的自负似乎是要求，我的小册子的每一行都应该专门描写他自己的特殊活动。在和同伴住在贝克街的那些年，我不止一次地观察到他在沉着镇静和好为人师的态度中隐藏着一种小小的虚荣。虽然如此，但我什么也没有说，只是坐在那里护理我的伤腿。我的腿以前曾经让阿富汗长滑膛枪子弹打穿过，尽管不妨碍我走路，但每逢天气变化，它就会酸痛。

"我的业务最近已经延伸到了欧洲大陆，"过了一会儿，福尔摩斯在石南科植物根老烟斗里装满烟丝，"上周福朗索瓦·勒·维拉尔就向我请教，你也许知道他最近在法国侦探界相当引人注目。他具备凯尔特人所有的敏锐直觉力，但他缺乏广博的确切学识，这对他技艺的进一步发展不可或缺。这是一桩有关遗嘱的案子，具有一些有趣的特征。我能够指点他的是两个类似的案子：一件是1857年里加市的案子，另一件是1871年圣路易市的案子。这两个案子已经向他暗示了正确的解决方案。这就是我今天早上收到的他感谢我帮助的信件。"

他一边说，一边把一张皱巴巴的外国信纸扔给我。我向下扫了一眼，发现有大量溢美之辞，随处可见"卓越出色"、"手段高超"和"行动有力"，这都证实了这个法国人热情洋溢的赞美。

"他像小学生对老师说话一样，"我说。

"噢，他把我的帮助评价得过高了，"夏洛克·福尔摩斯轻声说道，"他

"He has considerable gifts himself. He possesses two out of the three qualities necessary for the ideal detective. He has the power of observation and that of deduction. He is only wanting in knowledge, and that may come in time. He is now translating my small works into French."

"Your works?"

"Oh, didn't you know?" he cried, laughing. "Yes, I have been guilty of several monographs. They are all upon technical subjects. Here, for example, is one 'Upon the Distinction between the Ashes of the Various Tobaccos.' In it I enumerate a hundred and forty forms of cigar, cigarette, and pipe tobacco, with coloured plates **illustrating**[26] the difference in the ash. It is a point which is continually turning up in criminal trials, and which is sometimes of supreme importance as a clue. If you can say definitely, for example, that some murder had been done by a man who was smoking an Indian lunkah, it obviously narrows your field of search. To the trained eye there is as much difference between the black ash of a **Trichinopoly**[27] and the white fluff of bird's-eye as there is between a cabbage and a potato."

"You have an extraordinary genius for minutiae," I remarked.

"I appreciate their importance. Here is my **monograph**[28] upon the tracing of footsteps, with some remarks upon the uses of plaster of Paris as a preserver of impresses. Here, too, is a curious little work upon the influence of a trade upon the form of the hand, with **lithotypes**[29] of the hands of slaters, sailors, cork-cutters, compositors, weavers, and diamond-polishers. That is a matter of great practical interest to the scientific detective—especially in cases of unclaimed bodies, or in discovering the **antecedents**[30] of criminals. But I weary you with my hobby."

"Not at all," I answered earnestly. "It is of the greatest interest to me, especially since I have had the opportunity of observing your practical application of it. But you spoke just now of observation and deduction. Surely the one to some extent implies the other."

"Why, hardly," he answered, leaning back **luxuriously**[31] in his armchair and sending up thick blue wreaths from his pipe. "For example, observation shows me that you have been to the Wigmore Street Post-Office this morning, but deduction lets me know that when there you **dispatched**[32] a telegram."

自己也相当有才华。理想侦探必备的三种素质，他有两种。他有观察能力和演绎能力，只是缺乏知识，这他可以及时获得。他眼下正在把我的几篇小文译成法语。"

"你的作品？"

"噢，你不知道？"他大声笑道，"是的，我曾经不好意思写过几篇专论，都是技术方面的。比如，这篇《论各种烟草灰之间的区别》。在这篇专论里，我列举出140种雪茄、纸烟、烟斗丝的烟灰，配上彩色插图阐明烟灰的区别。这是在刑事审判中不断出现的一个要点，有时作为线索，具有最重要的特点。比如，如果你能明确地说某件谋杀案是由一个抽印度雪茄的人所为，显然就会缩小你的搜索范围。在训练有素的人看来，印度特里奇雪茄烟的黑灰和鸟眼烟的白灰之间的区别，完全像白菜和马铃薯之间的区别一样。"

"你对侦查的微小细节具有非凡的天赋，"我说。

"我意识到了它们的重要性。这是我对跟踪足迹的专论，一些地方还谈到了使用熟石膏保存印记的方法。这里还有一篇奇特小文，论述职业对手形的影响，附有石板瓦工、海员、软木切削工、排字工、织工和钻石雕刻工的手形石版图。这对科学侦探具有极大的实际意义——尤其是在无人认领的尸体和发现罪犯前科的案件中。可是，我的嗜好让你厌烦了吧。"

"一点也不，"我认真地回答说，"我对此怀有浓厚的兴趣，尤其是因为我曾经有机会观察过你的实际应用。不过，你刚才说到了观察和演绎。当然，在某种程度上，是两种方法的相互包含。"

"啊，几乎不会，"他非常舒适地靠在扶手椅里，从烟斗里吐出一圈圈浓浓的蓝烟回答说，"比如，观察向我表明，你今天早上曾经到过威格莫尔街邮局，但演绎却告诉我，你在那里什么时候发过一封电报。"

四签名

"Right!" said I. "Right on both points! But I confess that I don't see how you arrived at it. It was a sudden impulse upon my part, and I have mentioned it to no one."

"It is simplicity itself," he remarked, chuckling at my surprise—"so absurdly simple that an explanation is superfluous; and yet it may serve to define the limits of observation and of deduction. Observation tells me that you have a little reddish mould adhering to your instep. Just opposite the Wigmore Street Office they have taken up the pavement and thrown up some earth, which lies in such a way that it is difficult to avoid treading in it in entering. The earth is of this peculiar reddish tint which is found, as far as I know, nowhere else in the neighbourhood. So much is observation. The rest is deduction."

"How, then, did you deduce the telegram?"

"Why, of course I knew that you had not written a letter, since I sat opposite to you all morning. I see also in your open desk there that you have a sheet of stamps and a thick bundle of postcards. What could you go into the post-office for, then, but to send a wire? **Eliminate**[33] all other factors, and the one which remains must be the truth."

"In this case it certainly is so," I replied after a little thought. "The thing, however, is, as you say, of the simplest. Would you think me **impertinent**[34] if I were to put your theories to a more severe test?"

"On the contrary," he answered, "it would prevent me from taking a second dose of cocaine. I should be delighted to look into any problem which you might submit to me."

"I have heard you say it is difficult for a man to have any object in daily use without leaving the impress of his individuality upon it in such a way that a trained observer might read it. Now, I have here a watch which has recently come into my possession. Would you have the kindness to let me have an opinion upon the character or habits of the late owner?"

I handed him over the watch with some slight feeling of amusement in my heart, for the test was, as I thought, an impossible one, and I intended it as a lesson against the somewhat **dogmatic**[35] tone which he occasionally assumed. He balanced the watch in his hand, gazed hard at the dial, opened the back, and

"对！"我说，"两点都对！但是，我承认我不明白你是怎么得出这个结论的。那是我一时突然的冲动，我没有向任何人提起过。"

"这本身非常简单，"他对我的惊讶轻声笑道，"非常简单，不用解释，但解释可以详细说明观察和演绎之间的界限。观察告诉我，你的脚背上沾有一小块红土。威格莫尔街邮局对面修路，翻上来一些土，就那样堆在那里，走进邮局的人难免要踩上去。据我所知，这种特殊的红土，附近其他地方都找不到。这就是观察。其余的就是演绎。"

"那么，你是怎么演绎出那封电报的呢？"

"啊，我当然知道你没有写过一封信，因为我整个上午都坐在你对面。我也看到，你打开的桌子里有一张邮票和厚厚一捆明信片。那么，你走进邮局，除了发电报，还能做什么？排除所有其他因素，剩下的肯定就是事实真相。"

"的确是这样，"想了一会儿，我回答说，"然而，如你所说，这是最简单的一件事。如果我要将你的理论用在更加严格的试验上，你会认为我卤莽无礼吗？"

"正好相反，"他回答说，"这会使我不再注射第二次可卡因。我非常乐意研究你可能向我提出的任何问题。"

"我曾经听你说过，每个人都容易在任何一件日用品上留下个性特征的印记，这样训练有素的观察者可能一眼就会认出来。现在，我这里有一只最近得到的手表。你愿意帮忙让我了解一下手表前任主人的性格或习惯吗？"

我把手表递给他，心里感到有点儿好笑，因为我认为这个试验不能成立，并打算把这次试验作为对他偶尔有点武断口吻的一个教训。他在手里掂量着手表，死死地盯着表盘，打开后盖，先用肉眼，然后用高倍凸透镜仔细查看里面的机件。当最后他合上后盖，把手表还给我时，我禁不住对他垂头丧气

四签名

examined the works, first with his naked eyes and then with a powerful convex lens. I could hardly keep from smiling at his crestfallen face when he finally snapped the case to and handed it back.

"There are hardly any data," he remarked. "The watch has been recently cleaned, which robs me of my most suggestive facts."

"You are right," I answered. "It was cleaned before being sent to me."

In my heart I accused my companion of putting forward a most lame and impotent excuse to cover his failure. What data could he expect from an uncleaned watch?

"Though unsatisfactory, my research has not been entirely barren," he observed, staring up at the ceiling with dreamy, lack-lustre eyes. "Subject to your correction, I should judge that the watch belonged to your elder brother, who inherited it from your father."

"That you gather, no doubt, from the H. W. upon the back?"

"Quite so. The W. suggests your own name. The date of the watch is nearly fifty years back, and the **initials**[36] are as old as the watch: so it was made for the last generation. Jewellery usually descends to the eldest son, and he is most likely to have the same name as the father. Your father has, if I remember right, been dead many years. It has, therefore, been in the hands of your eldest brother."

"Right, so far," said I. "Anything else?"

"He was a man of untidy habits—very untidy and careless. He was left with good prospects, but he threw away his chances, lived for some time in poverty with occasional short intervals of prosperity, and finally, taking to drink, he died. That is all I can gather."

I sprang from my chair and limped impatiently about the room with considerable bitterness in my heart.

"This is unworthy of you, Holmes," I said. "I could not have believed that you would have descended to this. You cannot expect me to believe that you have read all this from his old watch! It is unkind and, to speak plainly, has a touch of **charlatanism**[37] in it."

"My dear doctor," said he kindly, "pray accept my apologies. Viewing the

的表情笑了起来。

"几乎没有任何资料，"他说，"这只手表最近已经擦净，擦去了最能引起我联想的那些事实根据。"

"你说得对，"我回答说，"这只手表是擦净后才送到了我的手里。"

我在心里责怪同伴居然提出一个极其蹩脚无力的借口来掩饰自己的失败。他能从一只没有清洁过的手表中指望到什么呢？

"尽管不能令人满意，但我的研究并不是完全没有结果，"他用模糊无神的眼睛望着天花板说，"愿听你的指正。我判断这只手表是你哥哥的，是他继承你父亲的。"

"你肯定是从后盖上的 H.W. 推断的吧？"

"正是这样。W. 表明是你自己的姓。这只手表的日期将近有 50 年了，而且词首大写字母和手表一样古老，所以这是为上一辈制的。珠宝通常传给长子，长子十有八九和父亲同名。如果我记得不错的话，你的父亲已经去世多年，于是这只手表传就到了你哥哥手里。"

"到目前为止说得不错，"我说，"还有什么？"

"他是一个邋遢的人——邋里邋遢，粗心大意。他本来有美好的前程，但他丢掉了一个个机会，有一段时间生活贫困，偶尔有过短暂的幸运，最后他酗酒而死。这就是我能推断的一切。"

我从椅子上跳起来，一瘸一拐在房间里急切地走来走去，心里充满了痛苦。

"福尔摩斯，你真卑劣，"我说，"我无法相信你居然会下作到这一步。你调查过我不幸哥哥的经历，现在假装用某种奇特的方法演绎出这一事实。你不能指望我相信你已经从他的旧表上看出了所有的一切！这样做不厚道，老实说，有点儿江湖骗子的味道。"

四签名

matter as an abstract problem, I had forgotten how personal and painful a thing it might be to you. I assure you, however, that I never even knew that you had a brother until you handed me the watch."

"Then how in the name of all that is wonderful did you get these facts? They are absolutely correct in every particular."

"Ah, that is good luck. I could only say what was the balance of probability. I did not at all expect to be so accurate."

"But it was not mere guesswork?"

"No, no: I never guess. It is a shocking habit—destructive to the logical **faculty**[38]. What seems strange to you is only so because you do not follow my train of thought or observe the small facts upon which large inferences may depend. For example, I began by stating that your brother was careless. When you observe the lower part of that watch-case you notice that it is not only **dinted**[39] in two places but it is cut and marked all over from the habit of keeping other hard objects, such as coins or keys, in the same pocket. Surely it is no great feat to assume that a man who treats a fifty-guinea watch so **cavalierly**[40] must be a careless man. Neither is it a very far-fetched inference that a man who inherits one article of such value is pretty well provided for in other respects."

I nodded to show that I followed his reasoning.

"It is very customary for **pawnbrokers**[41] in England, when they take a watch, to scratch the numbers of the ticket with a pin-point upon the inside of the case. It is more handy than a label as there is no risk of the number being lost or **transposed**[42]. There are no less than four such numbers visible to my lens on the inside of this case. Inference—that your brother was often at low water. Secondary inference—that he had occasional bursts of prosperity, or he could not have **redeemed**[43] the pledge. Finally, I ask you to look at the inner plate, which contains the keyhole. Look at the thousands of scratches all round the hole-marks where the key has slipped. What sober man's key could have scored those **grooves**[44]? But you will never see a drunkard's watch without them. He winds it at night, and he leaves these traces of his unsteady hand. Where is the mystery in all this?"

"我亲爱的医生,"他亲切地说,"请接受我的道歉。我把这件事看成了一个抽象问题,忘记了这可能对你是一件多么痛苦的私事。不过,我向你保证,在你递给我这只手表之前,我甚至从来不知道你还有一个哥哥。"

"那你究竟是怎么这样奇妙地得到这些事实的呢?这些事实每个细节都绝对正确。"

"啊,那是运气好。我只能说可能的情况是什么,根本没有指望那样准。"

"可是,这不仅仅是猜测吧?"

"不,不,我从不猜测。这是一种非常讨厌的习惯——对逻辑有害。你之所以感到奇怪,只是因为你没有理解我的思路,或者没有观察到大推论可能依赖的那些细小事实。比如,我开始时说过你的哥哥粗心大意。你观察这只表的表壳下部时,会注意到不仅两处有凹痕,而且到处都有划痕,这是因为他习惯把手表放在有硬币或钥匙这类硬东西的口袋里。对一只价值50畿尼的手表如此随便的人,一定是一个粗心大意的人,这样的设想肯定不是什么了不起的功绩。一个继承一件东西就如此贵重的人,在其他方面供养也差不多,这也不是非常牵强的推论吧。"

我点头表示理解他的推理。

"这对伦敦的典当商来说司空见惯:他们接受一只手表,就要用针尖把当票号码刻在表壳内侧。这比挂标签便利,绝不会有号码遗失或调换的危险。我在放大镜下可以在表壳内侧看到4个这类号码。推论——你的哥哥经常困窘。第二个推论——他偶尔会好上一阵,否则他就无法赎回抵押品了。最后,我请你看看这个含有钥匙孔的内盖。看看钥匙孔四周有几千道划痕——是钥匙划过的痕迹。神志清醒的人怎么能用钥匙划那些道道呢?但是,你会看到,酒鬼的手表没有一个不是这样。他夜里上发条,手不稳就会留下这些痕迹。所有这一切的诀窍在哪里呢?"

四签名

"It is as clear as daylight," I answered. "I regret the injustice which I did you. I should have had more faith in your marvellous faculty. May I ask whether you have any professional inquiry on foot at present?"

"None. Hence the cocaine. I cannot live without brainwork. What else is there to live for? Stand at the window here. Was ever such a **dreary**[45], dismal, unprofitable world? See how the yellow fog **swirls**[46] down the street and drifts across the dun-coloured houses. What could be more hopelessly **prosaic**[47] and material? What is the use of having powers, Doctor, when one has no field upon which to exert them? Crime is commonplace, existence is commonplace, and no qualities save those which are commonplace have any function upon earth."

I had opened my mouth to reply to this tirade when, with a crisp knock, our landlady entered, bearing a card upon the brass **salver**[48].

"A young lady for you, sir," she said, addressing my companion.

"Miss Mary Morstan," he read. "Hum! I have no recollection of the name. Ask the young lady to step up, Mrs. Hudson. Don't go, Doctor. I should prefer that you remain."

"这一清二楚,"我回答说。"我对冤枉你感到后悔。我应该对你的绝妙本领更有信心。请问你目前有正在进行的专业侦查活动吗?"

"一个也没有,所以才注射可卡因。没有脑力劳动,我就活不下去。除了这个,还有什么值得生活呢?站到这窗边。曾经有过如此凄凉、阴沉、徒劳的世界吗?看那黄雾沿街旋转而下,飘过那些暗褐色的房子。还有什么能比这更枯燥无味饱食终日令人绝望的吗?医生,英雄无用武之地,有能力又有什么用呢?犯罪是寻常之事,生存也是寻常之事,在这世界上,除了那些寻常之事,任何本领都不起作用。"

我张开嘴正要回答他这个激进言论,这时随着清脆的敲门声,我们的女房东走了进来,只见她端着一只铜盘,铜盘上放有一张名片。

"先生,一位小姐要见你,"她对我的同伴说。

"玛丽·摩斯坦小姐,"他念道,"嗯哼!我想不起来这个名字。哈得逊太太,请她上来。医生,别走,我希望你留下。"

Notes:
1. hypodermic syringe 皮下注射器
2. reconcile *vt.* 使和好；和解
3. nonchalant *adj.* 漠不关心的；无动于衷的
4. diffident *adj.* 缺乏自信的；羞怯的
5. exasperation *n.* 恼怒
6. languidly *adv.* 疲倦地；无力地
7. constitution *n.* 体格；体质；心理素质
8. vehemence *n.* 激烈；热心；强烈
9. transcendently *adv.* 卓越地；至高无上地
10. pathological *adj.* 病理学的；由疾病引起的
11. morbid *adj.* 疾病的；生病的；致病的
12. endow *vt.* 使（某人）天生具有（好资质、能力等）
13. stagnation *n.* 停滞
14. cryptogram *n.* 密码电文
15. exaltation *n.* 兴奋；得意洋洋
16. elopement *n.* 潜逃；私奔
17. Euclid *n.* 欧几里得（约公元前 3 世纪的古希腊数学家）
18. remonstrate *vt.* 告诫
19. tamper with *v.* 损害；篡改
20. unravel *v.* 拆开
21. pamphlet *n.* 小册子
22. didactic *adj.* 教导的；(指人) 学究式的；迂腐的
23. jezail *n.* 阿富汗长滑膛枪；吉赛尔步枪
24. brier *n.* 荆棘；野蔷薇；欧石南
25. profusion *n.* 大量；丰富
26. illustrate *vt.* 说明；阐明；表明
27. Trichinopoly *n.* 特里奇雪茄烟（一种两端开口的印度雪茄烟）
28. monograph *n.* 专著；专论
29. lithotype *n.* 石版印刷；版画
30. antecedent *n.* 发生在前的事；先例
31. luxuriously *adv.* 非常舒适地

32. dispatch *vt.* 发送

33. eliminate *vt.* 消除；排除；忽略

34. impertinent *adj.* 无礼的；莽撞的；不中肯的

35. dogmatic *adj.* 固执己见的；教条的；武断的

36. initial *n.* 首字母；大写字母

37. charlatanism *n.* 欺骗；庸医术；庸医的行为

38. faculty *n.* 能力；才能；技巧

39. dint *vt.* 击出凹痕

40. cavalierly *adv.* 像骑士般地，傲慢地

41. pawnbroker *n.* 当铺老板

42. transpose *vt.* 使变位；变换顺序

43. redeem *vt.* 用金钱赎回

44. groove *n.* 沟；槽；老一套；常规

45. dreary *adj.* 令人厌烦的；单调的；枯燥的

46. swirl *vi.* 旋转；打旋

47. prosaic *adj.* 无想像力的；无聊的；乏味的

48. salver *n.* 托盘；盘子

# Chapter 2

## THE STATEMENT OF THE CASE

# 第二章

## 案情陈述

Miss Morstan entered the room with a firm step and an outward **composure**[1] of manner. She was a blonde young lady, small, **dainty**[2], well gloved, and dressed in the most perfect taste. There was, however, a plainness and simplicity about her costume which bore with it a suggestion of limited means. The dress was a sombre grayish beige, untrimmed and **unbraided**[3], and she wore a small turban of the same dull hue, relieved only by a suspicion of white feather in the side. Her face had neither regularity of feature nor beauty of **complexion**[4], but her expression was sweet and amiable, and her large blue eyes were singularly spiritual and sympathetic. In an experience of women which extends over many nations and three separate continents, I have never looked upon a face which gave a clearer promise of a refined and sensitive nature. I could not but observe that as she took the seat which Sherlock Holmes placed for her, her lip trembled, her hand quivered, and she showed every sign of intense inward **agitation**[5].

"I have come to you, Mr. Holmes," she said, "because you once enabled my employer, Mrs. Cecil Forrester, to unravel a little domestic **complication**[6]. She was much impressed by your kindness and skill."

"Mrs. Cecil Forrester," he repeated thoughtfully. "I believe that I was of some slight service to her. The case, however, as I remember it, was a very simple one."

"She did not think so. But at least you cannot say the same of mine. I can hardly imagine anything more strange, more utterly inexplicable, than the situation in which I find myself."

Holmes rubbed his hands, and his eyes glistened. He leaned forward in his chair with an expression of extraordinary concentration upon his clear-cut, hawklike features.

"State your case," said he in brisk business tones.

I felt that my position was an embarrassing one. "You will, I am sure, excuse me," I said, rising from my chair.

To my surprise, the young lady held up her gloved hand to detain me. "If your friend," she said, "would be good enough to stop, he might be of **inestimable**[7] service to me."

摩斯坦小姐步伐坚定，外表沉着，走进了房间。她是一位金发碧眼、小巧玲珑的年轻女士，手套戴得严严实实，衣着完美，极有品位。然而，她的服装简单朴素，暗示她收入有限。她的衣服是暗灰色薄斜纹呢，没有装饰和镶边。她戴着一顶同样暗色的头巾式女帽，只是帽边插着少许白色羽毛作为调剂。她的脸庞既没有端庄的容貌，也没有漂亮的肤色，但她的表情温柔可爱，一双蓝蓝的大眼睛炯炯有神，和谐共鸣。我在见过的遍及三大洲许多国家的女人中，还从来没有见过这样一张更具优雅和灵敏气质的面容。我不禁观察起来，她在夏洛克·福尔摩斯指定的座位坐下时，嘴唇颤抖，一只手微微抖动，每种迹象都表明她内心紧张不安。

"福尔摩斯先生，我之所以来找你，"她说，"是因为你曾经为我的雇主塞西尔·弗里斯特太太解决过一桩小小的家庭纠纷。她对你的帮助和技能印象非常深刻。"

"塞西尔·弗里斯特太太，"他若有所思地重复道，"我想我对她有过微不足道的帮助。不过，我记得，那个案子非常简单。"

"她并不这样认为。但是，至少你不能说我的案子简单。我简直无法想象还有什么能比我自己的处境更奇特、更费解。"

福尔摩斯搓着手，两眼炯炯有神，在椅子上倾身向前，轮廓分明、雄鹰一样的脸上露出非常专注的神情。

"陈述一下你的案情，"他用公事公办的轻快语调说。

我感到自己的处境非常尴尬。

"我想我必须离开，"说着，我从椅子上站了起来。

让我吃惊的是，这位年轻女士举起戴着手套的手留住了我。

"如果你的朋友，"她说，"行行好留下来，他说不定对我有极大的帮助。"

四签名

I relapsed into my chair.

"Briefly," she continued, "the facts are these. My father was an officer in an Indian regiment, who sent me home when I was quite a child. My mother was dead, and I had no relative in England. I was placed, however, in a comfortable boarding establishment at Edinburgh, and there I remained until I was seventeen years of age. In the year 1878 my father, who was senior captain of his regiment, obtained twelve months' leave and came home. He telegraphed to me from London that he had arrived all safe and directed me to come down at once, giving the Langham Hotel as his address. His message, as I remember, was full of kindness and love. On reaching London I drove to the Langham and was informed that Captain Morstan was staying there, but that he had gone out the night before and had not returned. I waited all day without news of him. That night, on the advice of the manager of the hotel, I communicated with the police, and next morning we advertised in all the papers. Our inquiries led to no result; and from that day to this no word has ever been heard of my unfortunate father. He came home with his heart full of hope to find some peace, some comfort, and instead–"

She put her hand to her throat, and a choking sob cut short the sentence.

"The date?" asked Holmes, opening his notebook.

"He disappeared upon the third of December, 1878—nearly ten years ago."

"His luggage?"

"Remained at the hotel. There was nothing in it to suggest a clue—some clothes, some books, and a considerable number of curiosities from the Andaman Islands. He had been one of the officers in charge of the convict-guard there."

"Had he any friends in town?"

"Only one that we know of—Major Sholto, of his own regiment, the Thirty-fourth Bombay **Infantry**[8]. The major had retired some little time before and lived at Upper Norwood. We communicated

THE SIGN OF FOUR

我又坐回了椅子里。

"简单地说,"她接着说道,"情况是这样。我的父亲是印度军团的一名军官。我很小的时候,他就把我送回了国内。我的母亲已经去世,我在英国没有任何亲戚。不过,我还是被安排到了爱丁堡一所舒适的寄宿学校读书,(寄宿学校)一直到17岁。1878年,我的父亲担任团里资深上尉,所以获得了12个月假回国。他从伦敦给我发来电报说,他已经平安到达伦敦,盼咐我马上前来,给我的地址是朗汉姆旅馆。我还记得,他的电文充满了慈爱。一到伦敦,我就坐车赶往朗汉姆旅馆。那里的人告诉我说,摩斯坦上尉是住在那里,但他前一天夜里出去,还没有回来。我等了整整一天,没有他的消息。那天夜里,我听从旅馆经理的建议,报告了警方,并在第二天早上的所有报纸上登了寻人启事。我们的打听没有任何结果。从那天起到今天,始终没有听到不幸父亲的任何消息。他回国时,心里充满希望,想找到一些和平、一些安慰,可是——"

她把手放在咽喉上,抽噎声打断了她那句话。

"日期是?"福尔摩斯打开笔记本问道。

"他于1878年12月3日失踪——差不多10年了。"

"他的行李呢?"

"还在旅馆里。那里没有任何东西——一些衣服,几本书,还有相当多的安达曼群岛的古玩——可以作为线索。他曾经是那里负责看管囚犯的一名军官。"

"他在城里有什么朋友吗?"

"我们了解的只有一位——肖尔托少校,和他同在孟买第34步兵团。这名少校前段时间刚刚退役,住在上诺伍德。当然,我们和他联系过,但他连

with him, of course, but he did not even know that his brother officer was in England."

"A singular case," remarked Holmes.

"I have not yet described to you the most singular part. About six years ago—to be exact, upon the fourth of May, 1882—an advertisement appeared in the *Times* asking for the address of Miss Mary Morstan, and stating that it would be to her advantage to come forward. There was no name or address **appended**[9]. I had at that time just entered the family of Mrs. Cecil Forrester in the capacity of governess. By her advice I published my address in the advertisement column. The same day there arrived through the post a small cardboard box addressed to me, which I found to contain a very large and **lustrous**[10] pearl. No word of writing was enclosed. Since then every year upon the same date there has always appeared a similar box, containing a similar pearl, without any clue as to the sender. They have been pronounced by an expert to be of a rare variety and of considerable value. You can see for yourself that they are very handsome."

She opened a flat box as she spoke and showed me six of the finest pearls that I had ever seen.

"Your statement is most interesting," said Sherlock Holmes. "Has anything else occurred to you?"

"Yes, and no later than to-day. That is why I have come to you. This morning I received this letter, which you will perhaps read for yourself."

"Thank you," said Holmes. "The envelope, too, please. Post-mark, London, S. W. Date, July 7. Hum! Man's thumb-mark on corner—probably postman. Best quality paper. Envelopes at sixpence a packet. Particular man in his **stationery**[11]. No address.

*"Be at the third pillar from the left outside the Lyceum Theatre to-night at seven o'clock. If you are distrustful bring two friends. You are a wronged woman and shall have justice. Do not bring police. If you do, all will be in vain. Your unknown friend."*

自己的战友在英国都不知道。"

"一桩奇案，"福尔摩斯说。

"我还没有向你描述最奇特的部分呢。大约 6 年前——准确地说，就是 1882 年 5 月 4 日——《泰晤士报》上刊登了一则启事，征求玛丽·摩斯坦小姐的住址，并说如果她自告奋勇的话，会对她有利。没有附加任何名字和地址。我当时刚进塞西尔·弗里斯特太太家当家庭教师。根据她的建议，我在启事栏里登出了自己的住址。邮局当天就给我寄来了一只小纸盒，我发现里面装有一颗又大又亮的珍珠。上面没有附带一个字。从那以后，每年同一日期总会出现一只类似的盒子，里面装有一颗类似的珍珠，没有寄盒人的任何线索。一位行家曾经断言这些珍珠属珍稀品种，非常值钱。你们自己可以看到，它们很漂亮。"

她一边说，一边打开一只扁平盒子，让我看我从未见过的 6 颗最精美的珍珠。

"你的陈述非常有趣，"夏洛克·福尔摩斯，"你还遇到过其他情况吗？"

"是的，就在今天。这就是我来找你的原因。今天早上我收到了这封信。也许你可以自己看看。"

"谢谢你，"福尔摩斯说，"请把信封也给我。邮戳来自于伦敦西南区，日期 7 月 7 日。嗯哼！角上有男人的大拇指印——可能是邮递员的。上乘纸。6 便士一扎信封。写信人对信纸信封非常挑剔。没有地址。

今晚 7 点到莱森戏院外左数第 3 根柱子。如果你怀疑，就带两个朋友来。你是受到委屈的女人，要得到公道。不要带警察来。如果带，一切都是徒然。你不知名的朋友。

四签名

Well, really, this is a very pretty little mystery! What do you intend to do, Miss Morstan?"

"That is exactly what I want to ask you."

"Then we shall most certainly go—you and I and—yes, why Dr. Watson is the very man. Your correspondent says two friends. He and I have worked together before."

"But would he come?" she asked with something **appealing**[12] in her voice and expression.

"I shall be proud and happy," said I **fervently**[13], "if I can be of any service."

"You are both very kind," she answered. "I have led a retired life and have no friends whom I could appeal to. If I am here at six it will do, I suppose?"

"You must not be later," said Holmes. "There is one other point, however. Is this handwriting the same as that upon the pearl-box addresses?"

"I have them here," she answered, producing half a dozen pieces of paper.

"You are certainly a model client. You have the correct intuition. Let us see, now." He spread out the papers upon the table and gave little darting glances from one to the other. "They are disguised hands, except the letter," he said presently; "but there can be no question as to the authorship. See how the irrepressible Greek e will break out, and see the twirl of the final. They are undoubtedly by the same person. I should not like to suggest false hopes, Miss Morstan, but is there any resemblance between this hand and that of your father?"

"Nothing could be more unlike."

"I expected to hear you say so. We shall look out for you, then, at six. Pray allow me to keep the papers. I may look into the matter before then. It is only half-past three. *Au revoir*[14], then."

"*Au revoir*," said our visitor; and with a bright, kindly glance from one to the other of us, she replaced her pearl-box in her bosom and hurried away.

Standing at the window, I watched her walking **briskly**[15] down the street

啊，这真是一个非常迷人的小小谜团！摩斯坦小姐，你打算怎么做？"

"这正是我想要问你的事儿。"

"那我们一定得去——你和我，还有——啊，是的，华生医生正是我们需要的人。写信人说是两个朋友。他和我以前曾经在一起共过事。"

"可是，他愿意来吗？"她问，声音和表情都带着恳求。

"如果能帮上什么忙，"我热心地说，"我将非常自豪和高兴。"

"你们俩真好，"她回答说，"我曾经过着隐居生活，没有朋友可以求助。我6点到这里来，可以吧？"

"你不能再晚了，"福尔摩斯说，"不过，还有一点，这个笔迹和珍珠盒上的笔迹相同吗？"

"我都带来了，"她掏出6张纸回答说。

"你的确是一名模范客户。你具有正确的直觉。现在，让我们看看。"他把那些纸在桌子上展开，一张一张飞快地对比着看。"除了这封信，它们都是伪造的笔迹，"过了一会儿，他说，"但毫无疑问是同一个人写的。看这个希腊字母 e 控制不住要出格，再看最后的这个 s 旋转的样子。它们的确是同一个人写的。摩斯坦小姐，我不想提出虚假的希望，但这个笔迹和你父亲的笔迹有什么相似的地方吗？"

"绝不可能一样。"

"我就希望听到你这样说。那我们6点等你来。请允许我留下这些信纸。我可能要在此之前研究一下这件事。现在才3点半。那就再会。"

"再会，"我们的客人说。随后，她用愉快亲切的目光扫了我们一下，把珍珠盒放回怀里，匆匆而去。

我站在窗边，望着她脚步轻快地沿街而行，直到灰色女帽和白色羽毛在

四签名

until the gray turban and white feather were but a speck in the somber crowd.

"What a very attractive woman!" I exclaimed, turning to my companion.

He had lit his pipe again and was leaning back with drooping eyelids. "Is she?" he said **languidly**[16]; "I did not observe."

"You really are an automaton—a calculating machine," I cried. "There is something positively inhuman in you at times."

He smiled gently.

"It is of the first importance," he cried, "not to allow your judgment to be biased by personal qualities. A client is to me a mere unit, a factor in a problem. The emotional qualities are **antagonistic**[17] to clear reasoning. I assure you that the most winning woman I ever knew was hanged for poisoning three little children for their insurance-money, and the most repellent man of my acquaintance is a **philanthropist**[18] who has spent nearly a quarter of a million upon the London poor."

"In this case, however—"

"I never make exceptions. An exception disproves the rule. Have you ever had occasion to study character in handwriting? What do you make of this fellow's scribble?"

"It is **legible**[19] and regular," I answered. "A man of business habits and some force of character."

Holmes shook his head.

"Look at his long letters," he said. "They hardly rise above the common herd. That d might be an a, and that l an e. Men of character always differentiate their long letters, however illegibly they may write. There is vacillation in his k's and self-esteem in his capitals. I am going out now. I have some few references to make. Let me recommend this book one of the most remarkable ever penned. It is Winwood Reade's *Martyrdom of Man*. I shall be back in an hour."

I sat in the window with the volume in my hand, but my thoughts were far from the daring **speculations**[20] of the writer. My mind ran upon our late visitor—her smiles, the deep rich tones of her voice, the strange mystery which overhung her life. If she were seventeen at the time of her father's

昏暗的人群中仅仅成了一个斑点。

"多有魅力的女人啊！"我转向同伴大声说道。

他已经又点起了烟斗，靠回椅子，耷拉着眼皮。"是吗？"他无精打采地说，"我可没看出来。"

"你真是个机器人——一台计算机器！"我大声说道，"有时你确实没有人情味。"

他温和地微微一笑。

"至关重要的是，"他大声说道，"不要让你的判断受到个人品质的影响。客户对我仅仅是一个单位——是问题里的一种因素。情感和清晰推理是相互对立的。我可以明确告诉你，我曾经认识的最可爱的女人，为了获取保险金毒杀了3个小孩子而被绞死，而我认识的最令人反感的男人却是一名慈善家，他曾经为伦敦的穷人花了将近25万英镑。"

"不过，这次——"

"我从不容许有例外。例外会证明规律不成立。你曾经有机会研究过笔迹的特征吗？你对这个人的笔迹作何解释？"

"字迹清楚匀称，"我回答说，"是一个有办事干练和个性鲜明的人。"

福尔摩斯摇了摇头。

"看他那些长字母，"他说，"它们几乎都不高过一般的字母。那个d可能是a, l可能是e。个性鲜明的人无论写得多么潦草，长字母总会有所差别。他的k写得摇摆不定，大写字母显得自负。我现在要出去了。我要去查一些东西。让我推荐这本书——这是一本已经写出来的最不寻常的著作。那就是温伍德·里德写的《人类的牺牲》。我一小时后回来。"

我手里拿着书坐在窗前，但我的思想远离了作者的大胆推测，萦绕在刚才来的那个客人身上——她的微笑，她的深沉圆润的音调和笼罩她人生的奇

四签名

disappearance she must be seven-and-twenty now—a sweet age, when youth has lost its self-consciousness and become a little sobered by experience. So I sat and mused until such dangerous thoughts came into my head that I hurried away to my desk and plunged furiously into the latest treatise upon pathology. What was I, an army surgeon with a weak leg and a weaker banking account, that I should dare to think of such things? She was a unit, a factor—nothing more. If my future were black, it was better surely to face it like a man than to attempt to brighten it by mere **will-o'-the-wisps**[21] of the imagination.

异谜团。如果她在父亲失踪那年17岁，她现在肯定是27岁——这是甜蜜可爱的年龄，此时青春已经失去了拘谨，因经验而变得稍微清醒。我就那样坐在那里沉思默想，直到如此危险的思想闯入自己的脑海。于是，我匆匆走到桌边，飞快地扑到最近一篇有关病理学的论文上看了起来。我是何许人？我是一名陆军医生，一条腿软弱无力，银行存款更是没有多少，所以怎么敢想这种事儿？她是一个个体、一种因素——别的什么也不是。如果我的前途暗淡，肯定还不如像男子汉那样面对它，而不要试图只靠胡思乱想来看清它。

Notes:
1. composure *n.* 镇静；沉着
2. dainty *adj.* 娇俏的；优雅的
3. unbraid *vt.* 解开
4. complexion *n.* 肤色；面色
5. agitation *n.* 激动不安；焦虑
6. complication *n.*（出现的）困难；难题；〈医〉并发症
7. inestimable *adj.* 无价的；无法估计的
8. infantry *n.* 步兵；步兵团
9. append *vt.* 附加；添加
10. lustrous *adj.* 光亮的；有光泽的
11. stationery *n.* 文具；信纸
12. appealing *adj.* 吸引人的；恳求似的
13. fervently *adv.* 热心地；热诚地
14. au revoir *n.*〈法〉再会；再见
15. briskly *adv.* 轻快地；精神勃勃地
16. languidly *adv.* 疲倦地；无力地
17. antagonistic *adj.* 敌对的；对抗性的
18. philanthropist *n.* 慈善家
19. legible *adj.* 清晰的；易读的
20. speculation *n.* 思考；思索
21. will-o'-the-wisp 鬼火；虚幻的目标；引人入歧途的事物

# Chapter 3

IN QUEST OF A SOLUTION

# 第三章

寻求解决方案

It was half-past five before Holmes returned. He was bright, eager, and in excellent spirits, a mood which in his case **alternated with**[1] fits of the blackest depression.

"There is no great mystery in this matter," he said, taking the cup of tea which I had poured out for him; "the facts appear to admit of only one explanation."

"What! you have solved it already?"

"Well, that would be too much to say. I have discovered a suggestive fact, that is all. It is, however, very suggestive. The details are still to be added. I have just found, on consulting the back files of the *Times*, that Major Sholto, of Upper Norwood, late of the Thirty-fourth Bombay **Infantry**[2], died upon the twenty-eighth of April, 1882."

"I may be very obtuse, Holmes, but I fail to see what this suggests."

"No? You surprise me. Look at it in this way, then. Captain Morstan disappears. The only person in London whom he could have visited is Major Sholto. Major Sholto denies having heard that he was in London. Four years later Sholto dies. Within a week of his death Captain Morstan's daughter receives a valuable present, which is repeated from year to year and now **culminates**[3] in a letter which describes her as a wronged woman. What wrong can it refer to except this **deprivation**[4] of her father? And why should the presents begin immediately after Sholto's death unless it is that Sholto's heir knows something of the mystery and desires to make **compensation**[5]? Have you any alternative theory which will meet the facts?"

"But what a strange compensation! And how strangely made! Why, too, should he write a letter now, rather than six years ago? Again, the letter speaks of giving her justice. What justice can she have? It is too much to suppose that her father is still alive. There is no other injustice in her case that you know of."

"There are difficulties; there are certainly difficulties," said Sherlock Holmes pensively; "but our expedition of to-night will solve them all. Ah, here is a four-wheeler, and Miss Morstan is inside. Are you all ready? Then we had

福尔摩斯 5 点半才回来。他神情愉悦，迫不及待，兴高采烈。对他来说，这种情绪不时会与最糟糕的沮丧情绪交替出现。

"这个案子没有多大神秘，"他接住我给他倒的那杯茶说，"这些事实好像只有一种解释。"

"什么！你已经解决了吗？"

"啊，这样说一定很过分。我已经发现了一种可作参考的情况，仅此而已。不过，含义深远。那些细节还需要补充。我是在查阅《泰晤士报》过期合订本时刚刚发现，上诺伍德的前任孟买第 34 步兵团肖尔托少校死于 1882 年 4 月 28 日。"

"福尔摩斯，也许我非常迟钝，但我不明白这暗示着什么。"

"不明白？你真让我吃惊。那就这样去看。摩斯坦上尉失踪了。他在伦敦可能去拜访的人只有肖尔托少校。肖尔托少校否认听说过他在伦敦。4 年后，肖尔托去世。他死后不到一周，摩斯坦上尉的女儿就收到了一份贵重礼物，以后年年都收到。现在她又收到一封信，说她是一个受到委屈的女人。除了她丧父，还能指什么委屈呢？为什么肖尔托死后，礼物就马上开始寄给她？除非肖尔托的继承人知道其中的秘密，想要补偿。你还有其他推理来满足那些情况吗？"

"可是，这是多么奇特的补偿啊！方式又是多么奇特！还有，他为什么现在，而不是 6 年前写信？此外，信上还说要给她公道。她能得到什么公道呢？假如认为她的父亲还活着，那就太过分了。你又不了解她还受过什么委屈。"

"有困难，确实有困难，"夏洛克·福尔摩斯沉思着说，"但今晚我们的调查将会迎刃而解。啊，一辆四轮马车来了，摩斯坦小姐在里面。你都准备

better go down, for it is a little past the hour."

I picked up my hat and my heaviest stick, but I observed that Holmes took his revolver from his drawer and slipped it into his pocket. It was clear that he thought that our night's work might be a serious one.

Miss Morstan was **muffled**[6] in a dark cloak, and her sensitive face was composed but pale. She must have been more than woman if she did not feel some uneasiness at the strange **enterprise**[7] upon which we were embarking, yet her self-control was perfect, and she readily answered the few additional questions which Sherlock Holmes put to her.

"Major Sholto was a very particular friend of Papa's," she said. "His letters were full of **allusions**[8] to the major. He and Papa were in command of the troops at the Andaman Islands, so they were thrown a great deal together. By the way, a curious paper was found in Papa's desk which no one could understand. I don't suppose that it is of the slightest importance, but I thought you might care to see it, so I brought it with me. It is here."

Holmes unfolded the paper carefully and smoothed it out upon his knee. He then very methodically examined it all over with his double lens.

"It is paper of native Indian manufacture," he remarked. "It has at some time been pinned to a board. The **diagram**[9] upon it appears to be a plan of part of a large building with numerous halls, corridors, and passages. At one point is a small cross done in red ink, and above it is '3.37 from left,' in faded pencil-writing. In the left-hand corner is a curious **hieroglyphic**[10] like four crosses in a line with their arms touching. Beside it is written, in very rough and coarse characters, 'The sign of the four—Jonathan Small, Mahomet Singh, Abdullah Khan, Dost Akbar.' No, I confess that I do not see how this bears upon the matter. Yet it is evidently a document of importance. It has been kept carefully in a pocketbook, for the one side is as clean as the other."

"It was in his pocketbook that we found it."

"Preserve it carefully, then, Miss Morstan, for it may prove to be of use to us. I begin to suspect that this matter may turn out to be much deeper and more subtle than I at first supposed. I must reconsider my ideas."

He leaned back in the cab, and I could see by his drawn brow and his

好了吗？那我们最好下去，已经过点了。"

我拿起帽子和最重的手杖，但我观察到福尔摩斯从抽屉里拿出左轮手枪，悄悄放进了口袋。显然，他认为我们今晚的工作可能非常严峻。

摩斯坦小姐裹着黑色外衣，敏感的脸庞镇定而苍白。如果她对我们要从事的奇特计划没有什么不安的话，那她一定不是一般的女人。她完全能控制自己，对夏洛克·福尔摩斯另外提出的几个问题应答如流。

"肖尔托少校是爸爸的知己，"她说，"他的信里总是提到少校。他和爸爸指挥安达曼群岛的军队，所以他们常常在一起。顺便说一下，我在爸爸的书桌里发现一张没有人能看懂的怪纸。我想它无足轻重，但我想你也许想看一下，所以就随身带来了。就在这里。"

福尔摩斯小心翼翼地展开那张纸，在膝盖上抚平，然后用双倍放大镜有条不紊地细查了一遍。

"这是印度本地造纸，"他说，"曾经在木板上别过一段时间。纸上的图表看来是一座大建筑中一部分的平面图，带有许多大厅、走廊和通道。其中一处是红墨水画的小十字架，这上方用褪色铅笔写着'左起3.37'。左上角是一个奇怪的象形文字，就像一排四个相连的十字架。旁边用非常粗糙的笔法写着：'四签名——乔纳森·斯莫尔、穆罕默德·辛格、阿卜杜拉·汗、多斯特·阿克巴'。不，我承认，我看不出这和本案有何种关系。不过，这显然是一个重要文件。这张纸曾经在一个皮夹里仔细收藏过，因为两面都同样干净。"

"这是我们在他的皮夹里发现的。"

"摩斯坦小姐，要仔细保存，因为它可能对我们有用。我开始怀疑这个案子可能比我最初想的要深奥微妙得多。我必须重新考虑自己的想法。"

他向后靠在车座上，我从他皱起的额头和茫然的目光可以看出，他正在

vacant eye that he was thinking **intently**[11]. Miss Morstan and I chatted in an undertone about our present expedition and its possible outcome, but our companion maintained his **impenetrable**[12] reserve until the end of our journey.

It was a September evening and not yet seven o'clock, but the day had been a dreary one, and a dense **drizzly**[13] fog lay low upon the great city. Mud-coloured clouds drooped sadly over the muddy streets. Down the Strand the lamps were but misty **splotches**[14] of **diffused**[15] light which threw a feeble circular glimmer upon the slimy pavement. The yellow glare from the shop-windows streamed out into the steamy, vaporous air and threw a murky, shifting radiance across the crowded **thoroughfare**[16]. There was, to my mind, something eerie and ghostlike in the endless procession of faces which flitted across these narrow bars of light–sad faces and glad, haggard and merry. Like all humankind, they **flitted**[17] from the gloom into the light and so back into the gloom once more. I am not subject to impressions, but the dull, heavy evening, with the strange business upon which we were engaged, combined to make me nervous and depressed. I could see from Miss Morstan's manner that she was suffering from the same feeling. Holmes alone could **rise superior to**[18] petty influences. He held his open notebook upon his knee, and from time to time he jotted down figures and **memoranda**[19] in the light of his pocket-lantern.

At the Lyceum Theatre the crowds were already thick at the side-entrances. In front a continuous stream of **hansoms**[20] and four-wheelers were rattling up, **discharging**[21] their cargoes of shirt-fronted men and beshawled, bediamonded women. We had hardly reached the third pillar, which was our **rendezvous**[22], before a small, dark, brisk man in the dress of a coachman **accosted**[23] us.

"Are you the parties who come with Miss Morstan?" he asked.

"I am Miss Morstan, and these two gentlemen are my friends," said she.

He bent a pair of wonderfully **penetrating**[24] and questioning eyes upon us.

"You will excuse me, miss," he said with a certain **dogged**[25] manner, "but I was to ask you to give me your word that neither of your companions is a police-officer."

"I give you my word on that," she answered.

专心思考。摩斯坦小姐和我低声聊着我们目前的调查和可能的结果，但我们的同伴始终保持沉默，直到我们抵达旅程的终点，他都一声不吭。

这是9月的一个傍晚，还不到7点，天就阴沉沉的，毛毛细雨似的浓雾笼罩着这座大城市，泥土色的云暗淡地低垂在泥泞的街道上空。河滨马路的那些灯将微弱的环形光照在泥泞的人行道上，仅仅成了散光雾点。从橱窗照出的黄色灯光穿过雾蒙蒙的空气，将阴沉移动的光亮射过熙熙攘攘的大街。在我看来，源源不断的行人的脸上有一种像幽灵一样的怪诞东西。这些脸有喜有忧，有憔悴，也有欢乐，飞快地掠过这些狭窄的光柱。就像所有的人类一样，他们从黑暗飞快地进入光明，又从光明飞快地返回黑暗。我不会受到这些印象的影响，但这个灰暗阴沉的夜晚和我们要做的怪事，使我感到紧张和沮丧。我可以从摩斯坦小姐的举止看出，她也有同样的感觉。只有福尔摩斯不受小事的影响。他握着在膝盖上打开的笔记本，借助随身携带的小提灯的光亮，不时地匆匆记下一些数字和备忘录。

莱森戏院两边入口的观众已经水泄不通。戏院前面，双轮小马车和四轮马车源源不断丁丁当当开过来，卸下货物：穿着衬衣的男人和披着围巾、戴着钻石的女人。我们刚刚到达指定的第三根柱子，就有一个身材矮小、皮肤黝黑、行动轻快、穿着车夫服装的男人向我们打招呼。

"你们是和摩斯坦小姐一块来的那批人吗？"他问。

"我就是摩斯坦小姐，这两位先生是我的朋友，"她说。

他把一双非常敏锐和疑问的眼睛转向我们。

"小姐，对不起，"他用某种顽固的态度说，"但我要请你向我保证，你的同伴没有一名警官。"

"我可以向你保证，"她回答说。

四签名

He gave a shrill whistle, on which a street Arab led across a four-wheeler and opened the door. The man who had addressed us mounted to the box, while we took our places inside. We had hardly done so before the driver whipped up his horse, and we plunged away at a furious pace through the foggy streets.

The situation was a curious one. We were driving to an unknown place, on an unknown errand. Yet our invitation was either a complete hoax—which was an inconceivable **hypothesis**[26]—or else we had good reason to think that important issues might hang upon our journey. Miss Morstan's **demeanour**[27] was as resolute and collected as ever. I endeavoured to cheer and amuse her by **reminiscences**[28] of my adventures in Afghanistan; but, to tell the truth, I was myself so excited at our situation and so curious as to our destination that my stories were slightly involved. To this day she declares that I told her one moving **anecdote**[29] as to how a musket looked into my tent at the dead of night, and how I fired a double-barrelled tiger cub at it. At first I had some idea as to the direction in which we were driving; but soon, what with our pace, the fog, and my own limited knowledge of London, I lost my bearings and knew nothing save that we seemed to be going a very long way. Sherlock Holmes was never at fault, however, and he muttered the names as the cab rattled through squares and in and out by tortuous by-streets.

"Rochester Row," said he. "Now Vincent Square. Now we come out on the Vauxhall Bridge Road. We are making for the Surrey side apparently. Yes, I thought so. Now we are on the bridge. You can catch glimpses of the river."

We did indeed get a fleeting view of a stretch of the Thames, with the lamps shining upon the broad, silent water; but our cab dashed on and was soon involved in a **labyrinth**[30] of streets upon the other side.

"Wordsworth Road," said my companion. "Priory Road. Lark Hall Lane. Stockwell Place. Robert Street. Cold Harbour Lane. Our quest does not appear to take us to very fashionable regions."

We had indeed reached a questionable and **forbidding**[31] neighbourhood. Long lines of dull brick houses were only relieved by the coarse glare and tawdry brilliancy of public-houses at the corner. Then came rows of two-storied villas, each with a fronting of **miniature**[32] garden, and then again

他发出一声尖锐的口哨。一个街头流浪儿听到口哨，拉过一辆四轮马车，打开车门。那个和我们说话的人爬上车夫座，我们上车落座。我们一坐下来，马车夫就扬鞭策马。随后，我们飞快地穿过大雾弥漫的大街。

我们的处境非常奇特。我们正驶向一个未知的地方，也不知道要去做什么。可是，对我们的邀请要么完全是一场骗局——这是一种不可想象的假设——要么我们有充分理由认为，重要的结果说不定要看我们这次的旅程而定。摩斯坦小姐的举止仍然果断镇定。我尽力回忆自己在阿富汗冒险的经历，去逗她开心发笑。但是，说实话，我自己对我们的处境非常兴奋，也对我们的目的地非常好奇，所以我讲的故事也稍微受到了影响。直到今天，她还宣称我给她讲了一则动人的趣闻逸事，说的是一支滑膛枪如何在深夜伸进我的帐篷，我如何用一支双筒小老虎向它开火。起初，我对我们行驶的方向还有一些印象，可是不久，因为我们行进的速度、大雾，以及我自己对伦敦的有限了解，所以我迷失了方向，只知道我们的行程好像很长。无论如何，夏洛克·福尔摩斯都从来没有迷路。马车丁丁当当穿过一个个广场、出入一条条转弯抹角的胡同时，他都喃喃说出地名。

"罗彻斯特路，"他说，"现在是文森特广场。现在我们出来上了从沃克斯霍尔桥路，显然正走向萨里方向。是的，我想是这样。现在我们走上了桥面。你们可以瞥见河水。"

我们的确看到了飞快掠过的泰晤士河的一段风景，灯光照射在静静的宽阔水面上，但我们的马车向前飞奔，马上就进入了河对岸迷宫一样的街道。

"华兹华斯路，"我的同伴说，"小修道院路。拉克霍尔巷。斯托克维尔街。罗伯特街。冷港巷。看来并不是要把我们带到非常繁华的区域。"

我们的确已经到达了一个可疑又可怕的区域。一排排长长的阴暗砖房到

**interminable**[33] lines of new, staring brick buildings—the monster **tentacles**[34] which the giant city was throwing out into the country. At last the cab drew up at the third house in a new terrace. None of the other houses were inhabited, and that at which we stopped was as dark as its neighbours, save for a single glimmer in the kitchen-window. On our knocking, however, the door was instantly thrown open by a Hindoo servant, clad in a yellow turban, white loose-fitting clothes, and a yellow **sash**[35]. There was something strangely **incongruous**[36] in this Oriental figure framed in the commonplace doorway of a third-rate suburban dwelling-house.

"The sahib awaits you," said he, and even as he spoke, there came a high, piping voice from some inner room.

"Show them in to me, ***khitmutgar***[37]," it said. "Show them straight in to me."

了拐角才变成了粗鄙俗丽的酒店，随后是一排排两层楼的住宅（酒店），每幢楼前有一座小花园，接着又是一排排望不到边的显眼的新砖楼——是大城市向乡村伸出的一只只可怕触手。最后，马车停在这条新街的第3座房前。其他房子还没有人住。我们停车的房前，除了从厨房窗户透出的一线微弱闪光，也和其他房子一样黑暗。然而，我们敲门后，门马上就打开了，开门的是一个头裹黄色包头巾、身穿宽松白色衣服、腰系黄带子的印度仆人。这个三流郊区住宅的普通门口出现了这个东方仆人，有些奇怪，格格不入。

"老爷在等你们，"他说，甚至在他说话时，里屋就传来了高亢尖锐的声音。

"侍者，把他们领到我这里，"那个声音说，"把他们直接领到我这里。"

Notes:
1. alternate with 轮流；交换
2. infantry *n.* 步兵
3. culminate *vi.* 达到最高潮；告终；完结（in）
4. deprivation *n.* 被夺去；丧失；损失
5. compensation *n.* 补偿物；补偿；赔偿
6. muffle *vt.* 捂住
7. enterprise *n.* 企业；胆识
8. allusion *n.* 暗指
9. diagram *n.* 简图；图表
10. hieroglyphic *n.* 象形文字
11. intently *adv.* 专心地；集中地；专心地
12. impenetrable *adj.* 不接纳的；顽固的
13. drizzly *adj.* 下毛毛雨的
14. splotch *n.* 斑点
15. diffused *adj.* 散布的
16. thoroughfare *n.* 大道；大街
17. flit *vi.* 飞来飞去
18. rise superior to *v.* 不为所动；不受影响
19. memorandum *n.* 备忘录；便笺；摘要；非正式的记录
20. hansom *n.* （车夫驾驶台在后的）单马双轮双座马车
21. discharge *vt.* 卸下
22. rendezvous *n.* 约会的地点；公共聚会场所
23. accost *vt.* 走过去跟……讲话；跟……搭讪
24. penetrating *adj.* 穿透的；渗透的；锐利的
25. dogged *adj.* 顽固的；固执的
26. hypothesis *n.* 假设；前提
27. demeanour *n.* 行为；举止；态度
28. reminiscence *n.* 旧事；回忆
29. anecdote *n.* 趣闻；轶事
30. labyrinth *n.* 迷宫
31. forbidding *adj.* 可怕的；令人难亲近的

32. miniature garden *n.* 盆景；盆景园
33. interminable *adj.* 无止境的；无尽头的
34. tentacle *n.* 触器（手、须、角）；象触手的东西
35. sash *n.* 腰带；肩带
36. incongruous *adj.* 不协调的；不相称的
37. khidmatgar *n.* 〈印英〉男侍者

# Chapter 4

## THE STORY OF THE BALD-HEADED MAN

# 第四章

## 秃头人的故事

We followed the Indian down a sordid and common passage, ill-lit and worse furnished, until he came to a door upon the right, which he threw open. A blaze of yellow light streamed out upon us, and in the centre of the glare there stood a small man with a very high head, a bristle of red hair all round the fringe of it, and a bald, shining scalp which shot out from among it like a mountain-peak from fir-trees. He **writhed**[1] his hands together as he stood, and his features were in a **perpetual**[2] jerk—now smiling, now scowling, but never for an instant in repose. Nature had given him a pendulous lip, and a too visible line of yellow and irregular teeth, which he strove feebly to conceal by constantly passing his hand over the lower part of his face. In spite of his **obtrusive**[3] baldness he gave the impression of youth. In point of fact, he had just turned his thirtieth year.

"Your servant, Miss Morstan," he kept repeating in a thin, high voice. "Your servant, gentlemen. Pray step into my little sanctum. A small place, miss, but furnished to my own liking. An oasis of art in the howling desert of South London."

We were all astonished by the appearance of the apartment into which he invited us. In that sorry house it looked as out of place as a diamond of the first water in a setting of brass. The richest and glossiest of curtains and tapestries draped the walls, looped back here and there to expose some richly mounted painting or Oriental vase. The carpet was of **amber**[4] and black, so soft and so thick that the foot sank pleasantly into it, as into a bed of moss. Two great tiger-skins thrown **athwart**[5] it increased the suggestion of Eastern luxury, as did a huge **hookah**[6] which stood upon a mat in the corner. A lamp in the fashion of a silver dove was hung from an almost invisible golden wire in the centre of the room. As it burned it filled the air with a subtle and **aromatic**[7] odour.

"Mr. Thaddeus Sholto," said the little man, still jerking and smiling. "That is my name. You are Miss Morstan, of course. And these gentlemen—"

"This is Mr. Sherlock Holmes, and this Dr. Watson."

"A doctor, eh?" cried he, much excited. "Have you your **stethoscope**[8]? Might I ask you—would you have the kindness? I have **grave**[9] doubts as to my **mitral**[10] valve, if you would be so very good. The **aortic**[11] I may rely upon, but I should value your opinion upon the mitral."

我们跟随印度人，顺着一条肮脏普通、灯光昏暗、陈设糟糕的通道向前走。他走到右边的一个门前，推开门。一道黄色灯光射向我们，灯光中央站着一个矮小的男人，头很高，头四周是一圈又短又硬的红发，头顶又秃又亮，就像是冷杉树丛中冒出的山峰一样。他站在那里，扭动双手，面容一直在抽搐，时而微笑，时而皱眉，没有一刻平静过。他天生一张下垂的嘴唇，尽管他徒劳无益常常努力用手遮住脸的下半部，但参差不齐的黄牙还是显而易见。他明显秃顶，他给人的印象却年轻。实际上，他刚过30岁。

"摩斯坦小姐，愿为你效劳，"他一直用又细又高的声音重复说，"先生们，愿为你们效劳。请走进我这个小小密室。小姐，尽管地方小，却是按照我自己的爱好布置的。这是伦敦南郊荒凉沙漠中的一块艺术绿洲。"

我们都对他请我们走进的这个房间的外观非常惊讶。看上去它和这个蹩脚的房子格格不入，就像一颗最好品质的钻石镶在一个黄铜底座上似的。墙壁上挂着最华丽、最光泽的窗帘和挂毯，各处错落有致地露出装裱华丽的油画和东方花瓶。地毯呈琥珀色和黑色，又软又厚，脚踩上去非常舒适，就像踩在青苔地一样。两张横铺在地毯上的大虎皮更使人联想起了东方的华贵，犹如屋角草席上摆着大水烟壶引起的联想。房间中央有一根几乎看不见的金线，一盏银色鸽子式样的灯就挂在上面。当那盏灯亮起时，空气中就会充满淡淡的清香。

"撒迪厄斯·肖尔托先生，"这个矮小的男人说，仍然面容抽搐，微微含笑。"这是我的名字。你当然是摩斯坦小姐。这两位先生——"

"这位是夏洛克·福尔摩斯先生，这位是华生医生。"

"啊，一位医生？"他兴致勃勃，大声说道，"你带听诊器了吗？请问——你愿意帮忙吗？我对自己的二尖瓣严重怀疑，你是不是愿意行好。尽管可以依靠大动脉，但我应该重视你对我的二尖瓣的意见。"

四签名

I listened to his heart, as requested, but was unable to find anything amiss, save, indeed, that he was in an **ecstasy**[12] of fear, for he shivered from head to foot.

"It appears to be normal," I said. "You have no cause for uneasiness."

"You will excuse my anxiety, Miss Morstan," he remarked airily. "I am a great sufferer, and I have long had suspicions as to that valve. I am delighted to hear that they are **unwarranted**[13]. Had your father, Miss Morstan, refrained from throwing a strain upon his heart, he might have been alive now."

I could have struck the man across the face, so hot was I at this **callous**[14] and offhand reference to so delicate a matter. Miss Morstan sat down, and her face grew white to the lips.

"I knew in my heart that he was dead," said she.

"I can give you every information," said he; "and, what is more, I can do you justice; and I will, too, whatever Brother Bartholomew may say. I am so glad to have your friends here not only as an escort to you but also as witnesses to what I am about to do and say. The three of us can show a bold front to Brother Bartholomew. But let us have no outsiders—no police or officials. We can settle everything satisfactorily among ourselves without any interference. Nothing would annoy Brother Bartholomew more than any publicity."

He sat down upon a low settee and blinked at us inquiringly with his weak, watery blue eyes.

"For my part," said Holmes, "whatever you may choose to say will go no further."

I nodded to show my agreement.

"That is well! That is well!" said he. "May I offer you a glass of **Chianti**[15], Miss Morstan? Or of Tokay? I keep no other wines. Shall I open a flask? No? Well, then, I trust that you have no objection to tobacco-smoke, to the balsamic odour of the Eastern tobacco. I am a little nervous, and I find my hookah an invaluable **sedative**[16]."

He applied a taper to the great bowl, and the smoke bubbled merrily through the rose-water. We sat all three in a semicircle, with our heads

我应他的请求，听了听他的心脏，但找不出任何毛病，其实只发现他处在极端恐怖之中，因为他从头到脚浑身颤抖。

"似乎都正常，"我说，"你没有任何理由感到不安。"

"摩斯坦小姐，你要原谅我的焦虑，"他轻描淡写地说，"我是一个受大罪的人，早就对那个瓣膜产生了怀疑。我很高兴听说它们没有毛病。摩斯坦小姐，如果你的父亲没有损伤心脏，他说不定现在还活着。"

我对他这样无情草率提到如此微妙之事非常恼火，恨不能朝他的脸上打去。摩斯坦小姐坐下来，脸色一下白到了嘴唇。

"我心里明白他去世了，"她说。

"我可以告诉你所有的信息，"他说，"而且，重要的是，我还能公平对待你。无论巴塞洛缪哥可能说什么，我也一定会这样做。我很高兴你的两位朋友来这里，他们不仅是陪同你，而且对我要说的话和要做的事是见证人。我们三个可以勇敢面对巴塞洛缪哥。但是，我们绝不让外人参加——不要警察或官员。我们可以没有任何外人干涉，圆满解决所有的一切。如果宣扬出去，就会惹恼巴塞洛缪哥。"

他在低矮的长靠椅上坐下来，用有气无力、泪水汪汪的蓝眼睛探询似的对我们眨着。

"就我来说，"福尔摩斯说，"无论你可能想说什么，我都不会对别人说。"

我点头表示同意。

"那就好！那就好！"他说，"摩斯坦小姐，我可以给你一杯意大利基安蒂红葡萄酒？还是匈牙利托考伊白葡萄酒？我这里没有其他葡萄酒。我打开一瓶好吗？不？那好，我相信，你们不会反对这种烟草烟，不会反对东方烟草的香脂味吧。我有点儿紧张，后来我发现我的水烟壶起着不可估量的镇定作用。"

他用细蜡烛点上大水烟壶，随后烟从玫瑰水里欢快地冒了出来。我们三

四签名

advanced and our chins upon our hands, while the strange, jerky little fellow, with his high, shining head, puffed uneasily in the centre.

"When I first determined to make this communication to you," said he, "I might have given you my address; but I feared that you might disregard my request and bring unpleasant people with you. I took the liberty, therefore, of making an appointment in such a way that my man Williams might be able to see you first. I have complete confidence in his **discretion**[17], and he had orders, if he were dissatisfied, to proceed no further in the matter. You will excuse these **precautions**[18], but I am a man of somewhat retiring, and I might even say refined, tastes, and there is nothing more **unaesthetic**[19] than a policeman. I have a natural shrinking from all forms of rough materialism. I seldom come in contact with the rough crowd. I live, as you see, with some little atmosphere of elegance around me. I may call myself a patron of the arts. It is my weakness. The landscape is a genuine Corot, and though a **connoisseur**[20] might perhaps throw a doubt upon that Salvator Rosa, there cannot be the least question about the Bouguereau. I am partial to the modern French school."

"You will excuse me, Mr. Sholto," said Miss Morstan, "but I am here at your request to learn something which you desire to tell me. It is very late, and I should desire the interview to be as short as possible."

"At the best it must take some time," he answered; "for we shall certainly have to go to Norwood and see Brother Bartholomew. We shall all go and try if we can get the better of Brother Bartholomew. He is very angry with me for taking the course which has seemed right to me. I had quite high words with him last night. You cannot imagine what a terrible fellow he is when he is angry."

"If we are to go to Norwood, it would perhaps be as well to start at once," I ventured to remark.

He laughed until his ears were quite red.

"That would hardly do," he cried. "I don't know what he would say if I brought you in that sudden way. No, I must prepare you by showing you how we all stand to each other. In the first place, I must tell you that there are several points in the story of which I am myself ignorant. I can only lay the facts before

个围坐成半圆圈，头向前伸，两手支着下巴。这个奇怪而痉挛的矮小男人脑袋又高又亮，坐在我们中间，心神不安地吐着烟。

"当我最初决定和你联系时，"他说，"本可以把我的住址告诉你，但我怕你可能会不理会我的请求，给你招来厌恶的人。所以，我就冒昧预约，这样我的仆人威廉斯可能会先见到你们。我完全信任他的判断力，而且他得到吩咐，如果你们对他不满意的话，这件事就不要再继续进行下去了。你一定会理解这些预防措施，但我是一个有点儿不爱交际，甚至可以说附庸风雅的人，再没有比警察更缺乏审美力的人了。我天生会在一切形式的粗俗唯物主义面前退缩，很少和粗俗的人接触。你们可以看到，我生活的周围都带有一些小小的优雅氛围。我可以自称为艺术守护神。这是我的癖好。那幅风景画是柯罗的真迹。尽管一位鉴赏家也许会怀疑那幅萨尔瓦多·罗萨，但那幅布格罗不可能有任何问题。我对法国现代画派情有独钟。"

"对不起，肖尔托先生，"摩斯坦小姐说，"但我应邀来这里，是想听到你希望告诉我的一些事儿。时间很晚了，我希望我们的会见尽可能简短。"

"最理想的状态是，它还是要占用一些时间，"他回答说，"因为我们肯定还得去诺伍德见巴塞洛缪哥。我们都要去试一下，看我们是否能胜过他。他对我采取的自认为合理的行动非常生气。我昨晚和他大吵了一架。你们想象不出他生气时是一个多么可怕的家伙。"

"如果我们要去诺伍德，也许我们还是马上动身为好，"我冒昧说道。

他放声大笑，直笑得耳朵通红。

"那不行，"他大声说道，"如果突然那样带你们去，我不知道他会说什么。不，我必须向你们说明我们如何相互支持，以作好准备。首先，我必须告诉你们，这个故事里还有几点连我自己都不知道。我只能把我自己知道的那些

四签名

you as far as I know them myself.

"My father was, as you may have guessed, Major John Sholto, once of the Indian Army. He retired some eleven years ago and came to live at Pondicherry Lodge in Upper Norwood. He had prospered in India and brought back with him a considerable sum of money, a large collection of valuable curiosities, and a staff of native servants. With these advantages he bought himself a house, and lived in great luxury. My twin-brother Bartholomew and I were the only children.

"I very well remember the sensation which was caused by the disappearance of Captain Morstan. We read the details in the papers, and knowing that he had been a friend of our father's we discussed the case freely in his presence. He used to join in our **speculations**[21] as to what could have happened. Never for an instant did we suspect that he had the whole secret hidden in his own breast, that of all men he alone knew the fate of Arthur Morstan.

"We did know, however, that some mystery, some positive danger, overhung our father. He was very fearful of going out alone, and he always employed two **prize-fighters**[22] to act as porters at Pondicherry Lodge. Williams, who drove you to-night, was one of them. He was once lightweight champion of England. Our father would never tell us what it was he feared, but he had a most marked **aversion**[23] to men with wooden legs. On one occasion he actually fired his revolver at a wooden-legged man, who proved to be a harmless tradesman **canvassing for**[24] orders. We had to pay a large sum to hush the matter up. My brother and I used to think this a mere whim of my father's, but events have since led us to change our opinion.

"Early in 1882 my father received a letter from India which was a great shock to him. He nearly fainted at the breakfast-table when he opened it, and from that day he sickened to his death. What was in the letter we could never discover, but I could see as he held it that it was short and written in a scrawling hand. He had suffered for years from an enlarged **spleen**[25], but he now became rapidly worse, and towards the end of April we were informed that he was

情况摆在你们面前。

"你们可能已经猜到,我的父亲就是过去印度军队的约翰·肖尔托少校。他大约是 11 年前退休,来到上诺伍德的樱塘别墅居住。他在印度发了财,带回来相当可观的一笔钱、一大批贵重古玩和一群土著仆人。有了这些有利条件,他给自己买了一座房子,过着非常奢侈的生活。我和孪生兄弟巴塞洛缪是他仅有的孩子。

"我还非常清楚地记得摩斯坦上尉失踪引起的轰动。我们在报纸上看到过那些细节。我们知道他曾经是父亲的朋友,就无拘无束在他面前谈论这件事。他常常和我们一起推测这件事可能是怎么发生的。我们丝毫也没有怀疑他自己心里藏着这整个秘密——在所有人中,只有他知道阿瑟·摩斯坦的命运。

"然而,我们的确知道某种秘密——某种实际危险——笼罩着我们的父亲。他很怕独自出门,总是雇两个职业拳击手在樱塘别墅看门。今天为你们赶车的威廉斯就是其中一个。他曾经是英国轻量级冠军。我们的父亲从来不告诉我们他怕的是什么,但他极其厌恶装有木腿的人。有一次,他居然用左轮手枪向一个装有木腿的人开枪,后来证明那个人是一个没有恶意前来兜售订单的零售商。我们不得不赔了一大笔钱,才平息此事。我和哥哥过去总是以为这不过是父亲的一时兴致,但后来的一件件事使我们改变了看法。

"1882 年初,我的父亲收到了一封印度来信。这封信对他是一个巨大打击。他打开这封信后差点儿在早餐桌上晕倒,而且从那天起,他就一病不起。信里写什么,我们从来未能发现,但他拿着这封信时,我可以看到信很短,字迹潦草。他患脾肿大已有多年,但之后很快他就每况愈下。到 4 月底,医生

四签名

beyond all hope, and that he wished to make a last communication to us.

"When we entered his room he was propped up with pillows and breathing heavily. He **besought**[26] us to lock the door and to come upon either side of the bed. Then grasping our hands he made a remarkable statement to us in a voice which was broken as much by emotion as by pain. I shall try and give it to you in his own very words.

"'I have only one thing,' he said, 'which weighs upon my mind at this supreme moment. It is my treatment of poor Morstan's orphan. The cursed greed which has been my besetting sin through life has withheld from her the treasure, half at least of which should have been hers. And yet I have made no use of it myself, so blind and foolish a thing is avarice. The mere feeling of possession has been so dear to me that I could not bear to share it with another. See that chaplet tipped with pearls beside the quinine-bottle. Even that I could not bear to part with, although I had got it out with the design of sending it to her. You, my sons, will give her a fair share of the Agra treasure. But send her nothing—not even the **chaplet**[27]—until I am gone. After all, men have been as bad as this and have recovered.

"'I will tell you how Morstan died,' he continued. 'He had suffered for years from a weak heart, but he concealed it from every one. I alone knew it. When in India, he and I, through a remarkable chain of circumstances, came into possession of a considerable treasure. I brought it over to England, and on the night of Morstan's arrival he came straight over here to claim his share. He walked over from the station and was admitted by my faithful old Lal Chowdar, who is now dead. Morstan and I had a difference of opinion as to the division of the treasure, and we came to heated words. Morstan had sprung out of his chair in a paroxysm of anger, when he suddenly pressed his hand to his side, his face turned a dusky **hue**[28], and he fell backward, cutting his head against the corner of the treasure-chest. When I stooped over him I found, to my horror, that he was dead.

"'For a long time I sat half distracted, wondering what I should do. My first impulse was, of course, to call for assistance; but I could not but recognize that there was every chance that I would be accused of his murder. His death at

告诉我们说他完全没救了,他希望和我们最后谈一次。

"我们走进他的房间时,他用枕头靠坐起来,呼吸沉重。他恳求我们锁上门,到床两边来。随后,他握住我们的手,对我们讲了一件特别的事儿,他说话的声音因痛苦和激动而断断续续。我尽量用他自己的原话告诉你们。

"'在这个最后的时刻,只有一件事,'他说,'压在我心上。那就是我对待可怜的摩斯坦遗孤的态度。该死的贪心使我一生不断犯罪,使她无法得到那笔财宝,因为其中至少一半应该属于她。可是,我自己从来没有用过这笔财宝,贪婪真是盲目愚蠢的东西。纯粹占有的感觉对我是那样重要,所以我无法忍受和人分享。看到奎宁瓶旁边顶端上附加有珍珠的项圈了吧。我甚至舍不得放手,尽管我拿出来是想送给她。我的儿子们,你们要把阿格拉的财宝平分给她。但是,在我死前,不要给她任何东西——哪怕是那串项圈。毕竟来说,坏人也会良心发现的。

"'我要告诉你们摩斯坦是怎么死的,'他继续说道,'他多年来心脏衰弱,但他没有告诉任何人。只有我知道。在印度时,我和他经历过一系列非凡情况,得到了一笔可观的财宝。我把这笔财宝带到了英国。摩斯坦到达伦敦的那天晚上,直接来到这里要他应得的那份。他从车站步行走到这里,是忠实的老拉尔·乔达让他进来的,乔达现在已经死了。我和摩斯坦对平分财宝产生了不同意见,所以我们发生了激烈争吵。摩斯坦一怒之下从椅子上跳起来,这时他突然把手按在身体一侧,脸色变得暗黑,仰面跌倒,头撞在了宝箱的角上。让我惊恐的是,当我低头看他时,他已经死了。

"我坐了好一阵子,像精神失常似的,不知道该做什么。当然,我的第一个冲动就是请求帮助,但我不禁认识到我有可能会被指控为谋杀。他是在争吵中死去的,而且头上深长的伤口也对我不利。此外,官方调查时不可能

the moment of a quarrel, and the gash in his head, would be black against me. Again, an official inquiry could not be made without bringing out some facts about the treasure, which I was particularly anxious to keep secret. He had told me that no soul upon earth knew where he had gone. There seemed to be no necessity why any soul ever should know.

"'I was still pondering over the matter, when, looking up, I saw my servant, Lal Chowdar, in the doorway. He stole in and bolted the door behind him. "Do not fear, **sahib**[29]," he said; "no one need know that you have killed him. Let us hide him away, and who is the wiser?" "I did not kill him," said I. Lal Chowdar shook his head and smiled. "I heard it all, sahib," said he; "I heard you quarrel, and I heard the blow. But my lips are sealed. All are asleep in the house. Let us put him away together." That was enough to decide me. If my own servant could not believe my innocence, how could I hope to make it good before twelve foolish tradesmen in a jury-box? Lal Chowdar and I **disposed of**[30] the body that night, and within a few days the London papers were full of the mysterious disappearance of Captain Morstan. You will see from what I say that I can hardly be blamed in the matter. My fault lies in the fact that we concealed not only the body but also the treasure and that I have clung to Morstan's share as well as to my own. I wish you, therefore, to make **restitution**[31]. Put your ears down to my mouth. The treasure is hidden in—'

"At this instant a horrible change came over his expression; his eyes stared wildly, his jaw dropped, and he yelled in a voice which I can never forget, 'Keep him out! For Christ's sake keep him out!' We both stared round at the window behind us upon which his gaze was fixed. A face was looking in at us out of the darkness. We could see the whitening of the nose where it was pressed against the glass. It was a bearded, hairy face, with wild cruel eyes and an expression of concentrated **malevolence**[32]. My brother and I rushed towards the window, but the man was gone. When we returned to my father his head had dropped and his pulse had ceased to beat.

"We searched the garden that night but found no sign of the intruder save that just under the window a single footmark was visible in the flower-bed. But for that one trace, we might have thought that our imaginations had **conjured up**[33]

不说出有关财宝的一些情况。我对这尤其担忧,要保守秘密。他曾经告诉我说,世界上没有一个人知道他去了哪里。任何人似乎没有必要知道其中的原因。

"我还在沉思这件事,这时我抬起头,看到仆人拉尔·乔达站在门口。他偷偷走进来,在身后闩上了门。'老爷,不要怕,'他说,'谁也不必知道是你杀了他。让我们把他藏起来,谁会知道呢?''我没有杀他,'我说。拉尔·乔达摇摇头,微微一笑。'老爷,我都听见了,'他说,'我听见你们争吵,我还听见重击声。但是,我会守口如瓶。家里的人都睡着了。让我们一起把他搬走吧。'这足以判决我。如果我自己的仆人都不能相信我无罪,我还怎么能指望陪审席上的12个愚蠢的零售商宣告我无罪呢?拉尔·乔达和我当天夜里就处理掉了尸体。不到几天,伦敦报纸就登满了摩斯坦上尉神秘失踪的报道。从我说的情况,你们就会明白,我在这件事上绝不可能有过失。我的错误在于,我们不仅隐藏了尸体,而且隐藏了财宝,同时我既拿了自己那份,也拿了摩斯坦的那份,所以我希望你们去归还。把耳朵放到我的嘴边。财宝藏在——'

"这时,他的表情发生了可怕的变化,眼睛直瞪,下颚耷拉,用我永远难忘的声音尖声喊道:'让他出去!看在上帝的份上让他出去!'我们一起回头看到他的目光盯住的窗户。黑暗里有一张脸正在望着我们。我们可以看到他压在玻璃上变白的鼻子。一张胡子拉碴、毛茸茸的脸,眼睛疯狂冷酷,表情带着强烈的恶意。我和兄弟冲向窗户,但那个人已经不见了。当我回到父亲身边时,只见他的头已经耷拉,脉搏也已经停止了跳动。

"当天夜里,我们搜查了花园,但除了看到窗下花床里的一只脚印,没有发现这个闯入者的任何痕迹。要不是那个形迹,我们可能会以为那张疯狂残忍的脸是我们想象出来的。然而,我们马上又得到了一个更显著的证明,

that wild, fierce face. We soon, however, had another and a more striking proof that there were secret agencies at work all round us. The window of my father's room was found open in the morning, his cupboards and boxes had been rifled, and upon his chest was fixed a torn piece of paper with the words 'The sign of the four' scrawled across it. What the phrase meant or who our secret visitor may have been, we never knew. As far as we can judge, none of my father's property had been actually stolen, though everything had been turned out. My brother and I naturally associated this peculiar incident with the fear which **haunted**[34] my father during his life, but it is still a complete mystery to us."

The little man stopped to relight his hookah and puffed thoughtfully for a few moments. We had all sat absorbed, listening to his extraordinary narrative. At the short account of her father's death Miss Morstan had turned deadly white, and for a moment I feared that she was about to faint. She rallied, however, on drinking a glass of water which I quietly poured out for her from a Venetian carafe upon the side-table. Sherlock Holmes leaned back in his chair with an abstracted expression and the lids drawn low over his glittering eyes. As I glanced at him I could not but think how on that very day he had complained bitterly of the commonplaceness of life. Here at least was a problem which would tax his **sagacity**[35] to the utmost. Mr. Thaddeus Sholto looked from one to the other of us with an obvious pride at the effect which his story had produced and then continued between the puffs of his overgrown pipe.

"My brother and I," said he, "were, as you may imagine, much excited as to the treasure which my father had spoken of. For weeks and for months we dug and delved in every part of the garden without discovering its whereabouts. It was maddening to think that the hiding-place was on his very lips at the moment that he died. We could judge the splendour of the missing riches by the chaplet which he had taken out. Over this chaplet my brother Bartholomew and I had some little discussion. The pearls were evidently of great value, and he was averse to part with them, for, between friends, my brother was himself a little inclined to my father's fault. He thought, too, that if we parted with the chaplet it might give rise to gossip and finally bring us into trouble. It was all that I could do to persuade him to let me find out Miss Morstan's address and send her a **detached**[36] pearl at

就是我们周围有一些秘密机构正在行动。第二天早上,我们发现父亲房间的窗户敞开,他的橱柜和箱子都遭到了洗劫,他的箱子上钉着一张破纸,上面潦草地写着'四签名'这几个字。这几个字是什么意思、我们那个秘密客人是谁,我们从来都不知道。我们所能断定的是,尽管所有东西都被翻动过,但我父亲的财物居然没有被盗。我和兄弟自然就把这件怪事和父亲生前反复出现的恐惧联系起来,但这对我们还是一头雾水。"

这个矮小男人停下来,又点起了水烟壶,若有所思地吸了一会儿。我们都坐在那里,全神贯注地听他讲这个离奇的故事。听到对父亲死亡的短暂叙述,摩斯坦小姐脸色惨白。一时间,我怕她会晕倒。然而,等我默默地从靠墙桌子上的一只威尼斯式玻璃水瓶里给她倒了一杯水后,她又恢复了过来。夏洛克·福尔摩斯靠在椅子里神情发呆,眼皮耷拉着盖住闪亮的眼睛。我扫了他一眼,不禁想到,他今天还痛苦地抱怨人生是多么平庸。这里至少有一个问题将要最大可能利用他的聪明才智。撒迪厄斯·肖尔托先生看看我们这个,又瞧瞧那个,显然对自己的故事对我们产生的影响感到自豪,于是一边吸大水烟壶,一边接着说下去。

"你们可以想象,我和兄弟,"他说,"对父亲所说的财宝万分激动。我们在花园的各个地方都挖了几周、几个月,都没有发现财宝的下落。想到财宝的隐藏处竟然留在了他临终时的嘴里,真让人发疯。我们从他拿出的那个项圈就可以断定那笔遗失的财宝是多么壮观。我和哥哥巴塞洛缪曾经稍微讨论过这个项圈。这些珍珠显然价值巨大,他也不愿割舍,因为,朋友之间说说无妨,我的兄弟自己有点儿遗传了我父亲的毛病。他又想到,如果我们送掉那个项圈,可能会引起闲话,最后会给我们带来麻烦。我所能做的就是劝他让我找到摩斯坦小姐的住址,然后每隔一段固定时间给她寄一颗拆下来的

fixed intervals so that at least she might never feel **destitute**[37]."

"It was a kindly thought," said our companion earnestly; "it was extremely good of you."

The little man waved his hand **deprecatingly**[38].

"We were your trustees," he said; "that was the view which I took of it, though Brother Bartholomew could not altogether see it in that light. We had plenty of money ourselves. I desired no more. Besides, it would have been such bad taste to have treated a young lady in so scurvy a fashion. '*Le mauvais goût mène au crime.*' The French have a very neat way of putting these things. Our difference of opinion on this subject went so far that I thought it best to set up rooms for myself; so I left Pondicherry Lodge, taking the old *khitmutgar* and Williams with me. Yesterday, however, I learned that an event of extreme importance has occurred. The treasure has been discovered. I instantly communicated with Miss Morstan, and it only remains for us to drive out to Norwood and demand our share. I explained my views last night to Brother Bartholomew, so we shall be expected, if not welcome, visitors."

Mr. Thaddeus Sholto ceased and sat twitching on his luxurious settee. We all remained silent, with our thoughts upon the new development which the mysterious business had taken. Holmes was the first to spring to his feet.

"You have done well, sir, from first to last," said he. "It is possible that we may be able to make you some small return by throwing some light upon that which is still dark to you. But, as Miss Morstan remarked just now, it is late, and we had best put the matter through **without delay**[39]."

Our new acquaintance very deliberately coiled up the tube of his hookah and produced from behind a curtain a very long **befrogged**[40] topcoat with **astrakhan**[41] collar and cuffs. This he buttoned tightly up in spite of the extreme closeness of the night and finished his attire by putting on a rabbit-skin cap with hanging lappets which covered the ears, so that no part of him was visible save his mobile and peaky face.

"My health is somewhat fragile," he remarked as he led the way down the passage. "I am compelled to be a **valetudinarian**[42]."

珍珠,这样至少她就永远不会过穷日子了。"

"心眼真好,"我的同伴认真地说,"你这人特别好。"

这个矮小男人不以为然地挥了挥手。

"我们是你们的托管人,"他说,"这是我所持的观点,尽管巴塞洛缪哥不可能完全这样看。我们自己有很多钱。我不想要更多。再说,如此卑鄙对待这位年轻小姐一定会是低级趣味。'鄙俗乃罪恶之源。'法国人对这种事说得非常简洁明了。我们对这个话题意见分歧很大,所以我认为最好为自己另找房间住,于是就带着印度老仆人和威廉斯离开了樱塘别墅。然而,昨天我听说发生了一件极其重要的事儿。财宝已被发现。我马上和摩斯坦小姐取得了联系,只剩下我们驱车到诺伍德向他要我们那份财宝。我昨晚已经向巴塞洛缪哥解释过我的观点。所以即使我们不受欢迎,他也会希望我们去。"

撒迪厄斯·肖尔托先生结束谈话,坐在豪华靠背长椅上抽搐着。我们大家仍然沉默不语,思想都集中在这个神秘事件的新进展上。福尔摩斯首先站了起来。

"先生,你从头到尾做得都非常好,'他说,'也许我们能弄清你还不知道的事儿,对你进行一些小小的报答。但是,就像摩斯坦小姐刚才说的那样,时间不早了,我们最好赶快把这件事进行到底。"

我们的新朋友小心翼翼地卷起水烟壶烟管,从帘子后面拿出一件俄国羔皮领袖、饰有盘花钮扣的长夹大衣。尽管夜里特别闷热,但他还是扣紧钮扣,最后戴上兔皮帽子,帽子的垂片盖住了耳朵,因此除了他富有表情的瘦脸,他身体任何部分都看不见。

"我的健康状况不太好,"他领着我们顺着通道前行时说,"我被迫成了一个为健康状况过分担忧的人。"

四签名

Our cab was awaiting us outside, and our programme was evidently prearranged, for the driver started off at once at a rapid pace. Thaddeus Sholto talked incessantly in a voice which rose high above the rattle of the wheels.

"Bartholomew is a clever fellow," said he. "How do you think he found out where the treasure was? He had come to the conclusion that it was somewhere indoors, so he worked out all the cubic space of the house and made measurements everywhere so that not one inch should be unaccounted for. Among other things, he found that the height of the building was seventy-four feet, but on adding together the heights of all the separate rooms and making every allowance for the space between, which he ascertained by borings, he could not bring the total to more than seventy feet. There were four feet unaccounted for. These could only be at the top of the building. He knocked a hole, therefore, in the lath and plaster ceiling of the highest room, and there, sure enough, he came upon another little **garret**[43] above it, which had been sealed up and was known to no one.

In the centre stood the treasure-chest resting upon two rafters. He lowered it through the hole, and there it lies. He **computes**[44] the value of the jewels at not less than half a million sterling."

At the mention of this gigantic sum we all stared at one another open-eyed. Miss Morstan, could we **secure**[45] her rights, would change from a needy governess to the richest heiress in England. Surely it was the place of a loyal friend to rejoice at such news, yet I am ashamed to say that selfishness took me by the soul and that my heart turned as heavy as lead within me. I stammered out some few halting words of congratulation and then sat downcast, with my head drooped, deaf to the **babble**[46] of our new acquaintance. He was clearly a confirmed **hypochondriac**[47], and I was dreamily conscious that he was pouring forth **interminable**[48] trains of symptoms, and imploring information as to the composition and action of innumerable quack **nostrums**[49], some of which he bore about in a leather case in his pocket. I trust that he may not remember any of the answers which I gave him that night. Holmes declares that he overheard me caution him against the great danger of taking more than two drops of castor-oil, while I recommended **strychnine**[50] in large doses as a **sedative**[51].

我们的马车等在外面,对我们的出行显然预先作了安排,因为车夫马上出发,快速行驶起来。撒迪厄斯·肖尔托不停地说话,声音高过了车轮的卡嗒声。

"巴塞洛缪是一个聪明人,"他说,"你们认为他是如何找到财宝下落的呢?他最后得出结论,认为财宝藏在屋里某个地方,于是他算出了这座房子的所有体积,丈量了每个地方,每一英寸都计算在内。其中,他发现这座建筑高74英尺,但他把所有各个房间高度都加在一起,并通过钻孔确定并减去楼板厚度,总共不过70英尺。还有4英尺没有计入。这4英尺只能在房顶。因此,他在最高一层房间的板条和灰泥天花板上打了一个洞,果然在那里找到了一个无人知道的封闭小顶楼。那只财宝箱就放在天花板中央的两根橡木上。他把财宝箱从洞口取下来,财宝就在那里。他计算了一下,那些珠宝价值至少50万英镑。"

说到这个巨大金额,我们都瞪大眼睛,面面相觑。如果我们能让摩斯坦小姐获得自己的权利,她会从一个贫困的家庭教师一下变成英国最富的继承人。当然,忠实的朋友对这样的消息会非常高兴,但我非常惭愧地说,自私占有了我的灵魂,我心里沉得像有一块铅似的。我结结巴巴地说了几句祝贺的话,然后坐在那里垂头丧气,后来对新朋友说的话也充耳不闻。他显然是一个慢性忧郁症患者。我恍惚意识到他一口气说出了一连串症状,并从他的皮夹里拿出了无数秘方,恳求我对他这些秘方的成分和作用进行解释。我相信他可能没有记住我那天夜里对他的那些回答。福尔摩斯宣称他无意中听到我叮嘱他服用两滴以上蓖麻油有巨大危险,同时建议他服用大剂量士的宁作

However that may be, I was certainly relieved when our cab pulled up with a jerk and the coachman sprang down to open the door.

"This, Miss Morstan, is Pondicherry Lodge," said Mr. Thaddeus Sholto as he handed her out.

为镇定剂。无论可能是什么,当我们的马车颠簸了一下停下来,车夫跳下来,打开车门时,我确实松了口气。

"摩斯坦小姐,这就是樱塘别墅,"撒迪厄斯·肖尔托先生扶她下车时说。

Notes:
1. writhe *vt.* 缠结，缠绕
2. perpetual *adj.* 不断的；不停的
3. obtrusive *adj.* （难看得）刺眼的；过分炫耀的
4. amber *n.* 琥珀（色）
5. athwart *prep.* 横过；逆；相反
6. hookah *n.* 水烟袋
7. aromatic *adj.* 芳香的；有香味的
8. stethoscope *n.* 听诊器
9. grave *adj.* （指情况）严重的
10. mitral valve *n.* 僧帽瓣；二尖瓣
11. aortic *adj.* 大动脉的
12. ecstasy *n.* 恍惚忘形；精神昏迷
13. unwarranted *adj.* 没有根据的；无正当理由的
14. callous *adj.* 无情的；无感觉的（to）；无同情心的（to）
15. Chianti *n.* （意大利）基安蒂红葡萄酒
16. sedative *n.* 镇静药；镇静剂
17. discretion *n.* 慎重；谨慎；判断（力）；辨别（力）
18. precaution *n.* 谨慎；预防措施（方法）
19. unaesthetic *adj.* 无美感的；缺乏美感的
20. connoisseur *n.* 鉴赏家；鉴定家；行家
21. speculation *n.* 思考；推测
22. prize-fighter *n.* 职业拳击手
23. aversion *n.* 厌恶；讨厌；反感
24. canvass for 游说
25. spleen *n.* 脾（脏）
26. beseech *vt.* 哀求；恳求
27. chaplet *n.* 念珠；项圈
28. hue *n.* 色彩；色调
29. sahib *n.* 大人；老爷（旧时印度人对欧洲人的尊称）
30. dispose of 解决；处理；除掉
31. restitution *n.* 归还原主；赔偿；补偿

32. malevolence *n.* 恶意；恶毒；怨恨

33. conjure up 凭幻想做出；想象出

34. haunt *vt.* 缠住（某人）；常（在脑中）出现

35. sagacity *n.* 精明；精确的判断

36. detached *adj.* 孤立的；已拆下的

37. destitute *adj.* 赤贫的；贫苦的

38. deprecatingly *adv.* 不赞成地；恳求地

39. without delay 赶快；立刻

40. befrogged *adj.* 饰有盘花钮扣的

41. astrakhan *n.* 俄国羔皮；仿羊皮织物

42. valetudinarian *n.* 为健康过分担忧的人

43. garret *n.* 顶楼；阁楼

44. compute *vt.* 计算；估算

45. secure *vt.* 握紧；使安全；（使）获得

46. babble *n.* 听不清的声音；乱哄哄的说话声

47. hypochondriac *n.* 疑病（忧郁）症患者

48. interminable *adj.* 无止境的；冗长的

49. nostrum *n.* 骗人的疗法

50. strychnine *n.* 士的宁；马钱子碱

51. sedative *n.* 镇静药；镇静剂

# Chapter 5

## THE TRAGEDY OF PONDICHERRY LODGE

## 第五章

### 樱塘别墅惨案

It was nearly eleven o'clock when we reached this final stage of our night's adventures. We had left the damp fog of the great city behind us, and the night was fairly fine. A warm wind blew from the westward, and heavy clouds moved slowly across the sky, with half a moon peeping occasionally through the rifts. It was clear enough to see for some distance, but Thaddeus Sholto took down one of the side-lamps from the carriage to give us a better light upon our way.

Pondicherry Lodge stood in its own grounds and was girt round with a very high stone wall topped with broken glass. A single narrow iron-clamped door formed the only means of entrance. On this our guide knocked with a peculiar postman-like **rat-tat**[1].

"Who is there?" cried a gruff voice from within.

"It is I, McMurdo. You surely know my knock by this time."

There was a grumbling sound and a clanking and jarring of keys. The door swung heavily back, and a short, deep-chested man stood in the opening, with the yellow light of the lantern shining upon his **protruded**[2] face and twinkling, distrustful eyes.

"That you, Mr. Thaddeus? But who are the others? I had no orders about them from the master."

"No, McMurdo? You surprise me! I told my brother last night that I should bring some friends."

"He hain't been out o' his rooms to-day, Mr. Thaddeus, and I have no orders. You know very well that I must stick to regulations. I can let you in, but your friends they must just stop where they are."

This was an unexpected obstacle. Thaddeus Sholto looked about him in a perplexed and helpless manner.

"This is too bad of you, McMurdo!" he said. "If I **guarantee**[3] them, that is enough for you. There is the young lady, too. She cannot wait on the public road at this hour."

"Very sorry, Mr. Thaddeus," said the porter **inexorably**[4]. "Folk may be friends o' yours, and yet no friend o' the master's. He pays me well to do my duty, and my duty I'll do. I don't know none o' your friends."

当我们到达今晚冒险历程的这个最后阶段时,已经快 11 点了。我们已经把大城市的湿雾留在了身后,夜色相当晴朗。一阵暖风从西面吹来,乌云慢慢地移过天空,半圆的月亮偶尔透过云层的缝隙窥视。天清气朗,足以看到远处,但撒迪厄斯·肖尔托还是从马车上拿下一盏侧灯,更好地给我们照路。

樱塘别墅位于自己的场地,四周围着高高的石墙,墙头上插着碎玻璃。一扇狭窄的铁皮门是唯一的入口。我们的向导以邮递员的独特方式砰砰敲门。

"是谁呀?"一个粗暴的声音从里面问道。

"是我,麦克默多。你肯定知道这时候是我敲门。"

里面传来了抱怨声和钥匙的丁当声。门沉重地向后打开,随后一名个子矮小、胸部厚实的人站在门口,灯笼的黄色光亮照在他突出的脸上和两只闪烁多疑的眼睛上。

"撒迪厄斯先生,是你吗?可是,其他人都是谁?我没有得到主人对这些人的盼咐。"

"没有盼咐,麦克默多?你真让我吃惊!我昨晚告诉过哥哥说我要带几位朋友来。"

"撒迪厄斯先生,他今天没有出房间,我也没有得到任何盼咐。你非常清楚我必须遵守规矩。我可以让你进来,但你的朋友们必须呆在原地。"

这是意想不到的障碍。撒迪厄斯·肖尔托神情困惑,无奈地看了看四周。

"麦克默多,你太坏了!"他说,"如果我为他们担保,这就足够了。这里还有一位小姐,她现在不能待在大街上。"

"撒迪厄斯先生,非常抱歉,"守门人铁面无私地说,"这些人可能是你的朋友,但不是主人的朋友。他给我开的工钱不少,就是让我尽责,所以我一定要尽职。我不认识你的任何朋友。"

四签名

"Oh, yes you do, McMurdo," cried Sherlock Holmes **genially**[5]. "I don't think you can have forgotten me. Don't you remember that amateur who fought three rounds with you at Alison's rooms on the night of your benefit four years back?"

"Not Mr. Sherlock Holmes!" roared the prize-fighter. "God's truth! How could I have mistook you? If instead o' standin' there so quiet you had just stepped up and given me that cross-hit of yours under the jaw, I'd ha' known you without a question. Ah, you're one that has wasted your gifts, you have! You might have aimed high, if you had joined the fancy."

"You see, Watson, if all else fails me, I have still one of the scientific professions open to me," said Holmes, laughing. "Our friend won't keep us out in the cold now, I am sure."

"In you come, sir, in you come—you and your friends," he answered. "Very sorry, Mr. Thaddeus, but orders are very strict. Had to be certain of your friends before I let them in."

Inside, a gravel path wound through desolate grounds to a huge **clump**[6] of a house, square and prosaic, all plunged in shadow save where a moonbeam struck one corner and glimmered in a garret window. The vast size of the building, with its gloom and its deathly silence, struck a chill to the heart. Even Thaddeus Sholto seemed ill at ease, and the lantern quivered and rattled in his hand.

"I cannot understand it," he said. "There must be some mistake. I **distinctly**[7] told Bartholomew that we should be here, and yet there is no light in his window. I do not know what to make of it."

"Does he always guard the **premises**[8] in this way?" asked Holmes.

"Yes; he has followed my father's custom. He was the favourite son you know, and I sometimes think that my father may have told him more than he ever told me. That is Bartholomew's window up there where the moonshine strikes. It is quite bright, but there is no light from within, I think."

"None," said Holmes. "But I see the glint of a light in that little window beside the door."

"Ah, that is the housekeeper's room. That is where old Mrs.

"噢，不，你认识，麦克默多，"夏洛克·福尔摩斯和蔼地喊道，"我想你不可能忘了我吧。你不记得4年前你义赛那天夜里在艾莉森的场地和你打过3个回合的那个业余赛手了吗？"

"不会是夏洛克·福尔摩斯先生吧！"这个职业拳击手吼道，"天经地义！我怎么能认不出你呢？如果你不是安静地站在那里，而是干脆走上来给我的下颏一个钩拳，那我肯定就认识你了。啊，你是一个浪费了自己天才的人，浪费了！如果你继续那样的爱好，你说不定会目标高远。"

"华生，你明白，即使我其他所有的一切都失败，还有一种科学职业对我敞开，"福尔摩斯笑道，"我相信，我们的朋友不会现在让我们在外面挨冻。"

"进来，先生，进来——你和你的朋友们，"他回答说，"撒迪厄斯先生，非常抱歉，但主人命令很严。必须确信你的朋友是谁，我才能让他们进来。"

里面有一条碎石小路蜿蜒穿过荒凉的地面，通向隐在巨大树丛里的一座形状方正、平淡无奇的房子。房子都陷入阴影，只有一束月光照到房子的一角，在阁楼顶小窗闪烁。这样巨大的房子阴沉死寂，让人不寒而栗。就连撒迪厄斯·肖尔托都好像心神不安，所以灯笼在他手里颤抖作响。

"我不明白，"他说，"一定出了毛病。我清楚告诉过巴塞洛缪，我们要来这里，但他的窗户却没有灯光。我不知道对此作何解释。"

"他总是这样守卫房子吗？"福尔摩斯问道。

"是的，他遵循了我父亲的习惯。你知道，他是我父亲的爱子，我有时认为，我的父亲告诉他的话可能比告诉我的多。那上面月光照耀的就是巴塞洛缪的窗户。窗户相当亮，但我想里面没有灯光。"

"没有灯光，"福尔摩斯说，"但我看到门边那个小窗里有闪亮的灯光。"

"啊，那是女管家的房间，是伯恩斯通老太太坐的地方。她可以告诉我们所

四签名

Bernstone sits. She can tell us all about it. But perhaps you would not mind waiting here for a minute or two, for if we all go in together, and she has had no word of our coming, she may be alarmed. But, hush! what is that?"

He held up the lantern, and his hand shook until the circles of light flickered and wavered all round us. Miss Morstan seized my wrist, and we all stood, with thumping hearts, straining our ears. From the great black house there sounded through the silent night the saddest and most pitiful of sounds—the shrill, broken **whimpering**[9] of a frightened woman.

"It is Mrs. Bernstone," said Sholto. "She is the only woman in the house. Wait here. I shall be back in a moment."

He hurried for the door and knocked in his peculiar way. We could see a tall old woman admit him and sway with pleasure at the very sight of him.

"Oh, Mr. Thaddeus, sir, I am so glad you have come! I am so glad you have come, Mr. Thaddeus, sir!"

We heard her **reiterated**[10] rejoicings until the door was closed and her voice died away into a muffled **monotone**[11].

Our guide had left us the lantern. Holmes swung it slowly round and peered keenly at the house and at the great rubbish-heaps which cumbered the grounds. Miss Morstan and I stood together, and her hand was in mine. A wondrous subtle thing is love, for here were we two, who had never seen each other before that day, between whom no word or even look of affection had ever passed, and yet now in an hour of trouble our hands instinctively sought for each other. I have marvelled at it since, but at the time it seemed the most natural thing that I should go out to her so, and, as she has often told me, there was in her also the instinct to turn to me for comfort and protection. So we stood hand in hand like two children, and there was peace in our hearts for all the dark things that surrounded us.

"What a strange place!" she said, looking round.

"It looks as though all the moles in England had been let loose in it. I have seen something of the sort on the side of a hill near Ballarat, where the

有的一切。但是，也许你们不介意在这里等候一两分钟，因为如果我们都一块进去，而她事先没有得到我们要来的消息，也许她会惊慌。可是，嘘！那是什么？"

他举起灯笼，那只手抖动，直到光圈闪烁，在我们周围摇曳起来。摩斯坦小姐抓住我的手腕，我们都站在那里，心咚咚直跳，侧耳倾听。夜深人静，从这座巨大的黑房子里传来最伤心最可怜的声音——那是一个受惊女人断断续续、声音尖锐的呜咽。

"这是伯恩斯通太太的声音，"肖尔托说，"她是这座房子里唯一的女人。等在这里。我去去就来。"

他匆匆赶向门口，用特有的方式敲门。我们可以看到一位高个子老妇人一看到他，就把他让了进去，高兴得左右摇动。

"噢，撒迪厄斯先生，你来了真让人高兴！你来了真让人高兴，撒迪厄斯先生！"

我们听到她反复说这些喜庆话，直到门关上后，她的声音才渐渐消失，变成了受压抑似的单音。

向导给我们留下了灯笼。福尔摩斯慢慢地摇晃着，目光敏锐地窥视着房子和堆积在地上的大堆垃圾。我和摩斯坦小姐站在一起，她的手放在我的手里。爱情是一件奇妙敏感的东西，因为这里就我们俩，那天之前我们从来没有相互见过面，双方没有说过一句话，甚至没有传递过爱意的神情，而如今在危急时刻，我们的手本能地寻找对方。我对此曾经感到惊奇，但当时我那样向往她，仿佛是最自然的事儿，而且像她经常告诉我的那样，为了得到安慰和保护，她也本能地转向我。所以，我们像两个小孩子似的手拉手站在那里，对我们周围所有黑暗的东西内心平静。

"多么奇怪的一个地方！"她环顾四周说。

"好像英国所有的鼹鼠都已经放到了这里。我曾经在巴拉莱特附近的山

prospectors had been at work."

"And from the same cause," said Holmes. "These are the traces of the treasure-seekers. You must remember that they were six years looking for it. No wonder that the grounds look like a gravel-pit."

At that moment the door of the house burst open, and Thaddeus Sholto came running out, with his hands thrown forward and terror in his eyes.

"There is something amiss with Bartholomew!" he cried. "I am frightened! My nerves cannot stand it."

He was, indeed, half blubbering with fear, and his twitching, feeble face peeping out from the great astrakhan collar had the helpless, **appealing**[12] expression of a terrified child.

"Come into the house," said Holmes in his **crisp**[13], firm way.

"Yes, do!" pleaded Thaddeus Sholto. "I really do not feel equal to giving directions."

We all followed him into the housekeeper's room, which stood upon the left-hand side of the passage. The old woman was pacing up and down with a scared look and restless, picking fingers, but the sight of Miss Morstan appeared to have a **soothing**[14] effect upon her.

"God bless your sweet, calm face!" she cried with a hysterical sob. "It does me good to see you. Oh, but I have been sorely tried this day!"

Our companion patted her thin, work-worn hand and murmured some few words of kindly, womanly comfort which brought the colour back into the other's bloodless cheeks.

"Master has locked himself in and will not answer me," she explained. "All day I have waited to hear from him, for he often likes to be alone; but an hour ago I feared that something was amiss, so I went up and peeped through the keyhole. You must go up, Mr. Thaddeus—you must go up and look for yourself. I have seen Mr. Bartholomew Sholto in joy and in sorrow for ten long years, but I never saw him with such a face on him as that."

Sherlock Holmes took the lamp and led the way, for Thaddeus Sholto's teeth were chattering in his head. So shaken was he that I had to pass my hand under his arm as we went up the stairs, for his knees were trembling under

边看到过这种情景,因为那些探矿者曾经在那里工作过。"

"也是出于相同的原因,"福尔摩斯说。"这些是寻找财宝者留下的痕迹。你一定要记住,他们寻找了6年。难怪地面看上去像砂砾坑一样。"

这时,房门突然打开,撒迪厄斯·肖尔托跑出来,两手伸向前,眼里充满了恐惧。

"巴塞洛缪出事了!"他叫道,"吓死我了!我的神经受不了了。"

他的确吓得连哭带说,他从俄国羔皮大领子里露出的颤摇虚弱的脸上,带着像受到惊吓的小孩子那样无助的哀求神情。

"进屋,"福尔摩斯坚决干脆地说。

"对,进屋!"撒迪厄斯恳求道,"我真不知道怎么办。"

我们都跟随他走进位于通道左边的女管家的房间。老太太正带着恐惧的神情走来走去,手指不停地哆嗦着,但摩斯坦小姐的出现仿佛对她产生了安慰作用。

"上帝保佑你这张可爱镇静的脸!"她带着歇斯底里的哭诉喊道,"看到你,我好受了些。噢,我这一天真难熬啊!"

我们的同伴拍了拍她因劳作而磨损的瘦手,低声说了几句温和安慰的话,这使老太太苍白的脸颊又恢复了颜色。

"主人把自己锁进屋里,叫他也不给我开门,"她解释说,"我已经等了整整一天,想听到他的吩咐,因为他经常喜欢独自一人,但一小时前,我担心出了事,所以就上楼,透过钥匙孔向里看。你一定要上去,撒迪厄斯先生——你一定要上去亲自看一下。长达10年来,无论巴塞洛缪先生是喜是悲,我都看到过,但我从来没有看到过他这样的面孔。"

夏洛克·福尔摩斯提着灯在前面领路。撒迪厄斯·肖尔托牙齿得得打战,两膝颤抖,猛烈摇晃,所以上楼时,我不得不搀扶他。我们上楼时,福尔摩

him. Twice as we **ascended**[15], Holmes **whipped**[16] his lens out of his pocket and carefully examined marks which appeared to me to be mere shapeless **smudges**[17] of dust upon the cocoanut-matting which served as a stair-carpet. He walked slowly from step to step, holding the lamp low, and shooting keen glances to right and left. Miss Morstan had remained behind with the frightened housekeeper.

The third flight of stairs ended in a straight passage of some length, with a great picture in Indian **tapestry**[18] upon the right of it and three doors upon the left. Holmes advanced along it in the same slow and methodical way, while we kept close at his heels, with our long black shadows streaming backward down the corridor. The third door was that which we were seeking. Holmes knocked without receiving any answer, and then tried to turn the handle and force it open. It was locked on the inside, however, and by a broad and powerful bolt, as we could see when we set our lamp up against it. The key being turned, however, the hole was not entirely closed. Sherlock Holmes bent down to it and instantly rose again with a sharp intaking of the breath.

"There is something devilish in this, Watson," said he, more moved than I had ever before seen him. "What do you make of it?"

I stooped to the hole and recoiled in horror. Moonlight was streaming into the room, and it was bright with a vague and shifty radiance. Looking straight at me and suspended, as it were, in the air, for all beneath was in shadow, there hung a face—the very face of our companion Thaddeus. There was the same high, shining head, the same circular bristle of red hair, the same bloodless **countenance**[19]. The features were set, however, in a horrible smile, a fixed and unnatural grin, which in that still and moonlit room was more jarring to the nerves than any scowl or contortion. So like was the face to that of our little friend that I looked round at him to make sure that he was indeed with us. Then I recalled to mind that he had mentioned to us that his brother and he were twins.

"This is terrible!" I said to Holmes. "What is to be done?"

"The door must come down," he answered, and springing against it, he put all his weight upon the lock.

It creaked and groaned but did not yield. Together we flung ourselves upon

斯两次突然从口袋里拿出放大镜，仔细查看痕迹。在我看来，这不过是留在用作楼梯地毯的可可垫子上的不定形状的尘迹。他慢慢地拾级而上，把灯提得很低，敏锐地飞快扫视左右。摩斯坦小姐和惊恐的女管家留在后面。

第三段楼梯尽头是一条长长的笔直通道，右边挂着一条带有名画的印度挂毯，左边有三个门。福尔摩斯继续一边慢慢前进，一边系统观察。我们紧随其后，我们长长的黑影落在身后的走廊上。第三个门就是我们要找的那扇门。福尔摩斯敲门，没有得到任何回应。他又试着旋转门把手，强行打开门。然而，门从里面锁上了，而且当我们把灯靠近照时，可以看到还插着又宽又粗的门闩。不过，尽管钥匙扭转，但钥匙孔没有完全封闭。夏洛克·福尔摩斯弯腰贴近钥匙孔看了看，马上又站起来，突然倒吸了口气。

"华生，这里真可怕，"我以前从来没有看到过他这样激动过，他说，"你对此会作何解释？"

我弯腰从钥匙孔向里看，吓得连连后退。月光溪流般照进房间，房间因一种模糊变化的光辉而明亮。一张脸直盯着我，仿佛悬挂在空中，因为脸以下的所有部分都处在阴影里。这张脸正是我们的同伴撒迪厄斯的脸。同样又高又亮的秃顶，同样一圈短粗的红发，同样没有血色的面容。然而，面部表情固定，呈现出一种可怕的狞笑，一种固定奇异的露齿而笑。在这样静寂和月光照耀的房间里，这种笑容比愁眉苦脸或面部扭曲更让人毛骨悚然。那张脸和我们那个矮小朋友的脸如此相像，所以我回头想确定他的确和我们在一起。随后，我想起了他曾经对我们提起过他和哥哥是孪生兄弟。

"这真可怕！"我向福尔摩斯说，"该怎么办？"

"门一定要打开，"他回答说，然后扑到门上，把全身重量都压在了锁上。门嘎嘎吱吱响了一阵，但没有打开。我们再次一起扑上去，这次突然砰

it once more, and this time it gave way with a sudden snap, and we found ourselves within Bartholomew Sholto's chamber.

It appeared to have been fitted up as a chemical laboratory. A double line of glass-stoppered bottles was drawn up upon the wall opposite the door, and the table was littered over with Bunsen burners, test-tubes, and retorts. In the corners stood carboys of acid in wicker baskets. One of these appeared to leak or to have been broken, for a stream of dark-coloured liquid had trickled out from it, and the air was heavy with a peculiarly **pungent**[20], tarlike odour. A set of steps stood at one side of the room in the midst of a litter of lath and plaster, and above them there was an opening in the ceiling large enough for a man to pass through. At the foot of the steps a long coil of rope was thrown carelessly together.

By the table in a wooden armchair the master of the house was seated all in a heap, with his head sunk upon his left shoulder and that ghastly, **inscrutable**[21] smile upon his face. He was stiff and cold and had clearly been dead many hours. It seemed to me that not only his features but all his limbs were twisted and turned in the most fantastic fashion. By his hand upon the table there lay a peculiar instrument—a brown, close-grained stick, with a stone head like a hammer, rudely lashed on with coarse twine. Beside it was a torn sheet of notepaper with some words scrawled upon it. Holmes glanced at it and then handed it to me.

"You see," he said with a significant raising of the eyebrows.

In the light of the lantern I read with a thrill of horror, "The sign of the four."

"In God's name, what does it all mean?" I asked.

"It means murder," said he, stooping over the dead man. "Ah! I expected it. Look here!"

He pointed to what looked like a long dark thorn stuck in the skin just above the ear.

"It looks like a thorn," said I.

"It is a thorn. You may pick it out. But be careful, for it is poisoned."

I took it up between my finger and thumb. It came away from the skin so readily that hardly any mark was left behind. One tiny speck of blood showed where the **puncture**[22] had been.

的一声门开了,我们进入了巴塞洛缪的房间。

这个房间装备得像是化学试验室。门对面的墙上摆有两排带玻璃塞的瓶子。桌子上摆满了本生灯、试管和曲颈瓶。墙角放有一些柳条筐,柳条筐里放有大玻璃瓶的酸。其中一瓶好像已经破裂,因为一股黑色液体已经从中一滴一滴流了出来。空气中充满了一种特别刺鼻的柏油一般的气味。房间的一边在一堆板条和灰泥中放着一副折梯,梯子上方的天花板有一个口子,大得可以穿过一个人。梯子底部有一长卷绳子,随便扔在一起。

桌边一把扶手木椅上坐着房子的主人,只见他坐成一堆,头凹陷在左肩上,脸上带着可怕费解的微笑。他僵硬冰冷,显然已经死去好多小时了。在我看来,不仅他的容貌,而且他的四肢都扭曲,以最奇异的方式翻转。他放在桌子上的那只手边放着一个奇特的器具——一根纹理细密的褐色木棍带有像锤子一样的基岩,用粗麻绳拙劣地捆扎着。旁边放着一张破旧的信纸,上边潦草地写着几个字。福尔摩斯扫了一眼,然后把它递给了我。

"你看看,"他意味深长地扬了扬眉说。

在灯笼的光亮中,我胆战心惊地看到了"四签名"。

"看在上帝的份上,这一切是怎么回事?"我问道。

"这意味着谋杀,"他弯腰看着死者身上说。

"谋杀!不出我所料!瞧这里!"

他指着扎在尸体耳朵正上方的一根黑色长刺。

"好像是一根刺,"我说。

"是一根刺。你可以把它拔出来。但是,要小心,因为这根刺有毒。"

我用拇指和食指夹住把它拔了出来。刺很容易就离开了皮肤,几乎没有留下什么痕迹。一点小小的血斑表明刺曾经所在的地方。

四签名

"This is all an insoluble mystery to me," said I. "It grows darker instead of clearer."

"On the contrary," he answered, "it clears every instant. I only require a few missing links to have an entirely connected case."

We had almost forgotten our companion's presence since we entered the chamber. He was still standing in the doorway, the very picture of terror, wringing his hands and moaning to himself. Suddenly, however, he broke out into a sharp, **querulous**[23] cry.

"The treasure is gone!" he said. "They have robbed him of the treasure! There is the hole through which we lowered it. I helped him to do it! I was the last person who saw him! I left him here last night, and I heard him lock the door as I came downstairs."

"What time was that?"

"It was ten o'clock. And now he is dead, and the police will be called in, and I shall be suspected of having had a hand in it. Oh, yes, I am sure I shall. But you don't think so, gentlemen? Surely you don't think that it was I? Is it likely that I would have brought you here if it were I? Oh, dear! oh, dear! I know that I shall go mad!"

He jerked his arms and stamped his feet in a kind of **convulsive**[24] **frenzy**[25].

"You have no reason for fear, Mr. Sholto," said Holmes kindly, putting his hand upon his shoulder; "take my advice and drive down to the station to report the matter to the police. Offer to assist them in every way. We shall wait here until your return."

The little man obeyed in a **half-stupefied**[26] fashion, and we heard him stumbling down the stairs in the dark.

"这件事对我完全是一个不解之谜，"我说，"它变得越来越模糊，而不是越来越清晰。"

"正好相反，"他回答说，"它每一刻都变得更加清晰。我只缺少几个环节，就可以完全把这个案子连起来了。"

自从走进房间以来，我们差不多已经忘记了我们同伴的存在。他仍然站在门口，还是那种惊恐的样子，一边绞手，一边对自己呻吟。然而，他突然尖声怒喊起来。

"财宝不见了！"他说，"他们已经抢走了他的财宝！我们就是从那个洞口把财宝拿下来的。是我帮他拿下来的！我是最后看到他的一个人！我昨晚离开他下楼时还听到他锁门。"

"那是几点钟？"

"10点钟。现在他死了，警察肯定会来，我肯定会被怀疑插手了这件事。噢，是的，我肯定被怀疑。可是，你们不这样认为吧，先生们？你们肯定不会认为是我吧？如果是我的话，我还有可能带你们来这里吗？天哪！天哪！我知道自己要疯了！"

在一阵痉挛狂怒中，他又是甩臂，又是跺脚。

"肖尔托先生，你没有任何害怕的理由，"福尔摩斯把一只手放在他的肩上亲切地说，"听我的建议，坐车去警察局报案。主动在各方面协助他们，我们在这里等你回来。"

这个矮小的男人半是麻木言听计从，随后我们听到他跟跟跄跄在黑暗中走下楼梯。

四签名

Notes:
1. rat-tat *n.* 砰砰声
2. protrude *vt.* （使某物）伸出；（使某物）突出
3. guarantee *vt.* 保证；担保
4. inexorable *adj.* 铁面无私的；残酷无情的
5. genially *adv.* 亲切地；和蔼地
6. clump *n.* 团；块
7. distinctly *adv.* 清楚地
8. premise *n.* 房屋（及其附属建筑；地基等）
9. whimper *vi.* （微弱或惊恐地）啜泣；鸣咽
10. reiterated *adj.* 反复的；重复的
11. monotone *n.* 单调
12. appealing *adj.* 哀诉似的；恳求似的
13. crisp *adj.* 干净利落的；简明扼要的
14. soothing *adj.* 抚慰的；使人宽心的
15. ascend *vi.* 上升；攀登
16. whip *vt.* 突然拿取
17. smudge *n.* （尤指因擦而形成的）污迹；污斑
18. tapestry *n.* 挂毯
19. countenance *n.* 面容；表情
20. pungent *adj.* （味道或气味）有刺激味的；刺鼻的
21. inscrutable *adj.* 费解的；莫测高深的
22. puncture *n.* （尖物刺成的）小孔
23. querulous *adj.* 暴躁的
24. convulsive *adj.* 痉挛性的
25. frenzy *n.* 狂乱；极度的激动
26. stupefy *vt.* 使发呆；使惊讶

# Chapter 6

## SHERLOCK HOLMES GIVES A DEMONSTRATION

# 第六章
夏洛克·福尔摩斯论证

"Now, Watson," said Holmes, rubbing his hands, "we have half an hour to ourselves. Let us make good use of it. My case is, as I have told you, almost complete; but we must not err on the side of overconfidence. Simple as the case seems now, there may be something deeper underlying it."

"Simple!" I **ejaculated**[1].

"Surely," said he with something of the air of a clinical professor expounding to his class. "Just sit in the corner there, that your footprints may not complicate matters. Now to work! In the first place, how did these folk come and how did they go? The door has not been opened since last night. How of the window?" He carried the lamp across to it, muttering his observations aloud the while but addressing them to himself rather than to me. "Window is **snibbed**[2] on the inner side. Frame-work is solid. No hinges at the side. Let us open it. No water-pipe near. Roof quite out of reach. Yet a man has mounted by the window. It rained a little last night. Here is the print of a foot in mould upon the sill. And here is a circular muddy mark, and here again upon the floor, and here again by the table. See here, Watson! This is really a very pretty demonstration."

I looked at the round, well-defined muddy discs.

"That is not a foot-mark," said I.

"It is something much more valuable to us. It is the impression of a wooden stump. You see here on the sill is the boot-mark, a heavy boot with a broad metal heel, and beside it is the mark of the timber-toe."

"It is the wooden-legged man."

"Quite so. But there has been someone else—a very able and efficient ally. Could you scale that wall, Doctor?"

I looked out of the open window. The moon still shone brightly on that angle of the house. We were a good sixty feet from the ground, and, look where I would, I could see no foothold, nor as much as a **crevice**[3] in the brickwork.

"It is absolutely impossible," I answered.

"Without aid it is so. But suppose you had a friend up here who lowered you this good stout rope which I see in the corner, securing one end of it to

"好了，华生，"福尔摩斯搓着手说，"我们还有半小时。让我们好好利用。我已经告诉过你，这个案子差不多要完成了，但我们不要犯过于自信的错误。尽管这个案子现在似乎简单，但说不定其中藏有更深奥的东西。"

"简单！"我突然喊道。

"当然简单，"他带着临床教授对全体学生讲解的口气说，"请坐在屋角，以免你的脚印会乱上加乱。现在工作吧！首先，这些人是怎么来的，又是怎么走的？房门从昨晚以来就没有打开过。窗户怎么样？"他把灯提过窗边，出声嘀咕自己的观察意见，与其说是对我说话，不如说是自言自语。"窗户是从里面插上的，窗框非常坚固，两边没有合叶。让我们把它打开。附近没有水管。房顶离得相当远。可是，有人曾经通过窗户爬上过房顶。昨晚下过一点雨。窗台这里有一个泥脚印。这里也有一个圆形泥印，地板上也有一个，桌边还有一个。华生，看这里！这真是一个相当贴切的证据。"

我看着那些明确的圆泥印。

"这不是脚印，"我说。

"这是对我们有价值多的证据。这是一根木桩的压痕。你看这窗台上是靴印，一只带有宽铁后跟的沉重靴子，旁边是木脚印。"

"就是那个木腿人。"

"正是这样。可是，还有一个人——一个非常称职能干的同伙。医生，你能爬上那面墙吗？"

我从敞开的窗户向外看。月光仍然明亮地照在那个屋角。我们离地足有60英尺，而且从我所在的地方望去，我看到能落脚的地方，连一条砖缝也没有。

"这绝对不可能，"我回答说。

"没有人帮忙，是不可能。但是，假如这里有你的一位朋友，用我在屋角看

四签名

this great hook in the wall. Then, I think, if you were an active man, you might swarm up, wooden leg and all. You would depart, of course, in the same fashion, and your ally would draw up the rope, untie it from the hook, shut the window, snib it on the inside, and get away in the way that he originally came. As a minor point, it may be noted," he continued, fingering the rope, "that our wooden-legged friend, though a fair climber, was not a professional sailor. His hands were far from horny. My lens discloses more than one blood-mark, especially towards the end of the rope, from which I gather that he slipped down with such **velocity**[4] that he took the skin off his hands."

"This is all very well," said I; "but the thing becomes more unintelligible than ever. How about this mysterious ally? How came he into the room?"

"Yes, the ally!" repeated Holmes **pensively**[5]. "There are features of interest about this ally. He lifts the case from the regions of the commonplace. I fancy that this ally breaks fresh ground in the **annals**[6] of crime in this country—though parallel cases suggest themselves from India and, if my memory serves me, from Senegambia."

"How came he, then?" I reiterated. "The door is locked; the window is inaccessible. Was it through the chimney?"

"The grate is much too small," he answered. "I had already considered that possibility."

"How, then?" I persisted.

"You will not apply my precept," he said, shaking his head. "How often have I said to you that when you have **eliminated**[7] the impossible, whatever remains, however improbable, must be the truth? We know that he did not come through the door, the window, or the chimney. We also know that he could not have been concealed in the room, as there is no concealment possible. Where, then, did he come?"

"He came through the hole in the roof!" I cried.

"Of course he did. He must have done so. If you will have the kindness to hold the lamp for me, we shall now extend our researches to the room above–the secret room in which the treasure was found."

到的这条结实的粗绳的一头牢住墙上这个大钩把你放下来,又会怎么样。那么,我想,如果你是一个精力充沛的人,就是装着木腿也可以爬上去。你离开时当然也可以采取同样的方式,你的同伙会拉上来绳子,从钩子上解下来,关上窗户,从里面插上插销,然后从来路逃之夭夭。作为次要的一点,也可以注意到,"他用手指抚摸着绳子继续说道,"尽管我们那个木腿朋友爬墙水平还可以,但不是职业水手。他的手毫不粗糙。我用放大镜发现了不止一个血迹,尤其是在绳子末端。我由此推断,他在以这种速度向下滑时,把手上的皮肤都磨掉了。"

"这都很好,"我说,"但事情变得比先前更加莫名其妙。这个神秘的同谋怎么样了呢?他又是怎么进了这个房间?"

"对,那个同伙!"福尔摩斯沉思着重复道,"这个同伙的容貌特征非常有趣。他把这个案子提升到了不平凡的领域。我想这个同盟在这个国家的犯罪编年史上开辟了新的天地——尽管类似的案例本身暗示来自印度,如果我没有记错的话,是来自塞内冈比亚。"

"那他是怎么来的呢?"我反复问道,"门锁着,窗户又够不着。难道是通过烟囱?"

"壁炉太小了,"他回答说。"我已经考虑到了那种可能性。"

"那是怎么进来的呢?"我坚持问道。

"你不愿应用我的规则,"他摇了摇头说,"我曾经对你说过多少次,当你排除了不可能的因素后,无论剩下的是什么,无论是多么不可能,那一定就是事实真相吗?我们知道,他不是从门、窗和烟囱进来的。我们也知道他不可能藏在屋里,因为屋里没有可能藏身的地方。那他是什么时候进来的呢?"

"他是从房顶那个洞进来的!"我大声说道。

"他当然是从那个洞进来的。他肯定是那样做的。如果你帮忙为我提着灯,

四签名

He mounted the steps, and, seizing a rafter with either hand, he swung himself up into the **garret**[8]. Then, lying on his face, he reached down for the lamp and held it while I followed him.

The chamber in which we found ourselves was about ten feet one way and six the other. The floor was formed by the rafters, with thin lath and plaster between, so that in walking one had to step from beam to beam. The roof ran up to an apex and was evidently the inner shell of the true roof of the house. There was no furniture of any sort, and the **accumulated**[9] dust of years lay thick upon the floor.

"Here you are, you see," said Sherlock Holmes, putting his hand against the sloping wall. "This is a trapdoor which leads out on to the roof. I can press it back, and here is the roof itself, sloping at a gentle angle. This, then, is the way by which Number One entered. Let us see if we can find some other traces of his individuality?"

He held down the lamp to the floor, and as he did so I saw for the second time that night a startled, surprised look come over his face. For myself, as I followed his gaze, my skin was cold under my clothes. The floor was covered thickly with the prints of a naked foot—clear, well-defined, perfectly formed, but scarce half the size of those of an ordinary man.

"Holmes," I said in a whisper, "a child has done this horrid thing."

He had recovered his self-possession in an instant.

"I was **staggered**[10] for the moment," he said, "but the thing is quite natural. My memory failed me, or I should have been able to foretell it. There is nothing more to be learned here. Let us go down."

"What is your theory, then, as to those footmarks?" I asked eagerly when we had regained the lower room once more.

"My dear Watson, try a little analysis yourself," said he with a touch of impatience. "You know my methods. Apply them, and it will be instructive to compare results."

"I cannot conceive anything which will cover the facts," I answered.

"It will be clear enough to you soon," he said, in an offhand way. "I think

我们现在就会把研究伸展到上面的房间——就是到发现财宝的那个秘密房间。"

他登上梯子，然后两手轮替抓住橡木，翻身上了屋顶层，接着俯面伸手接过灯，我也随着他上去。

我们所在的这个房间大约有 10 英尺长、6 英尺宽。地板是由橡木架成的，中间铺着薄板条和灰泥。因此，我们行走时不得不从一根一根橡木上跨过去。屋顶呈尖顶状，显然是房子真正屋顶的内层。没有任何种类的家具，多年的积尘在地板上落了厚厚一层。

"给，你看，"夏洛克·福尔摩斯一只手按在斜墙上说，"这是通向屋顶外面的暗门。我可以推开这个暗门，这里就是坡度和缓的屋顶本身。那么，第一个人就是从这里进来的。让我们看看是否能找到他个人特征的一些其他痕迹。"

他垂下灯，照着地板。他这样做时，我那天晚上第二次看到他脸上掠过了惊骇诧异的表情。对我本人来说，我随着他的目光望去，不由浑身发冷。地板上到处是赤足脚印——清楚、明确、完整，但不足平常人脚的一半大。

"福尔摩斯，"我轻声说道。"一个小孩子做了这样恐怖的事儿。"

他马上恢复了沉着冷静。

"我暂时吃了一惊，"他说，"但这件事相当自然。我忘记了，否则我原来是能预测到的。这里没有什么可再了解的了。我们下去吧。"

"那你对那些脚印有什么推测呢？"当我们又回到下面屋里时，我迫不及待地问道。

"我亲爱的华生，你自己试着作点儿分析吧，"他有点儿不耐烦地回答说。"你知道我的方法。如果应用这些方法，比较各种结果就会有所启发。"

"我想不出任何可以涵盖那些情况的东西，"我回答说。

"你马上就会足够明白了，"他不假思索地说，"我想这里没有什么别的

that there is nothing else of importance here, but I will look."

He whipped out his lens and a tape measure and hurried about the room on his knees, measuring, comparing, examining, with his long thin nose only a few inches from the **planks**[11] and his beady eyes gleaming and deep-set like those of a bird. So swift, silent, and furtive were his movements, like those of a trained **bloodhound**[12] picking out a scent, that I could not but think what a terrible criminal he would have made had he turned his energy and **sagacity**[13] against the law instead of **exerting**[14] them in its defence. As he hunted about, he kept muttering to himself, and finally he broke out into a loud crow of delight.

"We are certainly in luck," said he. "We ought to have very little trouble now. Number One has had the misfortune to tread in the creosote. You can see the outline of the edge of his small foot here at the side of this evil-smelling mess. The carboy has been cracked, you see, and the stuff has leaked out."

"What then?" I asked.

"Why, we have got him, that's all," said he.

"I know a dog that would follow that scent to the world's end. If a pack can track a trailed herring across a shire, how far can a specially trained hound follow so pungent a smell as this? It sounds like a sum in the **rule of three**[15]. The answer should give us the— But hallo! here are the **accredited**[16] representatives of the law."

Heavy steps and the **clamour**[17] of loud voices were audible from below, and the hall door shut with a loud crash.

"Before they come," said Holmes, "just put your hand here on this poor fellow's arm, and here on his leg. What do you feel?"

"The muscles are as hard as a board," I answered.

"Quite so. They are in a state of extreme contraction, far exceeding the usual rigor mortis. Coupled with this distortion of the face, this **Hippocratic**[18] smile, or 'risus sardonicus,' as the old writers called it, what conclusion would it suggest to your mind?"

"Death from some powerful vegetable alkaloid," I answered, "some

重要东西了，但我还要看看。"

他突然拿出放大镜和卷尺，跪在地上，在房间里匆匆行动起来，测量、比较和检查，细长的鼻子离地板只有几英寸，圆溜溜亮闪闪深陷的眼睛和鸟眼一样。他的动作如此迅速、寂静和鬼祟，就像训练有素正在寻找踪迹的警犬似的，所以我不禁想到，如果他把精力和睿智用于对抗法律而不是努力维护法律，他就会变成一个多么可怕的罪犯！他一边四处搜索，一边不断喃喃自语，最后突然发出了一阵响亮的欢叫。

"我们确实走运，"他说，"我们现在不应该有多少麻烦了。第一个人不幸踩在了木馏油上。你可以看到，在这乱七八糟难闻的东西旁边有他的小脚印的轮廓。你明白，大玻璃瓶已经破裂，里面的东西流了出来。"

"那又怎么样？"我问道。

"啊，我们已经抓住他了，"他说。

"我知道，一只狗会顺着气味找到天涯海角。如果一群猎犬能穿过一个郡追踪到一条被跟踪的鲱鱼，那么一条经过特殊训练的猎犬追踪这么强烈的气味能追多远呢？这听上去就像是比例运算法中的算术题。公认的法律代表们来了。"

下面传来了沉重的脚步声、谈话声，以及门厅响亮的关门声。

"在他们到来之前，"福尔摩斯说，"请把手放在这个可怜人的胳膊上，还有他这条腿上。你感觉如何？"

"肌肉坚硬得像木板一样，"我回答说。

"正是这样。它们处于极端收缩的状态，远远超过普通的尸僵。加上这种面部的扭曲，这种希波克拉底式样的微笑，或者老作家所称的'痉笑'，这会使你想起什么结论呢？"

"因某种强烈的植物性生物碱而死，"我回答说，"某种类似马钱子碱、

**strychnine**[19]-like substance which would produce tetanus."

"That was the idea which occurred to me the instant I saw the drawn muscles of the face. On getting into the room I at once looked for the means by which the poison had entered the system. As you saw, I discovered a thorn which had been driven or shot with no great force into the scalp. You observe that the part struck was that which would be turned towards the hole in the ceiling if the man were erect in his chair. Now examine this thorn."

I took it up gingerly and held it in the light of the lantern. It was long, sharp, and black, with a glazed look near the point as though some **gummy**[20] substance had dried upon it. The **blunt**[21] end had been trimmed and rounded off with a knife.

"Is that an English thorn?" he asked.

"No, it certainly is not."

"With all these data you should be able to draw some just inference. But here are the regulars, so the **auxiliary**[22] forces may beat a retreat."

As he spoke, the steps which had been coming nearer sounded loudly on the passage, and a very stout, portly man in a gray suit strode heavily into the room. He was red-faced, burly, and **plethoric**[23], with a pair of very small twinkling eyes which looked keenly out from between swollen and puffy pouches. He was closely followed by an inspector in uniform and by the still **palpitating**[24] Thaddeus Sholto.

"Here's a business!" he cried in a muffled, **husky**[25] voice. "Here's a pretty business! But who are all these? Why, the house seems to be as full as a rabbit-**warren**[26]!"

"I think you must recollect me, Mr. Athelney Jones," said Holmes quietly.

"Why, of course I do!" he **wheezed**[27]. "It's Mr. Sherlock Holmes, the theorist. Remember you! I'll never forget how you lectured us all on causes and inferences and effects in the Bishopgate jewel case. It's true you set us on the right track; but you'll own now that it was more by good luck than good guidance."

能造成破伤风的物质。"

"一看到他面部肌肉收缩,我就想到了这一点。走进房间后,我马上寻找毒物进入体内的途径。像你看到的那样,我发现一根刺不费多大力气就扎进或射入了他的头皮。你观察到,如果那个人直坐在椅子上,被击中的部位一定是朝向天花板的那个洞。现在仔细检查这根刺。"

我小心翼翼地把它拿起来,对着灯光看。这根刺又长又尖又黑,尖端附近有一层发亮的光泽,好像某种胶质的东西干在了上面。钝端被刀子修整成了圆形。

"那是英国刺吗?"他问道。

"不,肯定不是。"

"有了所有这些资料,你应该能得出某种合理的结论。但是,正规军来了,所以辅助部队可以撤退了。"

他说话时,越来越近的脚步声响彻在走廊上。一个非常壮实的灰衣胖子脚步沉重地走进了房间。他脸色发红,身材魁梧,血气旺盛,一双非常小的闪烁的眼睛从肿胀鼓起的眼泡之间向外敏锐地望着。他后面紧跟着一位穿制服的警官和仍在颤抖的撒迪厄斯·肖尔托。

"有事干了!"他用压抑沙哑的声音喊道。"这是一桩漂亮的案子!可这些人都是谁?啊,这房子里好像养兔场满满当当!"

"阿塞尔尼·琼斯先生,我想你一定还记得我,"福尔摩斯平静地说。

"啊,我当然记得!"他喘息着说,"你是理论家夏洛克·福尔摩斯先生。记得你!我永远不会忘记你在主教门珍宝案中如何向我们讲述起因、推论和结果。你确实把我们引入了正道,但你现在要承认,那是靠运气好,而不是指导好。"

四签名

"It was a piece of very simple reasoning."

"Oh, come, now, come! Never be ashamed to own up. But what is all this? Bad business! Bad business! Stern facts here—no room for theories. How lucky that I happened to be out at Norwood over another case! I was at the station when the message arrived. What d'you think the man died of?"

"Oh, this is hardly a case for me to theorize over," said Holmes dryly.

"No, no. Still, we can't deny that you hit the nail on the head sometimes. Dear me! Door locked, I understand. Jewels worth half a million missing. How was the window?"

"Fastened; but there are steps on the sill."

"Well, well, if it was fastened the steps could have nothing to do with the matter. That's common sense. Man might have died in a fit; but then the jewels are missing. Ha! I have a theory. These flashes come upon me at times.—Just step outside, Sergeant, and you, Mr. Sholto. Your friend can remain.—What do you think of this, Holmes? Sholto was, on his own confession, with his brother last night. The brother died in a fit, on which Sholto walked off with the treasure? How's that?"

"On which the dead man very considerately got up and locked the door on the inside."

"Hum! There's a flaw there. Let us apply common sense to the matter. This Thaddeus Sholto was with his brother; there was a quarrel: so much we know. The brother is dead and the jewels are gone. So much also we know. No one saw the brother from the time Thaddeus left him. His bed had not been slept in. Thaddeus is evidently in a most disturbed state of mind. His appearance is—well, not attractive. You see that I am weaving my web round Thaddeus. The net begins to close upon him."

"You are not quite in possession of the facts yet," said Holmes. "This splinter of wood, which I have every reason to believe to be poisoned, was in the man's scalp where you still see the mark; this card, inscribed as you see it, was on the table, and beside it lay this rather curious stone-headed instrument. How does all that fit into your theory?"

"那是一个非常简单的推理。"

"噢，得了，好了，算了！千万不要不好意思爽快承认。可这一切是怎么回事？太糟了！太糟了！严峻的事实都摆在这里——没有推测的空间。多么运气，我正好为了另一个案子到诺伍德来！消息来时，我正在局里。你认为这个人是怎么死的？"

"噢，这个案子几乎不需要我推理，"福尔摩斯枯燥无味地回答说。

"对，对。尽管如此，但我们不能否认，你有时正中要害。天哪！我明白，门锁着。价值50万英镑的珠宝丢失了。窗户是怎么回事？"

"窗户闩着，但窗台上有脚印。"

"好了，好了。如果窗户闩着，那些脚印可能就和这个案子没有任何关系。这是常识。这个人也许死于疾病发作，另一方面那些珠宝又不翼而飞。哈！我有了一种推测。有时我会产生这些灵感。——警官，请出去，还有你，肖尔托先生。你的朋友可以留下来。——福尔摩斯先生，你认为这是怎么回事？肖尔托自己承认昨晚和他的哥哥在一起。他的哥哥死于疾病发作，肖尔托就拿走了珠宝。这个想法怎么样？"

"死者生前考虑非常周到，起来从里面锁上了门。"

"嗯哼！这里有漏洞。让我们运用常识来对待这件事。这个撒迪厄斯·肖尔特曾经和他的哥哥在一起，他们发生过一场争吵，这我们知道。哥哥死了，珠宝丢了。这我们也知道。撒迪厄斯离开他后，没有人再看到过他的哥哥。他的床也没有人再睡过。撒迪厄斯显然处在极度不安的精神状态。他的外貌——也没有吸引力。你看我在撒迪厄斯四周布下了网。这张网开始对他收紧。"

"你还没有完全掌握那些情况，"福尔摩斯说，"我完全有理由相信这个木刺有毒，插进了死者的头皮，你仍会看到那个痕迹。你看，这张卡片是这

"Confirms it in every respect," said the fat detective **pompously**[28]. "House is full of Indian curiosities. Thaddeus brought this up, and if this splinter be poisonous Thaddeus may as well have made murderous use of it as any other man. The card is some **hocus-pocus**[29]—a blind, as like as not. The only question is, how did he depart? Ah, of course, here is a hole in the roof."

With great activity, considering his bulk, he sprang up the steps and squeezed through into the garret, and immediately afterwards we heard his exulting voice **proclaiming**[30] that he had found the trapdoor.

"He can find something," remarked Holmes, shrugging his shoulders; "he has occasional glimmerings of reason. *Il n'y a pas des sots si incommodes que ceux qui ont de l'esprit*!"

"You see!" said Athelney Jones, reappearing down the steps again; "facts are better than theories, after all. My view of the case is confirmed. There is a trapdoor communicating with the roof, and it is partly open."

"It was I who opened it."

"Oh, indeed! You did notice it, then?" He seemed a little **crestfallen**[31] at the discovery. "Well, whoever noticed it, it shows how our gentleman got away. Inspector!"

"Yes, sir," from the passage.

"Ask Mr. Sholto to step this way. —Mr. Sholto, it is my duty to inform you that anything which you may say will be used against you. I arrest you in the Queen's name as being concerned in the death of your brother."

"There, now! Didn't I tell you!" cried the poor little man, throwing out his hands and looking from one to the other of us.

"Don't trouble yourself about it, Mr. Sholto," said Holmes; "I think that I can engage to clear you of the charge."

"Don't promise too much, Mr. Theorist, don't promise too much!" snapped the detective. "You may find it a harder matter than you think."

"Not only will I clear him, Mr. Jones, but I will make you a free present of the name and description of one of the two people who were in this room last night. His name, I have every reason to believe, is Jonathan Small. He

样题写，放在桌子上，桌边还放着这根相当古怪的镶石工具。所有这一切是怎么适应你的理论呢？"

"各方面都会进一步证实，"这个胖侦探神气活现地说，"房子里都是印度古玩。撒迪厄斯提出了这一点，如果这个木刺有毒，撒迪厄斯可能也会和任何其他人一样利用它杀人。这张卡片是一种诡计——很可能是一种障眼法。唯一的问题是，他是怎么离开的呢？啊，当然，这个顶上有一个洞。"

他身体笨重，费了很大劲儿，才爬上梯子，挤过去，进入顶楼。随后，我们马上听到他欢叫着宣布说，他已经找到了暗门。

"他能发现一些东西，"福尔摩斯耸了耸肩说，"他偶尔也有理智的闪光。没有头脑的笨蛋更难相处！"

"你看！"阿塞尔尼·琼斯又从梯子上下来后说，"毕竟事实胜于理论。我对这个案子的看法得到了进一步证实。有一个暗门和屋顶相通，而且暗门部分打开。"

"暗门是我打开的。"

"噢，的确是！那你的确注意到了暗门吗？"他好像对这个发现有点儿垂头丧气，"啊，无论是谁注意到的，这都说明了我们那位先生是怎么逃走的。警官！"

走廊里传来了一个声音："是的，先生。"

"请肖尔托先生这边走。——肖尔托先生，我的责任就是告诉你，你说的任何话都可能对你不利。我以女王的名义逮捕你，因为你和你哥哥的死亡有牵连。"

"好了，好了！我不是告诉过你嘛！"这个可怜的矮小男人伸出双手，看看我们这个，瞧瞧我们那个。

"肖尔托先生，不要自寻烦恼，"福尔摩斯说，"我想我可以清除对你的指控。"

"理论家先生，不要承诺太多了，"这位侦探厉声说道，"你可能会发现这件事比你想的要难。"

"琼斯先生，我不仅要证明他无罪，而且要免费给你提供昨晚到这个房间的其中一人的姓名和特征。我有充分理由相信，他的名字叫乔纳森·斯莫尔。

四签名

is a poorly educated man, small, active, with his right leg off, and wearing a wooden stump which is worn away upon the inner side. His left boot has a coarse, square-toed sole, with an iron band round the heel. He is a middle-aged man, much sunburned, and has been a convict. These few indications may be of some assistance to you, coupled with the fact that there is a good deal of skin missing from the palm of his hand. The other man—"

"Ah! the other man?" asked Athelney Jones in a sneering voice, but impressed none the less, as I could easily see, by the **precision**[32] of the other's manner.

"Is a rather curious person," said Sherlock Holmes, turning upon his heel. "I hope before very long to be able to introduce you to the pair of them. A word with you, Watson."

He led me out to the head of the stair.

"This unexpected occurrence," he said, "has caused us rather to lose sight of the original purpose of our journey."

"I have just been thinking so," I answered; "it is not right that Miss Morstan should remain in this **stricken**[33] house."

"No. You must escort her home. She lives with Mrs. Cecil Forrester in Lower Camberwell, so it is not very far. I will wait for you here if you will drive out again. Or perhaps you are too tired?"

"By no means. I don't think I could rest until I know more of this fantastic business. I have seen something of the rough side of life, but I give you my word that this quick succession of strange surprises to-night has shaken my nerve completely. I should like, however, to see the matter through with you, now that I have got so far."

"Your presence will be of great service to me," he answered. "We shall work the case out independently and leave this fellow Jones to exult over any mare's-nest which he may choose to construct. When you have dropped Miss Morstan, I wish you to go on to No. 3 Pinchin Lane, down near the water's edge at Lambeth. The third house on the right-hand side is a bird-stuffer's; Sherman is the name. You will see a weasel holding a young rabbit in the window. Knock old Sherman up and tell him, with my compliments, that I want Toby at once. You will bring Toby back in the cab with you."

他受教育程度不高，矮小，灵活，右腿截去，安了一只木腿，木腿里侧已经磨损，左靴下面有一个粗糙的方形脚掌，后跟周围钉着铁箍。他是中年人，皮肤晒得黝黑，曾经当过囚犯。这几个迹象，加上他的手掌上有好多脱皮这一事实，可能对你有某种帮助。另一个人——"

"啊！另一个人？"阿塞尔尼·琼斯用轻蔑的声音问道，但我可以轻易看出，对方侦查的精确仍然深深打动了他。

"是一个相当古怪的人，"夏洛克·福尔摩斯转过身说，"我希望不久之后就能把这两个人介绍给你。华生，和你说句话。"

他把我领到楼梯口。

"这个意外事件，"他说，"已经使我们有点儿忘记了我们此行原来的目的。"

"我刚才一直在这样想，"我回答说，"摩斯坦小姐留在这个倒霉的房子里不合适。"

"对。你必须护送她回家。她和塞西尔·弗里斯特太太住在下坎伯威尔，所以离这里不很远。如果你愿意再驾车外出，我可以在这里等你。要么你可能太累了吧？"

"一点不累。我想，我要等了解到这件怪事的更多情况，才能休息。尽管我曾经见过生活艰难的一面，但我告诉你，今晚这一连串迅速发生的咄咄怪事，已经彻底动摇了我的勇气。然而，既然已经到了这个地步，我愿意和你一起了结这个案子。"

"你在场会对我有极大帮助，"他回答说。"我们要独立破这个案子，让琼斯这个人为他可能决定建造的不切实际的东西狂喜吧。你送完摩斯坦小姐后，我希望你到朗伯斯区河边附近的品钦巷3号去一下。一个做鸟类标本的在右边第三个房子。名字叫谢尔曼。你会看到窗户上画着一只黄鼠狼抓着一只小兔子。把老谢尔曼叫起来，告诉他，我问候他，马上要托比。你要坐车把托比带回来。"

四签名

"A dog, I suppose."

"Yes, a queer **mongrel**[34] with a most amazing power of scent. I would rather have Toby's help than that of the whole detective force of London."

"I shall bring him then," said I. "It is one now. I ought to be back before three if I can get a fresh horse."

"And I," said Holmes, "shall see what I can learn from Mrs. Bernstone and from the Indian servant, who, Mr. Thaddeus tells me, sleeps in the next garret. Then I shall study the great Jones's methods and listen to his not too delicate **sarcasms**[35]."

"'*Wir sind gewohnt, dass die Menschen verhönen was sie nicht verstehen.*'

"Goethe is always **pithy**[36]."

"我想，是一只狗吧。"

"是的，是一只奇特的杂种狗，嗅觉能力极其惊人。我宁愿让托比帮忙，也不愿让伦敦的所有侦探帮忙。"

"那我就把它带回来，"我说，"现在已经一点了。如果我能找到一匹马，3点前就应该赶回来。"

福尔摩斯说，"我还要看看能从伯恩斯通太太和印度仆人那里听到什么情况。撒迪厄斯先生告诉我说，那个仆人睡在隔壁的顶楼。随后，我要研究伟大琼斯的方法，听听他不太得体的挖苦。"

"'我们已经习以为常，有些人对他们不了解的事物偏要说三道四。'

"歌德总是简明扼要。"

四签名

Notes:
1. ejaculate *vt.* 突然说出
2. snib *vt.* 闩上（门或窗户）
3. crevice *n.*（尤指岩石的）裂缝；缺口
4. velocity *n.* 速度
5. pensively *adv.* 沉思地
6. annals *n.* 历史记录
7. eliminate *vt.* 排除
8. garret *n.* 顶楼；阁楼
9. accumulated *adj.* 堆积的；累积的
10. stagger *vt.* 使……感到震惊
11. plank *n.*（厚）木板
12. bloodhound *n.* 一种大侦探犬
13. sagacity *n.* 精明；精确的判断
14. exert *vt.* 运用；发挥
15. rule of three 比例法
16. accredited *adj.* 可接受的；可信任的；公认的
17. clamour *n.* 喧闹；大声的要求或抗议
18. Hippocratic *adj.* 希波克拉提斯的
19. strychnine *n.* 士的宁；马钱子碱
20. gummy *adj.* 胶粘的；粘性的；含有树胶的
21. blunt *adj.* 钝的
22. auxiliary *adj.* 辅助的
23. plethoric *adj.* 多血症的
24. palpitate *vi.* 颤动；发抖
25. husky *adj.* 喉咙发干的；嗓子哑的
26. rabbit-warren *n.* 养兔场
27. wheeze *vi.* 喘息；发出呼哧呼哧的喘息声
28. pompously *adv.* 傲慢地
29. hocus-pocus *n.* 哄骗；戏弄
30. proclaim *vt.* 正式宣布
31. crestfallen *adj.* 沮丧的；垂头丧气的

32. precision *n.* 精确度；准确（性）
33. stricken *adj.* 受灾的；遭损害的
34. mongrel *n.* 杂种狗
35. sarcasm *n.* 讥讽；讽刺；挖苦
36. pithy *adj.* 简练的；精辟的

# Chapter 7

## THE EPISODE OF THE BARREL

## 第七章

### 木桶的插曲

The police had brought a cab with them, and in this I escorted Miss Morstan back to her home. After the angelic fashion of women, she had borne trouble with a calm face as long as there was someone weaker than herself to support, and I had found her bright and **placid**[1] by the side of the frightened housekeeper. In the cab, however, she first turned faint and then burst into a passion of weeping—so sorely had she been tried by the adventures of the night. She has told me since that she thought me cold and distant upon that journey. She little guessed the struggle within my breast, or the effort of self-restraint which held me back. My sympathies and my love went out to her, even as my hand had in the garden. I felt that years of the **conventionalities**[2] of life could not teach me to know her sweet, brave nature as had this one day of strange experiences. Yet there were two thoughts which sealed the words of affection upon my lips. She was weak and helpless, shaken in mind and nerve. It was to take her at a disadvantage to obtrude love upon her at such a time. Worse still, she was rich. If Holmes's researches were successful, she would be an heiress. Was it fair, was it honourable, that a half-pay surgeon should take such advantage of an intimacy which chance had brought about? Might she not look upon me as a mere **vulgar**[3] fortune-seeker? I could not bear to risk that such a thought should cross her mind. This Agra treasure **intervened**[4] like an impassable barrier between us.

It was nearly two o'clock when we reached Mrs. Cecil Forrester's. The servants had retired hours ago, but Mrs. Forrester had been so interested by the strange message which Miss Morstan had received that she had sat up in the hope of her return. She opened the door herself, a middle-aged, graceful woman, and it gave me joy to see how tenderly her arm stole round the other's waist and how motherly was the voice in which she greeted her. She was clearly no mere paid **dependant**[5] but an honoured friend. I was introduced, and Mrs. Forrester earnestly begged me to step in and tell her our adventures. I explained, however, the importance of my errand and promised faithfully to call and report any progress which we might make with the case. As we drove away I stole a glance back, and I still seem to see that little group on the step—the two graceful, clinging figures, the half-

警察带来了一辆马车，于是我就坐进去，护送摩斯坦小姐回家。她按照女人天使般的风范，只要有比她更脆弱的人需要支持，她就会面色平静，忍受艰难。我发现她在惊恐的女管家身边欢快而平静。然而，她坐进马车后，先是变得无精打采，然后突然哭了起来。经过一夜的冒险经历，她经受了痛苦的考验。之后，她告诉我说，她认为我那一路上冷淡疏远。她完全没有想到我内心的斗争，也完全没有想到我用了多大自制力才控制住自己。甚至在花园里握手时，我就对她流露出了同情和爱。我感到，多年的人生惯例无法教会我知道她在这一天奇特经历中表现出的可爱勇敢的天性。然而，有两种想法封住了我的嘴，说不出情爱的话语。她软弱无助，思想上和神经上受到了震动。这种时候把爱情强加给她，那会是攻其不备。更糟的是，她有钱。如果福尔摩斯的研究成功，她就会成为继承人。一个拿半薪的外科医生利用这样凑巧的机会和她亲近，这公平吗？这体面吗？她会把我看成是一个纯粹的粗俗的淘金者吗？我不能忍受冒着让她产生这种想法的危险。这笔阿格拉财宝就像我们之间一道无法逾越的障碍。

我们到达塞西尔·弗里斯特太太家里时，差不多已经两点了。仆人们已经入睡几个小时了，但弗里斯特太太对摩斯坦小姐接到怪信这件事非常关心，所以她熬夜，希望摩斯坦小姐回来。是她亲自开门。她是一位优雅得体的中年女人。看到她是多么体贴地悄悄用胳膊搂着摩斯坦小姐的腰，听到她问候小姐时声音多么像母亲那样慈爱，这让我非常高兴。显然，摩斯坦小姐绝不仅仅是一个受雇用的人，而是一位受尊重的朋友。摩斯坦小姐介绍我后，弗里斯特太太诚恳请我进来，并把我们的奇遇告诉了她。然而，我解释我此行的重要性，并忠实答应会拜访她，汇报我们对案情的进展情况。我们驱车离开时，我偷偷回头瞥了一眼，仿佛看到两个紧紧依偎站在台阶上的优美身影、半开的房门、从

opened door, the hall-light shining through stained glass, the barometer, and the bright stair-rods. It was soothing to catch even that passing glimpse of a **tranquil**[6] English home in the midst of the wild, dark business which had absorbed us.

And the more I thought of what had happened, the wilder and darker it grew. I reviewed the whole extraordinary **sequence**[7] of events as I rattled on through the silent, gas-lit streets. There was the original problem: that at least was pretty clear now. The death of Captain Morstan, the sending of the pearls, the advertisement, the letter—we had had light upon all those events. They had only led us, however, to a deeper and far more tragic mystery. The Indian treasure, the curious plan found among Morstan's baggage, the strange scene at Major Sholto's death, the rediscovery of the treasure immediately followed by the murder of the discoverer, the very **singular**[8] accompaniments to the crime, the footsteps, the remarkable weapons, the words upon the card, corresponding with those upon Captain Morstan's chart—here was indeed a **labyrinth**[9] in which a man less singularly **endowed**[10] than my fellow-lodger might well despair of ever finding the clue.

Pinchin Lane was a row of shabby, two-storied brick houses in the lower quarter of Lambeth. I had to knock for some time at No. 3 before I could make any impression. At last, however, there was the glint of a candle behind the blind, and a face looked out at the upper window.

"Go on, you drunken **vagabond**[11]," said the face. "If you kick up any more row, I'll open the kennels and let out forty-three dogs upon you."

"If you'll let one out, it's just what I have come for," said I.

"Go on!" yelled the voice. "So help me gracious, I have a wiper in this bag, and I'll drop it on your 'ead if you don't hook it!"

"But I want a dog," I cried.

"I won't be argued with!" shouted Mr. Sherman. "Now stand clear; for when I say 'three,' down goes the wiper."

"Mr. Sherlock Holmes—" I began; but the words had a most magical effect, for the window instantly slammed down, and within a minute the door was unbarred and open. Mr. Sherman was a lanky, lean old man, with stooping

彩色玻璃射出来的门厅灯光、晴雨表，以及楼梯栏杆。在吸引我们的这个野蛮黑暗的事件中，即使飞快地看一眼宁静的英国家庭，也会让人宽心。

我对发生的情况越想越觉得野蛮黑暗。当马车咯哒咯哒穿过煤气灯照射的寂静街道时，我又回顾了一下整个奇异事件的进展。最初的问题至少现在相当清楚了。摩斯坦上尉之死、寄来的珍珠、那则启事和那封信——我们对所有那些事件都已经清楚了。然而，那些事件却把我们引向了更深入、更悲惨的迷案。印度的财宝、摩斯坦上尉行李中发现的古怪平面图、肖尔托少校临死时的奇异场景、财宝的重新发现、紧随其后发现财宝者的被害、伴随犯罪发生的那些怪事、那些脚印、异常的凶器，以及卡片上与摩斯坦上尉的图表上一致的文字——这的确像迷宫一样，如果没有和我的同房者那样奇异的天赋，就可能完全没有信心找到线索。

品钦巷位于朗伯斯区的较低区域，是一排破旧的两层砖房。我敲3号门敲了一段时间，才有人应声。然而，最后百叶窗后面出现了闪烁的烛光，一张脸从上面的窗户露出来。

"走开，你这喝醉的流浪汉，"那张脸说，"如果你再吵闹，我就打开狗窝，放出43条狗咬你。"

"如果你放出一条狗，我就是冲这个来的，"我说。

"走开！"那个声音大叫着说，"天哪，我这袋子里有一块抹布，如果你不赶快离开，我就扔到你的头上！"

"可我要狗，"我又叫道。

"我不和你争吵！"谢尔曼先生喊道，"马上站开。我说到'三'，就扔抹布。"

"夏洛克·福尔摩斯先生——"我开口说道，但这几个字具有极其迷人的效果，因为窗户立刻关上，不到一分钟就拔去门闩，打开了门。谢尔曼先

shoulders, a stringy neck, and blue-tinted glasses.

"A friend of Mr. Sherlock is always welcome," said he. "Step in, sir. Keep clear of the **badger**[12], for he bites. Ah, naughty, naughty; would you take a nip at the gentleman?" This to a stoat which thrust its wicked head and red eyes between the bars of its cage. "Don't mind that, sir; it's only a slowworm. It hain't got no fangs, so I gives it the run o' the room, for it keeps the beetles down. You must not mind my bein' just a little short wi' you at first, for I'm guyed at by the children, and there's many a one just comes down this lane to knock me up. What was it that Mr. Sherlock Holmes wanted, sir?"

"He wanted a dog of yours."

"Ah! that would be Toby."

"Yes, Toby was the name."

"Toby lives at No. 7 on the left here."

He moved slowly forward with his candle among the queer animal family which he had gathered round him. In the uncertain, shadowy light I could see dimly that there were glancing, glimmering eyes peeping down at us from every cranny and corner. Even the **rafters**[13] above our heads were lined by solemn fowls, who lazily shifted their weight from one leg to the other as our voices disturbed their slumbers.

Toby proved to be an ugly, long-haired, **lop-eared**[14] creature, half **spaniel**[15] and half **lurcher**[16], brown and white in colour, with a very clumsy, **waddling**[17] gait. It accepted, after some hesitation, a lump of sugar which the old naturalist handed to me, and, having thus sealed an alliance, it followed me to the cab and made no difficulties about accompanying me. It had just struck three on the Palace clock when I found myself back once more at Pondicherry Lodge. The ex-prize-fighter McMurdo had, I found, been arrested as an **accessory**[18], and both he and Mr. Sholto had been marched off to the station. Two constables guarded the narrow gate, but they allowed me to pass with the dog on my mentioning the detective's name.

Holmes was standing on the doorstep with his hands in his pockets, smoking his pipe.

生是一个身体瘦长的老头，肩膀耷拉，脖子青筋暴露，戴着蓝光眼镜。

"福尔摩斯先生的朋友一向受欢迎，"他说，"进来吧，先生。避开那只獾，它会咬人。啊，小讨厌，小讨厌，你会咬这位先生吗？"这是对一只白鼬说的，因为它从笼子的铁条之间伸出了邪恶的脑袋和两只红眼睛。"先生，不要管它，这不过是一只蛇蜥，没有毒牙，我让它在房间里跑动，它会吃掉甲虫。我起先对你有点儿粗暴无礼，不要介意，因为我常常受到孩子们戏弄，有许多孩子到这条小巷把我敲醒。夏洛克·福尔摩斯先生想要的是什么，先生？"

"他要你的一条狗。"

"啊！那一定是托比。"

"对，就是托比这个名字。"

"托比住在这左边7号。"

他端着蜡烛慢慢向前走，走在他收集来的那些奇怪动物之中。在朦胧不定的光线中，我可以隐约看到每个裂缝和角落都有闪烁的眼睛在窥视着我们。就连我们头顶的椽子也落了一排暗黑色的家禽。它们懒洋洋地把身体重量从一只爪子换到另一只爪子上，因为我们的声音打搅了它们的睡眠。

原来托比是一条模样丑陋的长毛垂耳狗，一半是西班牙狗，一半是潜猎犬，毛色棕白相间，走起路来笨手笨脚、摇摇晃晃。它犹豫了一阵，接受了老博物学家递给我的一块糖，这样就结成了同盟。它跟随我上了马车，毫无困难地陪伴着我。我又回到樱塘别墅时，王宫的时钟刚刚敲过了3点。我发现，那个曾经当过职业拳击手的麦克默多已经作为从犯被捕，他和肖尔托先生都被押解到了警察局。两名警察把守着狭窄的大门，但我一提到侦探的名字，他们就让我带狗通过。

福尔摩斯正站在门阶上，两手插在口袋里，抽着烟斗。

"Ah, you have him there!" said he. "Good dog, then! Athelney Jones has gone. We have had an **immense**[19] display of energy since you left. He has arrested not only friend Thaddeus but the gatekeeper, the housekeeper, and the Indian servant. We have the place to ourselves but for a sergeant upstairs. Leave the dog here and come up."

We tied Toby to the hall table and reascended the stairs. The room was as we had left it, save that a sheet had been draped over the central figure. A weary-looking police-sergeant reclined in the corner.

"Lend me your bull's eye, Sergeant," said my companion. "Now tie this bit of card round my neck, so as to hang it in front of me. Thank you. Now I must kick off my boots and stockings. Just you carry them down with you, Watson. I am going to do a little climbing. And dip my handkerchief into the creosote. That will do. Now come up into the garret with me for a moment."

We clambered up through the hole. Holmes turned his light once more upon the footsteps in the dust.

"I wish you particularly to notice these footmarks," he said. "Do you observe anything **noteworthy**[20] about them?"

"They belong," I said, "to a child or a small woman."

"Apart from their size, though. Is there nothing else?"

"They appear to be much as other footmarks."

"Not at all. Look here! This is the print of a right foot in the dust. Now I make one with my naked foot beside it. What is the chief difference?"

"Your toes are all cramped together. The other print has each toe distinctly divided."

"Quite so. That is the point. Bear that in mind. Now, would you kindly step over to that flap-window and smell the edge of the woodwork? I shall stay over here, as I have this handkerchief in my hand."

I did as he directed and was instantly conscious of a strong **tarry**[21] smell.

"That is where he put his foot in getting out. If you can trace him, I should think that Toby will have no difficulty. Now run downstairs, loose the dog, and look out for Blondin."

"啊,你带它来了!"他说,"真是好狗!阿塞尔尼·琼斯已经走了。你离开后,我们大干了一场。他不仅逮捕了朋友撒迪厄斯,而且逮捕了看门人、女管家和印度仆人。除了楼上的一名警官,这地方归我们所有。把狗留在这里,上来吧。"

我们把托比拴在门厅的桌腿上,又继续上楼。房间像我们离开时一样,只是在房间中央的死者身上蒙了一个床单。一位神情疲惫的警官斜靠在屋角。

"警官,把你的牛眼灯借我用一下,"我的同伴说,"现在把这个卡片系在我的脖子上,以便它挂在我前面。谢谢。现在我必须脱掉靴子和长袜。华生,请你把它们带下楼。我要向上稍微爬点儿。然后,把我的手帕在木馏油里浸一下。行了。现在和我一起上顶楼去一会儿。"

我们从洞口爬了上去。福尔摩斯又一次把灯光照在灰尘里的脚印上。

"我希望你特别注意这些脚印,"他说,"你观察到它们有什么值得注意的情况吗?"

"这是一个孩子或小女人的脚印,"我说。

"不过,除了脚印的大小,还有别的什么吗?"

"它们似乎和其他脚印差不多一样。"

"根本不一样。看这里!这是灰尘里的一只右脚印。现在我在它旁边用光脚印上一个。主要区别是什么?"

"你的脚趾都紧扣在一起。另一个脚印的各个脚趾都明显分开。"

"正是这样。这就是要点。记住这一点。现在,请你走到那个吊窗边,闻一下木框边好吗?我站在这边,因为我手里拿着这块手帕。"

我按照他的吩咐去闻了闻,马上感觉到一股强烈的焦油味。

"这是他出去时脚踩的地方。如果你能闻出他的气味,我想托比就不会有任何困难。现在跑下楼,放开那条狗,然后去搜捕布朗丁。"

四签名

By the time that I got out into the grounds Sherlock Holmes was on the roof, and I could see him like an enormous glow-worm crawling very slowly along the ridge. I lost sight of him behind a stack of chimneys, but he presently reappeared and then vanished once more upon the opposite side. When I made my way round there I found him seated at one of the corner eaves.

"That you, Watson?" he cried.

"Yes."

"This is the place. What is that black thing down there?"

"A water-barrel."

"Top on it?"

"Yes."

"No sign of a ladder?"

"No."

"**Confound**[22] the fellow! It's a most breakneck place. I ought to be able to come down where he could climb up. The water-pipe feels pretty firm. Here goes, anyhow."

There was a scuffling of feet, and the lantern began to come steadily down the side of the wall. Then with a light spring he came on to the barrel, and from there to the earth.

"It was easy to follow him," he said, drawing on his stockings and boots. "Tiles were loosened the whole way along, and in his hurry he had dropped this. It confirms my **diagnosis**[23], as you doctors express it."

The object which he held up to me was a small pocket or pouch woven out of coloured grasses and with a few tawdry beads strung round it. In shape and size it was not unlike a cigarette-case. Inside were half a dozen spines of dark wood, sharp at one end and rounded at the other, like that which had struck Bartholomew Sholto.

"They are hellish things," said he. "Look out that you don't **prick**[24]

我出门，走进空地时，夏洛克·福尔摩斯上了屋顶。我可以看到他像一只大萤火虫似的沿着屋顶慢慢爬行。他爬到一排烟囱后面就不见了，但他马上又重新出现，随后再次消失在对面。当我绕到那里时，发现他坐在房檐的一角。

"是你吗，华生？"他喊道。

"是。"

"就是这个地方。下面那个黑东西是什么？"

"是一只水桶。"

"上面有盖子吗？"

"有。"

"没有梯子的迹象吗？"

"没有。"

"这家伙真该死！这是一个极其危险的地方。他能从这里爬上来，我就能从这里爬下去。这个水管感觉相当结实。不管怎样，从这里下来。"

一阵拖步行走的声音响过之后，灯笼开始顺着墙边稳稳地降了下来。随后，他轻轻跳落在水桶上，又从水桶跳到了地上。

"跟踪他并不难，"他一边穿长袜和靴子，一边说。"这整个一路都被踩松了，而且他慌乱中掉下了这个东西。像你们医生说的那样，它进一步证实了我的诊断。"

他举起来给我看的那个东西是一个用彩色草编成的小袋或烟荷包，四周挂着几颗俗气的珠子。形状和大小像一只烟盒。里边有6根黑木刺，一头是尖的，另一头是圆的，就像刺中巴塞洛缪·肖尔托那根一样。

"这是恶魔般可怕的东西，"他说，"留神不要刺着你自己。我得到这些东西非常高兴，因为这可能是他拥有的全部凶器。你我不久以后就不怕皮肤

四签名

yourself. I'm delighted to have them, for the chances are that they are all he has. There is the less fear of you or me finding one in our skin before long. I would sooner face a Martini bullet, myself. Are you game for a six-mile **trudge**[25], Watson?"

"Certainly," I answered.

"Your leg will stand it?"

"Oh, yes."

"Here you are, doggy! Good old Toby! Smell it, Toby, smell it!" He pushed the creosote handkerchief under the dog's nose, while the creature stood with its fluffy legs separated, and with a most comical cock to its head, like a connoisseur sniffing the **bouquet**[26] of a famous **vintage**[27]. Holmes then threw the handkerchief to a distance, fastened a stout cord to the mongrel's collar, and led him to the foot of the water-barrel. The creature instantly broke into a succession of high, **tremulous**[28] yelps and, with his nose on the ground and his tail in the air, pattered off upon the trail at a pace which strained his leash and kept us at the top of our speed.

The east had been gradually whitening, and we could now see some distance in the cold gray light. The square, massive house, with its black, empty windows and high, bare walls, towered up, sad and **forlorn**[29], behind us. Our course led right across the grounds, in and out among the trenches and pits with which they were scarred and intersected. The whole place, with its scattered dirt-heaps and ill-grown shrubs, had a blighted, ill-omened look which harmonized with the black tragedy which hung over it.

On reaching the boundary wall Toby ran along, whining eagerly, underneath its shadow, and stopped finally in a corner screened by a young beech. Where the two walls joined, several bricks had been loosened, and the crevices left were worn down and rounded upon the lower side, as though they had frequently been used as a ladder. Holmes clambered up, and taking the dog from me he dropped it over upon the other side.

"There's the print of Wooden-leg's hand," he remarked as I mounted up beside him. "You see the slight **smudge**[30] of blood upon the white plaster. What a lucky thing it is that we have had no very heavy rain since yesterday! The

上扎这种东西了。我自己宁愿面对马帝尼枪子弹。华生，你有胆量跋涉6英里吗？"

"当然有，"我回答说。

"你的腿受得了吗？"

"噢，是的。"

"给，狗狗！好心的老托比！闻闻这个，托比，闻闻这个！"他把浸过木馏油的手帕推到狗的鼻子下面。狗分开毛茸茸的腿站在那里，极其滑稽地歪着脑袋，就像行家在闻著名葡萄酒的芳香一样。随后，福尔摩斯把手帕扔到远处，在这条杂种狗的项圈上系了一根结实的绳索，牵着它来到水桶边。狗突然马上发出一连串高亢颤抖的狂叫，鼻子贴在地上，尾巴朝天，跟踪气味嗒嗒一路快跑。绳索绷紧，使我们全速飞奔。

东方渐渐发白，我们在寒冷的灰光中可以看到远处。那座正方形的大房子，窗户漆黑空洞，墙壁又高又秃，暗淡凄凉，耸立在我们背后。我们的路线向右穿过房屋四周的空地，在纵横交错的沟渠和深坑之间出出进进。整个地方分散堆着土堆，灌木丛生，参差不齐，有一种衰落、不祥的景象，与笼罩在这里的惨案相互一致。

托比一到达那里，就顺着围墙跑了起来，同时在围墙的阴影里迫不及待地低声哀叫，最后在一棵小山毛榉树遮挡的墙角停下来。在两面墙会合的地方，好几块砖已经松动，留下的裂缝磨损，较低的那边已经磨圆，好像它们常被用作爬墙的梯子。福尔摩斯爬上去，从我手里接过狗，从另一边把它放了下去。

"这里有木腿人的手印，"我爬到他身边时，他说，"你看到白色灰泥上的血迹了吧。昨天以来没有任何大雨，是多么幸运！尽管隔了28小时，但

四签名

scent will lie upon the road in spite of their eight-and-twenty hours' start."

I confess that I had my doubts myself when I reflected upon the great traffic which had passed along the London road in the interval. My fears were soon appeased, however. Toby never hesitated or **swerved**[31] but waddled on in his peculiar rolling fashion. Clearly the **pungent**[32] smell of the **creosote**[33] rose high above all other **contending**[34] scents.

"Do not imagine," said Holmes, "that I depend for my success in this case upon the mere chance of one of these fellows having put his foot in the chemical. I have knowledge now which would enable me to trace them in many different ways. This, however, is the readiest, and, since fortune has put it into our hands, I should be culpable if I neglected it. It has, however, prevented the case from becoming the pretty little intellectual problem which it at one time promised to be. There might have been some credit to be gained out of it but for this too **palpable**[35] clue."

"There is credit, and to spare," said I. "I assure you, Holmes, that I marvel at the means by which you obtain your results in this case even more than I did in the Jefferson Hope murder. The thing seems to me to be deeper and more inexplicable. How, for example, could you describe with such confidence the wooden-legged man?"

"**Pshaw**[36], my dear boy! it was simplicity itself. I don't wish to be theatrical. It is all patent and above-board. Two officers who are in command of a convict-guard learn an important secret as to buried treasure. A map is drawn for them by an Englishman named Jonathan Small. You remember that we saw the name upon the chart in Captain Morstan's possession. He had signed it in behalf of himself and his associates—the sign of the four, as he somewhat dramatically called it. Aided by this chart, the officers–or one of them–gets the treasure and brings it to England, leaving, we will suppose, some condition under which he received it unfulfilled. Now, then, why did not Jonathan Small get the treasure himself? The answer is obvious. The chart is dated at a time when Morstan was brought into close association with convicts. Jonathan Small did not get the treasure because he and his associates were themselves convicts and could not get away."

气味会留在路上。"

我承认，回想这段时间伦敦道路上经过的巨大交通量时，我一直有疑虑。然而，我的种种担心马上得到了平息。托比毫不犹豫，也从不改变方向，而是以它自己独特的滚动方式蹒跚向前。显然，木馏油强烈的气味超过了所有其他的气味。

"不要认为，"福尔摩斯说，"我在这个案子上取得成功，仅仅是依靠其中一个家伙把脚踩到化学药品这个机会。我现在知道能使我追踪他们的许多不同方法。然而，这是最现成的方法，而且，既然幸运女神把这个方法放进了我们的手里，如果我们忽视，我就应该受到谴责。不过，这个案子不再像它一度那样需要动点脑子。要不是这个过于明显的线索，我们可能会因此得到一些赞许。"

"有赞许，而且不少，"我说，"福尔摩斯，我向你保证，我对你在这个案子里用的方法比我在杰斐逊·霍普谋杀案里用的方法取得的结果更惊奇。在我看来，这件事似乎更加深刻、更加神秘。比如，你怎么能这样自信地形容那个木腿人呢？"

"啐，我的老伙计！这件事本身非常简单。我不想夸张。这一切都显而易见、光明正大。两个指挥看守囚犯的军官获悉一个藏宝的重要秘密。一个名叫乔纳森·斯莫尔的英国人为他们画了一张图。你记得我们看到过摩斯坦上尉持有的图上有这个名字。他代表自己和同伙们签了名——四签名，他这样叫有点儿引人注目。在这张图的帮助下，这两个军官——或者其中一个人——得到了财宝，带回了英国。我们可以设想，他得到财宝后，没有履行当初约定的某个条件。那么，为什么乔纳森·斯莫尔自己没有得到财宝呢？这个答案显而易见。那张图表的日期正是摩斯坦和囚犯们密切接触的时候。乔纳森·斯莫尔之所以没有得到财宝，是因为他和同伙都是囚犯，无法逃脱。"

四签名

"But this is mere speculation," said I.

"It is more than that. It is the only **hypothesis**[37] which covers the facts. Let us see how it fits in with the **sequel**[38]. Major Sholto remains at peace for some years, happy in the possession of his treasure. Then he receives a letter from India which gives him a great fright. What was that?"

"A letter to say that the men whom he had wronged had been set free."

"Or had escaped. That is much more likely, for he would have known what their term of imprisonment was. It would not have been a surprise to him. What does he do then? He guards himself against a wooden-legged man—a white man, mark you, for he mistakes a white tradesman for him and actually fires a pistol at him. Now, only one white man's name is on the chart. The others are Hindoos or Mohammedans. There is no other white man. Therefore we may say with confidence that the wooden-legged man is identical with Jonathan Small. Does the reasoning strike you as being faulty?"

"No: it is clear and **concise**[39]."

"Well, now, let us put ourselves in the place of Jonathan Small. Let us look at it from his point of view. He comes to England with the double idea of regaining what he would consider to be his rights and of having his revenge upon the man who had wronged him. He found out where Sholto lived, and very possibly he established communications with someone inside the house. There is this **butler**[40], Lal Rao, whom we have not seen. Mrs. Bernstone gives him far from a good character. Small could not find out, however, where the treasure was hid, for no one ever knew save the major and one faithful servant who had died. Suddenly Small learns that the major is on his deathbed. In a frenzy lest the secret of the treasure die with him, he **runs the gauntlet**[41] of the guards, makes his way to the dying man's window, and is only **deterred**[42] from entering by the presence of his two sons. Mad with hate, however, against the dead man, he enters the room that night, searches his private papers in the hope of discovering some **memorandum**[43] relating to the treasure, and finally leaves a **memento**[44] of his visit in the short inscription upon the card. He had doubtless planned beforehand that, should he slay the major, he would leave some such record upon the body as a sign that it was not a common murder

"可是，这仅仅是推测，"我说。

"这不仅仅是推测，而是涉及那些情况的唯一假设。让我们看看这个假设和结局如何吻合。肖尔托少校占有财宝后心花怒放，安居了几年。后来，他收到了印度寄来的一封信，这封信让他大惊失色。这是怎么回事呢？"

"信上说，他曾经冤枉过的那些人已被释放了。"

"或者说已经逃跑了。这之所以更有可能，是因为他知道他们的刑期是多少，否则他就不会吃惊了。那他做了什么呢？他提防木腿人——请你注意，木腿人是一个白人，因为他错把一个白种商人当成了那个人，居然拿手枪向那个人开了一枪。现在，图表上只有一个白种人的名字。其余的都是印度人或伊斯兰教徒。没有任何其他的白种人。所以，我们可以充满自信地说，这个木腿人就是乔纳森·斯莫尔。你认为这种推理错误吗？"

"不，这既清晰又简明。"

"那好吧，让我们站在乔纳森·斯莫尔的立场，从他的观点看一下这件事。他来英国有双重目的：一是重新得到他认为应有的权利，二是向曾经冤枉他的人报仇。他查明了肖尔托住在哪里，很有可能他还和那座房子的某个人建立了联系。这个男仆叫拉尔·拉奥，我们还没有见过。伯恩斯通太太说他绝不是好人。不过，斯莫尔没有找到藏宝的地方，因为除了少校和一个已经死去的忠实仆人，谁也不知道。斯莫尔突然听说少校生命垂危。狂乱之中，唯恐藏宝的秘密随着少校消逝，他就冒着被卫兵交叉射击的危险，跑到垂死者的窗前。只是因为少校的两个儿子在场，他才没有进去。然而，他对死者恨得发疯，当天夜里就进入那个房间，搜寻私人文件，希望发现和财宝有关的一些备忘录，最后在卡片上简短留言，作为对他来访的纪念。毫无疑问，他已经事先作好了计划，如果他要杀死少校，就会在尸体边留下这种记录，表

but, from the point of view of the four associates, something in the nature of an act of justice. **Whimsical**[45] and **bizarre**[46] conceits of this kind are common enough in the annals of crime and usually afford valuable indications as to the criminal. Do you follow all this?"

"Very clearly."

"Now what could Jonathan small do? He could only continue to keep a secret watch upon the efforts made to find the treasure. Possibly he leaves England and only comes back at intervals. Then comes the discovery of the garret, and he is instantly informed of it. We again trace the presence of some **confederate**[47] in the household. Jonathan, with his wooden leg, is utterly unable to reach the lofty room of Bartholomew Sholto. He takes with him, however, a rather curious associate, who gets over this difficulty but dips his naked foot into creosote, whence come Toby, and a six-mile limp for a half-pay officer with a damaged tendo Achillis."

"But it was the associate and not Jonathan who committed the crime."

"Quite so. And rather to Jonathan's disgust, to judge by the way he stamped about when he got into the room. He bore no **grudge**[48] against Bartholomew Sholto and would have preferred if he could have been simply bound and gagged. He did not wish to put his head in a halter. There was no help for it, however: the savage instincts of his companion had broken out, and the poison had done its work: so Jonathan Small left his record, lowered the treasure-box to the ground, and followed it himself. That was the train of events as far as I can **decipher**[49] them. Of course, as to his personal appearance, he must be middle-aged and must be sunburned after serving his time in such an oven as the Andamans. His height is readily calculated from the length of his stride, and we know that he was bearded. His hairiness was the one point which impressed itself upon Thaddeus Sholto when he saw him at the window. I don't know that there is anything else."

"The associate?"

"Ah, well, there is no great mystery in that. But you will know all about it soon enough. How sweet the morning air is! See how that one little cloud floats like a pink feather from some gigantic **flamingo**[50]. Now the red rim of the sun

明这不是一起普通谋杀，而从四个同伙的观点来看是类似正义的行为。这种异想天开和稀奇古怪的个人意见在犯罪编年史上司空见惯，通常还会提供有关罪犯的重要情况。这一切你都清楚吗？"

"非常清楚。"

"现在，乔纳森·斯莫尔能做什么呢？他只能继续秘密监视别人寻找财宝的种种努力。他可能会离开英国，只是隔一段时间才回来。后来传来顶楼发现财宝的消息，马上就有人告诉了他。我们又一次追踪到那个房子里有帮凶。乔纳森装着木腿，完全不可能爬上巴塞洛缪·肖尔托高高的房间。然而，他带了一个相当古怪的同伙。这个同伙克服了这种困难，但把赤脚浸在了木馏油里，因此才来了托比，并使一名脚筋受伤的半薪军官一瘸一拐走了6英里。"

"可犯罪的是那个同伙，而不是乔纳森。"

"正是这样。从乔纳森走进房间时来回踩脚的样子判断，他对此相当反感，对巴塞洛缪·肖尔托没有任何怨恨，如果可能，他宁愿只把巴塞洛缪·肖尔托捆起来堵上嘴，不想作茧自缚。然而，这无济于事：同伙的野蛮本性已经爆发，毒药已经发挥作用，因此乔纳森·斯莫尔留下了记录，把财宝箱放到了地上，然后自己也跟了下来。这就是我所能解释的那一连串事件。当然，至于他个人的外貌，他一定是中年人，在烤箱一样热的安达曼岛服刑之后一定晒得黝黑。他的身高从他步幅的长度不难计算出来。我们知道他留着络腮胡。撒迪厄斯·肖尔托在窗口看到了他的多毛状态，这一点给肖尔托留下了深刻印象。其他还有什么，我就不知道了。"

"那个同伙呢？"

"啊，这没有多大神秘。你马上就会知道所有的一切。早晨的空气是多么新鲜！看那朵小小的云彩像巨大火烈鸟的一根粉红色的羽毛飘浮。现在，

pushes itself over the London cloud-bank. It shines on a good many folk, but on none, I dare bet, who are on a stranger errand than you and I. How small we feel with our petty ambitions and strivings in the presence of the great elemental forces of Nature! Are you well up in your Jean Paul?"

"Fairly so. I worked back to him through Carlyle."

"That was like following the brook to the parent lake. He makes one curious but profound remark. It is that the chief proof of man's real greatness lies in his **perception**[51] of his own smallness. It argues, you see, a power of comparison and of appreciation which is in itself a proof of nobility. There is much food for thought in Richter. You have not a pistol, have you?"

"I have my stick."

"It is just possible that we may need something of the sort if we get to their lair. Jonathan I shall leave to you, but if the other turns nasty I shall shoot him dead."

He took out his revolver as he spoke, and, having loaded two of the chambers, he put it back into the right-hand pocket of his jacket.

We had during this time been following the guidance of Toby down the half-rural villa-lined roads which lead to the **metropolis**[52]. Now, however, we were beginning to come among continuous streets, where labourers and dockmen were already astir, and slatternly women were taking down shutters and brushing door-steps. At the square-topped corner public-houses business was just beginning, and rough-looking men were emerging, rubbing their sleeves across their beards after their morning wet. Strange dogs **sauntered**[53] up and stared wonderingly at us as we passed, but our inimitable Toby looked neither to the right nor to the left but **trotted**[54] onward with his nose to the ground and an occasional eager whine which spoke of a hot scent.

We had traversed Streatham, Brixton, Camberwell, and now found ourselves in Kennington Lane, having borne away through the side streets to the east of the Oval. The men whom we pursued seemed to have taken a curiously zigzag road, with the idea probably of escaping observation. They

太阳的红边越过了伦敦的云层。太阳照在了好多人身上,但我敢打赌,谁也没有你我肩负的使命奇特。我们感到自己的小小抱负和奋斗在伟大的自然力面前是多么渺小!你对让·保罗了解吗?"

"算是吧。我是通过卡莱尔才了解他的。"

"这就像顺着小溪找到母亲湖一样。他说了一句奇特而又深刻的话。人类真正伟大的主要证明在于他能感知到自己的渺小。你明白,这表明了比较和鉴赏的力量,这种力量本身就是一个高贵的证明。里希特尔的作品里有许多精神食粮。你没有带手枪,对吗?"

"我有手杖。"

"如果我们到达他们的老巢,就可能需要这种东西。我要把乔纳森交给你,但如果另一个人对我们有危险,我就开枪打死他。"

他一边说,一边掏出左轮手枪,然后装上两颗子弹,又放回到夹克的右口袋。

这段时间,我们一直跟随托比,走在通往伦敦的路上,两边是半乡村式的别墅。然而,现在我们开始来到了人流不断的大街。劳工和码头工人已经活动起来,衣着不整的女人们正在放下百叶窗打扫门阶。街角正方形房顶的酒馆刚刚开始营业。模样粗野的男人们正走出来,用袖子擦着早晨喝过酒后沾湿的胡子。我们经过时,一些陌生的狗跑上来,奇怪地望着我们,但我们无与伦比的托比毫不左顾右盼,而是用鼻子冲着地,跑步向前,偶尔急切地低声哀叫,这说明气味强烈。

我们已经穿过了斯特里森区、布里克斯顿区、坎伯威尔区,穿过那些小街,来到奥弗尔区东边,到达了肯宁顿巷。我们追寻的那些人好像走的是奇怪的弯弯曲曲的路,也许是想避开有人注意。如果有平行的小街,他们就绝不走

had never kept to the main road if a **parallel**[55] side street would serve their turn. At the foot of Kennington Lane they had edged away to the left through Bond Street and Miles Street. Where the latter street turns into Knight's Place, Toby ceased to advance but began to run backward and forward with one ear cocked and the other drooping, the very picture of **canine**[56] indecision. Then he waddled round in circles, looking up to us from time to time, as if to ask for sympathy in his embarrassment.

"What the deuce is the matter with the dog?" **growled**[57] Holmes. "They surely would not take a cab or go off in a balloon."

"Perhaps they stood here for some time," I suggested.

"Ah! it's all right. He's off again," said my companion in a tone of relief.

He was indeed off, for after sniffing round again he suddenly made up his mind and darted away with an energy and determination such as he had not yet shown. The scent appeared to be much hotter than before, for he had not even to put his nose on the ground but tugged at his leash and tried to break into a run. I could see by the gleam in Holmes's eyes that he thought we were nearing the end of our journey.

Our course now ran down Nine Elms until we came to Broderick and Nelson's large timber-yard just past the White Eagle tavern. Here the dog, frantic with excitement, turned down through the side gate into the enclosure, where the sawyers were already at work. On the dog raced through sawdust and shavings, down an alley, round a passage, between two wood-piles, and finally, with a triumphant yelp, sprang upon a large barrel which still stood upon the **hand-trolley**[58] on which it had been brought. With **lolling**[59] tongue and blinking eyes Toby stood upon the **cask**[60], looking from one to the other of us for some sign of appreciation. The staves of the barrel and the wheels of the trolley were smeared with a dark liquid, and the whole air was heavy with the smell of creosote.

Sherlock Holmes and I looked blankly at each other and then burst **simultaneously**[61] into an uncontrollable fit of laughter.

大路。到了肯宁顿巷尽头,他们转向左侧,穿过证券街和迈尔斯街。托比从迈尔斯街转入骑士街后,停止前进,只是开始来回跑动,一只耳朵竖起,另一只耳朵下垂,一副犹豫不定的样子。随后,它又摇摇摆摆转了几圈,抬起头,不时地望着我们,仿佛是在困窘中请求同情。

"这只狗到底是怎么回事?"福尔摩斯吼道,"他们肯定不会乘出租马车,也不会乘坐气球逃跑。"

"他们可能在这里站过一段时间,"我建议说。

"啊,好了。它又走了,"我的同伴用放心的口气说。

狗的确又走了起来,四处闻了一阵,突然下定决心,以前所未有的劲头和决心飞跑。气味似乎要比先前强烈得多,因为它甚至不必鼻子着地,而是用力拖着绳索,尽力奔跑。我从福尔摩斯两眼发亮可以看出,他认为我们快要接近旅程的终点了。

我们现在的路线是沿着九榆树飞奔而下,直至来到白鹰酒店附近的布罗德里克和纳尔逊大木场。到了这里,这条狗兴奋发狂,通过侧门跑进了锯木工人已在工作的围场。这条狗继续飞跑过锯屑和刨花,穿过一条胡同,绕过两个木堆之间的过道,最后胜利地欢叫一声纵身跳上仍放在手推车上的一只大木桶。托比伸着舌头,眨着眼睛,站在木桶上,看看我们这个,又瞧瞧我们那个,想看到某种赞赏的迹象。木桶的桶板和手推车的轮子都沾有一种黑色液体,整个空气中弥漫着木馏油的浓重气味。

我和夏洛克·福尔摩斯茫然对视,然后不约而同爆发出一阵无法控制的大笑。

四签名

Notes:
1. placid *adj.* 平静的；温和的
2. conventionality *n.* 常规；惯例
3. vulgar *adj.* 庸俗的
4. intervene *vi.* 插进；介入；介于
5. dependant *n.* 受赡养者；受扶养的家属
6. tranquil *adj.* 安静的；宁静的
7. sequence *n.* 有关联的一组事物；一连串
8. singular *adj.* 单独的；异常的；奇特的
9. labyrinth *n.* 迷宫
10. endow *vt.* 使（某人）天生具有
11. vagabond *n.* 流浪者；游手好闲者
12. badger *n.* 獾
13. rafter *n.* 椽
14. lop-eared *adj.* 垂耳的
15. spaniel *n.* 长耳垂毛狗；西班牙猎犬
16. lurcher *n.* 杂种猎狗
17. waddle *vi.* （像鸭子一样）摇摇摆摆地走
18. accessory *n.* 同谋；帮凶；包庇犯
19. immense *adj.* 极大的；巨大的
20. noteworthy *adj.* 值得注意的；重要的
21. tarry *adj.* 柏油的
22. confound *vt.* 可恶；让……死掉
23. diagnosis *n.* 诊断
24. prick *vt.* 刺；扎
25. trudge *n.* 跋涉；长途疲劳的步行
26. bouquet *n.* （酒的）芳香
27. vintage *n.* 酒；(=vintage wine，特指某年某地所产的) 美酒
28. tremulous *adj.* 颤抖的；打颤的
29. forlorn *adj.* 凄凉的；被弃置的；荒凉的
30. smudge *n.* 污点；污迹
31. swerve *vi.* 改变方向；改变目的

32. pungent *adj.* 有刺激味的；刺鼻的

33. creosote *n.* 杂芬油；木馏油；碳酸

34. contend *vi.* 争夺；竞争

35. palpable *adj.* 明显的

36. pshaw *int.* 啐！哼！（表示不耐烦、轻蔑时的叫声）

37. hypothesis *n.* 假设；前提

38. sequel *n.* 结果；结局

39. concise *adj.* 简明的

40. butler *n.* 男管家

41. run the gauntlet 受到两面夹攻；交叉射击

42. deter *vt.* 阻止；制止

43. memorandum *n.* 备忘录；便函

44. memento *n.* 纪念品；令人回忆的东西

45. whimsical *adj.* 异想天开的；古怪的

46. bizarre *adj.* 奇形怪状的；怪诞的

47. confederate *n.* 同伙；合谋者

48. grudge *n.* 不满；怨恨

49. decipher *vt.* 破译；辨认

50. flamingo *n.* 火烈鸟

51. perception *n.* 感知；认识

52. metropolis *n.* 一国的主要城市（不一定是首都）

53. saunter *vi.* 漫步；闲逛

54. trot *vi.* 小跑；急走

55. parallel *adj.* 平行的；类似的

56. canine *adj.* 犬的

57. growl *vt.* 低声咆哮着说

58. hand-trolley 手摇车；货仓车

59. loll *vi.* 下垂；伸出

60. cask *n.* 桶；容器

61. simultaneously *adv.* 同时地；一齐

四签名

# Chapter 8

## THE BAKER STREET IRREGULARS

# 第八章

## 贝克街的非正规军

"What now?" I asked. "Toby has lost his character for **infallibility**[1]."

"He acted according to his lights," said Holmes, lifting him down from the barrel and walking him out of the timber-yard. "If you consider how much creosote is carted about London in one day, it is no great wonder that our trail should have been crossed. It is much used now, especially for the seasoning of wood. Poor Toby is not to blame."

"We must get on the main scent again, I suppose."

"Yes. And, fortunately, we have no distance to go. Evidently what puzzled the dog at the corner of Knight's Place was that there were two different trails running in opposite directions. We took the wrong one. It only remains to follow the other."

There was no difficulty about this. On leading Toby to the place where he had committed his fault, he cast about in a wide circle and finally dashed off in a fresh direction.

"We must take care that he does not now bring us to the place where the creosote-barrel came from," I observed.

"I had thought of that. But you notice that he keeps on the pavement, whereas the barrel passed down the roadway. No, we are on the true scent now."

It tended down towards the riverside, running through Belmont Place and Prince's Street. At the end of Broad Street it ran right down to the water's edge, where there was a small wooden **wharf**[2]. Toby led us to the very edge of this and there stood whining, looking out on the dark current beyond.

"We are out of luck," said Holmes. "They have taken to a boat here."

Several small punts and skiffs were lying about in the water and on the edge of the wharf. We took Toby round to each in turn, but though he sniffed earnestly he made no sign.

Close to the rude **landing-stage**[3] was a small brick house, with a wooden **placard**[4] slung out through the second window. "Mordecai Smith" was printed across it in large letters, and, underneath, "Boats to hire by the hour or day." A second **inscription**[5] above the door informed us that a steam **launch**[6] was kept—a statement which was confirmed by a great pile of coke upon the jetty. Sherlock Holmes looked slowly round, and his face assumed an **ominous**[7] expression.

"现在怎么办?"我问道,"托比已经失去了它万无一失的能力。"

"托比是根据它自己的感觉行事,"说着,福尔摩斯把它从木桶上抱下来,牵着它走出了木场。"如果你考虑一下伦敦一天运输多少木馏油,就不会对我们的道路受阻大惊小怪了。现在很多地方都使用木馏油,尤其是用于风干木料。不应该责怪可怜的托比。"

"我想,我们必须再次找到那主要的气味。"

"是的。再说,幸亏我们走不了多远。显然,骑士街拐角让那条狗困惑的是有两条不同的路走向了相反的方向。我们走错了路。剩下的只有走另一条路。"

要做到这一点,没有任何困难。我们牵着托比回到了它原来出错的地方。它搜索了一大圈,最后朝一个新的方向奔去。

"我们必须当心,它现在不会带我们去木馏油桶所来的那个地方,"我说。

"我已经想到了这一点。但是,你注意它是走在人行道上,木桶则是顺着车道走。不,我们现在找的气味没错。"

它穿过贝尔蒙路和王子街,奔向河边。到了布罗德街尽头,它直接跑到水边,那里有一个小小的木码头。托比把我们领到这个码头边上,站在那里望着远处昏暗的水流,低声哀鸣。

"我们点儿背,"福尔摩斯说。"他们已经从这里上船了。"

好几只小平底船和单人小艇停在水里和码头。我们把托比依次带到各只船上。可是,尽管它认真地嗅着,却没有任何表示。

靠近简陋的栈桥处有一座小砖房,第二个窗口挂出一块木牌,上面用印刷体大字母写着"莫迪凯·史密斯",下面则是"船只出租,按小时或天计价"。门上方的第二行字告诉我们,备有汽艇——码头上的一大堆焦炭进一步证实了这个说法。夏洛克·福尔摩斯慢慢地环顾四周,脸上露出了不祥的表情。

"This looks bad," said he. "These fellows are sharper than I expected. They seem to have covered their tracks. There has, I fear, been **preconcerted**[8] management here."

He was approaching the door of the house, when it opened, and a little curly-headed lad of six came running out, followed by a **stoutish**[9], red-faced woman with a large sponge in her hand.

"You come back and be washed, Jack," she shouted. "Come back, you young **imp**[10]; for if your father comes home and finds you like that he'll let us hear of it."

"Dear little chap!" said Holmes strategically. "What a rosy-cheeked young rascal! Now, Jack, is there anything you would like?"

The youth **pondered**[11] for a moment.

"I'd like a shillin'," said he.

"Nothing you would like better?"

"I'd like two shillin' better," the **prodigy**[12] answered after some thought.

"Here you are, then! Catch! —A fine child, Mrs. Smith!"

"Lor' bless you, sir, he is that, and forward. He gets a'most too much for me to manage, 'specially when my man is away days at a time."

"Away, is he?" said Holmes in a disappointed voice. "I am sorry for that, for I wanted to speak to Mr. Smith."

"He's been away since yesterday mornin', sir, and, truth to tell, I am beginnin' to feel frightened about him. But if it was about a boat, sir, maybe I could serve as well."

"I wanted to hire his steam launch."

"Why, bless you, sir, it is in the steam launch that he has gone. That's what puzzles me; for I know there ain't more coals in her than would take her to about Woolwich and back. If he's been away in the barge I'd ha' thought nothin'; for many a time a job has taken him as far as Gravesend, and then if there was much doin' there he might ha' stayed over. But what good is a steam launch without coals?"

"He might have bought some at a wharf down the river."

"He might, sir, but it weren't his way. Many a time I've heard him call out

"这看来很糟,"他说。"这些家伙比我预料的要狡猾。他们似乎早已掩盖了自己的足迹。我怕,这里事先早有安排。"

他正要接近房门,这时门开了,一个鬈发的6岁小男孩跑了出来,后面跟着的是一个满面红光的胖女人,手里拿着一大块海绵。

"杰克,你回来洗洗!"她喊道,"回来,你这小淘气鬼!要是你爸爸回家发现你这样,他一定会揍你的。"

"可爱的小家伙!"福尔摩斯策略地说,"脸蛋多么红润的小淘气!好了,杰克,你想要什么东西吗?"

小孩子想了一会儿。

"我想要一先令,"他说。

"你不想要更好的东西吗?"

"我更想要两先令,"这个神童想了一会儿,回答说。

"那给你!接住!——史密斯太太,他是一个好孩子!"

"先生,上帝保佑你,他是好孩子,而且早熟。我都快管不住他了,尤其是我的老公一不在家就是好几天。"

"他不在家?"福尔摩斯用失望的声音说,"我对此非常遗憾,因为我本来是想对史密斯先生说话。"

"先生,他昨天早上以来就不在家了。说实话,我开始为他担惊受怕。不过,先生,如要租船,也许我也可以效力。"

"我想要租他的汽艇。"

"啊,先生,愿上帝保佑你,他就是坐汽艇走的。这就是让我困惑的地方,因为我知道船上的煤不够去伍尔维奇来回烧。如果他坐驳船离开,我就什么也不会想了,因为一项工作常常要好多次把他带到格雷夫森德那样远的地方去。再说,如果要做的活多,说不定他还会在那里过夜。可是,汽艇没有煤有什么用呢?"

"他可以在河下游的码头买一些煤。"

四签名

at the prices they charge for a few odd bags. Besides, I don't like that wooden-legged man, wi' his ugly face and **outlandish**[13] talk. What did he want always knockin' about here for?"

"A wooden-legged man?" said Holmes with bland surprise.

"Yes, sir, a brown, monkey-faced chap that's called more'n once for my old man. It was him that roused him up yesternight, and, what's more, my man knew he was comin', for he had steam up in the launch. I tell you straight, sir, I don't feel easy in my mind about it."

"But, my dear Mrs. Smith," said Holmes, shrugging his shoulders, "you are frightening yourself about nothing. How could you possibly tell that it was the wooden-legged man who came in the night? I don't quite understand how you can be so sure."

"His voice, sir. I knew his voice, which is kind o' thick and foggy. He tapped at the **winder**[14]—about three it would be. 'Show a leg, matey,' says he: 'time to turn out guard.' My old man woke up Jim—that's my eldest—and away they went without so much as a word to me. I could hear the wooden leg clackin' on the stones."

"And was this wooden-legged man alone?"

"Couldn't say, I am sure, sir. I didn't hear no one else."

"I am sorry, Mrs. Smith, for I wanted a steam launch, and I have heard good reports of the—Let me see, what is her name?"

"The *Aurora*, sir."

"Ah! She's not that old green launch with a yellow line, very broad in the beam?"

"No, indeed. She's as trim a little thing as any on the river. She's been fresh painted, black with two red **streaks**[15]."

"Thanks. I hope that you will hear soon from Mr. Smith. I am going down the river, and if I should see anything of the Aurora I shall let him know that you are uneasy. A black funnel, you say?"

"No, sir. Black with a white band."

"Ah, of course. It was the sides which were black. Good-morning, Mrs. Smith. There is a boatman here with a **wherry**[16], Watson. We shall take it and

"先生，尽管他可以买，但这不是他的做法。我曾经多次听到他大声说才几袋零散的煤，就要价那么高。此外，我不喜欢那个木腿人，他的脸丑陋，说话一股洋味。他总是跑到这里想干什么？"

"木腿人？"福尔摩斯冷漠而又惊讶地问道。

"是的，先生，是一个棕色皮肤、猴脸模样的家伙，他不止一次来找我的老公。昨晚就是他把我的老公叫醒的。还有，我的老公知道他要来，因为他让汽艇有了蒸汽。先生，我老实告诉你，我对这件事总是不放心。"

"可是，我亲爱的史密斯太太，"福尔摩斯耸耸肩说，"你是在没事儿吓唬自己。你怎么可能知道夜里来的是那个木腿人？我不大明白你怎么能那样肯定。"

"先生，是他的声音。我知道他的声音，他的声音有点儿沙哑模糊。他轻轻敲了敲窗户——大约是3点。'伙计，快起床，'他说。'该出去警戒了。'我的老公叫醒吉姆——那是我的大儿子——然后他们二话没对我说就走了。我可以听见那只木腿走在石头上发出的咯哒咯哒声。"

"就这个木腿人一个人吗？"

"先生，这我可说不准。我没有听到有其他人。"

"史密斯太太，对不起，因为我想租一只汽艇，早就听说过这只——让我想想，这只船叫什么名字来着？"

"'曙光女神号'，先生。"

"啊！不就是那只带有黄线、船梁很宽的绿色旧汽艇吗？"

"不，的确不是。它像河上任何小船一样整洁，刷过漆，黑色船身带有两道红色条纹。"

"谢谢。我希望你很快就会听到史密斯先生的消息。我要顺河而下，如果我看到'曙光女神号'，我就会告诉他说你很担心。你说，是黑色烟窗吗？"

"不是，先生。是带有白镶条的黑色烟窗。"

"啊，当然。船边是黑色的。史密斯太太，再见。华生，这里有船夫划着舢板。"

cross the river."

"The main thing with people of that sort," said Holmes as we sat in the sheets of the wherry, "is never to let them think that their information can be of the slightest importance to you. If you do they will instantly shut up like an oyster. If you listen to them under protest, as it were, you are very likely to get what you want."

"Our course now seems pretty clear," said I.

"What would you do, then?"

"I would engage a launch and go down the river on the track of the *Aurora*."

"My dear fellow, it would be a **colossal**[17] task. She may have touched at any wharf on either side of the stream between here and Greenwich. Below the bridge there is a perfect labyrinth of landing-places for miles. It would take you days and days to exhaust them if you set about it alone."

"Employ the police, then."

"No. I shall probably call Athelney Jones in at the last moment. He is not a bad fellow, and I should not like to do anything which would injure him professionally. But I have a fancy for working it out myself, now that we have gone so far."

"Could we advertise, then, asking for information from wharfingers?"

"Worse and worse! Our men would know that the chase was hot at their heels, and they would be off out of the country. As it is, they are likely enough to leave, but as long as they think they are perfectly safe they will be in no hurry. Jones's energy will be of use to us there, for his view of the case is sure to push itself into the daily press, and the runaways will think that everyone is off on the wrong scent."

"What are we to do, then?" I asked as we landed near Millbank **Penitentiary**[18].

"Take this hansom, drive home, have some breakfast, and get an hour's sleep. It is quite on the **cards**[19] that we may be afoot to-night again. Stop at a telegraph office, cabby! We will keep Toby, for he may be of use to us yet."

我们乘舢板过河。"

"和这种人打交道，重要的是，"我们一边坐船，福尔摩斯一边说，"绝不要让他们认为他们的消息可能对你有哪怕一丁点的重要性。如果你那样做，他们马上就会守口如瓶。如果你好像极不愿意听他们说，你十有八九会得到你想要的东西。"

"我们的计划现在似乎相当清楚了，"我说。

"那你要怎么做？"

"我要雇一只汽艇顺河而下，追踪'曙光女神号'。"

"老伙计，这将是一项巨大任务。这只船可能靠在从这里到格林威治之间河流两岸的任何一个码头。桥下那里方圆几英里都是上岸的地方，完全像迷宫一样。如果你单独着手，要详尽研究需要花费你好多天。"

"那就请警察。"

"不。在紧要关头，我也许会叫阿塞尔尼·琼斯。他这人不错，我不想在专业上做任何伤害他的事儿。但是，既然我们已经进行到了这个地步，我就很想自己来解决这件事。"

"那么，我们可以登启事，向码头老板征求信息吗？"

"那会越来越糟！我们要找的那些人就会知道，我们正在对他们紧追不舍，他们就要离开这个国家。实际上，他们很有可能会离开，但只要他们认为自己平安无事，就会不慌不忙。琼斯的行动会对我们有用，因为他对本案的看法肯定会每天见报，所以这些亡命徒会以为大家都追错了方向。"

"那我们要怎么办？"当我们在密尔班克感化院附近上岸时，我问道。

"乘坐这辆马车回去吃早饭，然后睡一小时。很可能我们今晚又要走路。车夫，在电报局门口停一下。我们要把托比留在那里，因为说不定它对我们还有用。"

We pulled up at the Great Peter Street Post-Office, and Holmes **dispatched**[20] his wire.

"Whom do you think that is to?" he asked as we resumed our journey.

"I am sure I don't know."

"You remember the Baker Street division of the detective police force whom I employed in the Jefferson Hope case?"

"Well," said I, laughing.

"This is just the case where they might be invaluable. If they fail I have other resources, but I shall try them first. That wire was to my dirty little lieutenant, Wiggins, and I expect that he and his gang will be with us before we have finished our breakfast."

It was between eight and nine o'clock now, and I was conscious of a strong reaction after the successive excitements of the night. I was limp and weary, befogged in mind and **fatigued**[21] in body. I had not the professional enthusiasm which carried my companion on, nor could I look at the matter as a mere abstract intellectual problem. As far as the death of Bartholomew Sholto went, I had heard little good of him and could feel no intense **antipathy**[22] to his murderers. The treasure, however, was a different matter. That, or part of it, belonged rightfully to Miss Morstan. While there was a chance of recovering it I was ready to devote my life to the one object. True, if I found it, it would probably put her forever beyond my reach. Yet it would be a petty and selfish love which would be influenced by such a thought as that. If Holmes could work to find the criminals, I had a tenfold stronger reason to urge me on to find the treasure.

A bath at Baker Street and a complete change freshened me up wonderfully. When I came down to our room I found the breakfast laid and Holmes pouring out the coffee.

"Here it is," said he, laughing and pointing to an open newspaper. "The energetic Jones and the **ubiquitous**[23] reporter have fixed it up between them. But you have had enough of the case. Better have your ham and eggs first."

I took the paper from him and read the short notice, which was headed "Mysterious Business at Upper Norwood."

我们在大彼得街邮局停下来，福尔摩斯发了一封电报。

"你认为这是发给谁的呢？"我们又开始上路时，他问道。

"我肯定不知道。"

"你还记得我在杰斐逊·霍普一案中雇用的侦探部队贝克街分队吗？"

"噢，"我笑道。

"他们可能正好非常有用。如果他们失败，我还有其他办法，但我要先让他们试一下。那封电报是发给我那个脏兮兮的小中尉威金斯的，我料想，在我们吃完早饭之前，他和他那帮人就会来我们这里。"

现在是八九点钟，而在一夜连续兴奋之后，我意识到一种强烈的反应。我浑身乏力，脑子糊涂，筋疲力尽。我没有那种支持同伴前进的职业热情，也无法把这件事看成是纯粹抽象的智力问题。就巴塞洛缪·肖尔托死亡来说，我听到有关他的好话不多，所以对杀害他的那些凶手不可能有任何强烈的憎恶。然而，财宝则另当别论。这笔财宝——或部分财宝——理所应当属于摩斯坦小姐。只要有机会找回财宝，我情愿奉献自己的生命。诚然，如果我找到财宝，那可能会把她置于我永远够不到的地方。不过，如果爱情受到这种想法的影响，就会渺小自私。如果福尔摩斯能经过努力找到那些罪犯，我就更有 10 倍的理由促使自己继续寻找财宝。

我在贝克街沐浴更衣，顿时神清气爽。我下楼来到我们的房间时，发现早饭已经摆好，福尔摩斯正在倒咖啡。

"给，"他一边笑，一边指着一张打开的报纸说，"精力充沛的琼斯和无所不在的记者已经搞定了这个案子。但是，你已经对这个案子感到厌烦了。最好还是先吃你的火腿蛋。"

我从他手里接过报纸，读上面那个简短介绍，标题是《上诺伍德的神秘案件》。

四签名

*About twelve o'clock last night [said the Standard] Mr. Bartholomew Sholto, of Pondicherry Lodge, Upper Norwood, was found dead in his room under circumstances which point to **foul play**[24]. As far as we can learn, no actual traces of violence were found upon Mr. Sholto's person, but a valuable collection of Indian gems which the deceased gentleman had inherited from his father has been carried off. The discovery was first made by Mr. Sherlock Holmes and Dr. Watson, who had called at the house with Mr. Thaddeus Sholto, brother of the deceased. By a singular piece of good fortune, Mr. Athelney Jones, the well-known member of the detective police force, happened to be at the Norwood police station and was on the ground within half an hour of the first alarm. His trained and experienced faculties were at once directed towards the **detection**[25] of the criminals, with the **gratifying**[26] result that the brother, Thaddeus Sholto, has already been arrested, together with the housekeeper, Mrs. Bernstone, an Indian butler named Lal Rao, and a porter, or gatekeeper, named McMurdo. It is quite certain that the thief or thieves were well acquainted with the house, for Mr. Jones's well-known technical knowledge and his powers of **minute**[27] observation have enabled him to prove conclusively that the miscreants could not have entered by the door or by the window but must have made their way across the roof of the building, and so through a trapdoor into a room which communicated with that in which the body was found. This fact, which has been very clearly made out, proves conclusively that it was no mere **haphazard**[28] burglary. The prompt and energetic action of the officers of the law shows the great advantage of the presence on such occasions of a single vigorous and masterful mind. We cannot but think that it supplies an argument to those who would wish to see our detectives more de-centralized, and so brought into closer and more effective touch with the cases which it is their duty to investigate.*

"Isn't it **gorgeous**[29]!" said Holmes, grinning over his coffee cup. "What do you think of it?"

"I think that we have had a close shave ourselves of being arrested for the crime."

"So do I. I wouldn't answer for our safety now if he should happen to have

昨晚大约 12 点发现上诺伍德樱塘别墅的巴塞洛缪·肖尔托先生在他的房间死亡，情况表明是谋杀。据我们所能了解，没有在肖尔托先生身上发现任何实际的暴力痕迹，但死者继承他父亲的一批贵重的印度宝石已被人拿走。首先发现这件事的是死者的弟弟撒迪厄斯·肖尔托先生，以及前来访问死者的夏洛克·福尔摩斯先生和华生医生。异常侥幸的是，侦探部队的著名成员阿塞尔尼·琼斯先生正好在上诺伍德警察局，所以接警后不到半小时就赶到了现场。他训练有素，经验丰富，马上侦查到了那些罪犯，取得了满意结果，死者的弟弟撒迪厄斯·肖尔托已经被捕，一块被捕的还有女管家伯恩斯通太太、名叫拉尔·拉奥的印度仆人和名叫麦克默多的门房或看门人。完全肯定的是，这名或多名窃贼对这座房子非常熟悉，因为琼斯先生清晰明了的技术知识和细致入微的观察能力已经使他能最后证明，罪犯不可能是从门窗，肯定是从屋顶，通过一个暗门，进入那个与发现尸体相通的房间。这个已经一目了然的事实最后证明，这绝不仅仅是偶然的入室盗窃案。警探们迅速积极的行动表明，在这种情况下，一位精力充沛、巧妙熟练的人在场会有多么大的好处。我们不能不认为，有些人希望看到我们的侦探更加分散，以便更加密切有效地接触和他们职责有关的案件调查，这样做就向他们证实了这一点。

"好极了！"福尔摩斯一边喝咖啡，一边咧嘴笑道，"你对这件事有什么看法？"

"我想我们也差点儿被当成凶手被捕。"

"我也这么想。如果他正好又心血来潮，我现在就无法保证我们的安全了。"

四签名

another of his attacks of energy."

At this moment there was a loud ring at the bell, and I could hear Mrs. Hudson, our landlady, raising her voice in a wail of **expostulation**[30] and dismay.

"By heavens, Holmes," I said, half rising, "I believe that they are really after us."

"No, it's not quite so bad as that. It is the unofficial force—the Baker Street irregulars."

As he spoke, there came a swift pattering of naked feet upon the stairs, a clatter of high voices, and in rushed a dozen dirty and ragged little street Arabs. There was some show of discipline among them, despite their **tumultuous**[31] entry, for they instantly drew up in line and stood facing us with expectant faces. One of their number, taller and older than the others, stood forward with an air of lounging superiority which was very funny in such a disreputable little scarecrow.

"Got your message, sir," said he, "and brought 'em on sharp. Three bob and a tanner for tickets."

"Here you are," said Holmes, producing some silver. "In future they can report to you, Wiggins, and you to me. I cannot have the house invaded in this way. However, it is just as well that you should all hear the instructions. I want to find the whereabouts of a steam launch called the *Aurora*, owner Mordecai Smith, black with two red streaks, **funnel**[32] black with a white band. She is down the river somewhere. I want one boy to be at Mordecai Smith's landing-stage opposite Millbank to say if the boat comes back. You must divide it out among yourselves and do both banks thoroughly. Let me know the moment you have news. Is that all clear?"

"Yes, guv'nor," said Wiggins.

"The old scale of pay, and a guinea to the boy who finds the boat. Here's a day in advance. Now off you go!"

He handed them a shilling each, and away they buzzed down the stairs, and I saw them a moment later streaming down the street.

"If the launch is above water they will find her," said Holmes as he rose

正在这时,门铃大声响起,随后我可以听到我们的女房东哈得逊太太因劝告和惊慌而抬高了声音。

"天哪,福尔摩斯,"我半站起来说,"我相信他们真的在追我们。"

"不,还没有糟糕到那种地步。这是非官方部队——贝克街的非正规军。"

在他说话的当儿,楼梯上就传来了赤脚飞走的啪嗒声和大声喧哗。随后,冲进来十几个蓬头垢面、衣衫褴褛的街头流浪儿。尽管他们闹哄哄地进来,但他们还是表现出一些纪律性,因为他们马上站成一排,一脸期待,面向我们站立。其中一名个子较高,年龄较大,站到前面,一副懒散的优越神情,这在这样一群衣衫褴褛的小孩中非常滑稽。

"先生,接到你的命令,"他说,"就马上带他们来了。车票3先令6便士。"

"给,"福尔摩斯掏出一些银币说,"威金斯,以后他们可以向你报告,然后你对我报告。我不能让房间闯进这么多人。不过,这样也好,你们都应该听到我的命令。我要找到一只名叫'曙光女神号'的汽艇的下落,船主叫莫迪凯·史密斯,船身黑中带两条红色条纹,烟囱黑中带有一条白道。这只船在河下游的某个地方。我要一个男孩守在密尔班克感化院对岸莫迪凯·史密斯的栈桥边,看船回不回来。你们必须分散开来,彻底守在两岸。一有消息,就告诉我。都听明白了吗?"

"明白了,老板,"威金斯说。

"报酬还是老规矩,给找到船的那个男孩一畿尼。这是提前给你们的一天工资。好了,你们走吧!"

他递给他们每人一先令。随后,他们蜂拥着跑下了楼梯。我看到他们不一会儿就鱼贯走向了大街。

"如果这只船浮在水上,他们就会找到它,"福尔摩斯一边从桌边站起来,

from the table and lit his pipe. "They can go everywhere, see everything, overhear everyone. I expect to hear before evening that they have spotted her. In the meanwhile, we can do nothing but await results. We cannot pick up the broken trail until we find either the *Aurora* or Mr. Mordecai Smith."

"Toby could eat these scraps, I dare say. Are you going to bed, Holmes?"

"No: I am not tired. I have a curious **constitution**[33]. I never remember feeling tired by work, though idleness exhausts me completely. I am going to smoke and to think over this queer business to which my fair client has introduced us. If ever man had an easy task, this of ours ought to be. Wooden-legged men are not so common, but the other man must, I should think, be absolutely unique."

"That other man again!"

"I have no wish to make a mystery of him to you, anyway. But you must have formed your own opinion. Now, do consider the data. Diminutive footmarks, toes never fettered by boots, naked feet, stone-headed wooden **mace**[34], great **agility**[35], small poisoned darts. What do you make of all this?"

"A savage!" I exclaimed. "Perhaps one of those Indians who were the associates of Jonathan Small."

"Hardly that," said he. "When first I saw signs of strange weapons I was inclined to think so, but the remarkable character of the footmarks caused me to reconsider my views. Some of the inhabitants of the Indian **Peninsula**[36] are small men, but none could have left such marks as that. The Hindoo proper has long and thin feet. The sandal-wearing Mohammedan has the great toe well separated from the others because the thong is commonly passed between. These little darts, too, could only be shot in one way. They are from a blow-pipe. Now, then, where are we to find our savage?"

"South America," I **hazarded**[37].

He stretched his hand up and took down a bulky volume from the shelf.

"This is the first volume of a **gazetteer**[38] which is now being published. It may be looked upon as the very latest authority.

点起烟斗，一边说。"他们哪里都可以去，什么人都可以见到，什么话都可以偷听。我预料，傍晚之前就会听到他们发现汽艇的消息。在此期间，我们只能等待结果。我们要等找到'曙光女神号'或莫迪凯·史密斯，才能得到中断的线索。"

"我敢说，托比可以吃这些残羹剩饭。福尔摩斯，你要上床睡觉吗？"

"不，我不累。我有不寻常的体质。我工作时从来想不起累，懒散倒会让我筋疲力尽。我要抽烟，仔细考虑漂亮的客户让我们办的这个奇案。如果有什么容易办的事儿，我们这个案子就应该是。木腿人并不是那样常见，但我想另一个人一定是绝无仅有。"

"又是另一个人！"

"反正，我对你绝不想把他神秘化。不过，你一定已经形成了自己的看法。现在，请考虑一下那些材料。小小的脚印、从未穿过靴子的脚趾、赤脚、一端装有石头的木棒、行动极其敏捷、小毒飞镖。你对所有这一切作何解释呢？"

"野人！"我大声喊道，"可能是和乔纳森·斯莫尔同伙的一个印度人。"

"几乎不可能，"他说，"我第一次看到奇怪武器的迹象时，也这样认为，但那些脚印的显著特征使我重新考虑自己的观点。尽管印度半岛的一些居民个子矮小，但谁也不可能留下这样的脚印。真正印度人的脚瘦长。穿凉鞋的伊斯兰教徒因为鞋带常常缚在趾缝间，所以大脚趾和其他脚趾完全分开。这些小飞镖也只能以一种方式发射，就是从吹管里发射。那么，我们要去哪里找野人呢？"

"南美洲，"我冒昧地说。

他伸出一只手，从书架上取下了一本厚书。

"这是现在出版的地名辞典的第一卷，可以看作是最新的权威著作。我

What have we here?

"*Andaman Islands, situated 340 miles to the north of Sumatra, in the Bay of Bengal.*"

Hum! hum! What's all this? Moist climate, coral reefs, sharks, Port Blair, convict barracks, Rutland Island, cottonwoods—Ah, here we are!

"*The **aborigines**[39] of the Andaman Islands may perhaps claim the distinction of being the smallest race upon this earth, though some **anthropologists**[40] prefer the Bushmen of Africa, the Digger Indians of America, and the Terra del Fuegians. The average height is rather below four feet, although many full-grown adults may be found who are very much smaller than this. They are a fierce, morose, and intractable people, though capable of forming most devoted friendships when their confidence has once been gained.*"

Mark that, Watson. Now, then listen to this.

"*They are naturally **hideous**[41], having large, **misshapen**[42] heads, small fierce eyes, and distorted features. Their feet and hands, however, are remarkably small. So **intractable**[43] and fierce are they, that all the efforts of the British officials have failed to win them over in any degree. They have always been a terror to shipwrecked crews, braining the survivors with their stone-headed clubs or shooting them with their poisoned arrows. These massacres are **invariably**[44] concluded by a cannibal feast.*"

Nice, **amiable**[45] people, Watson! If this fellow had been left to his own unaided devices, this affair might have taken an even more **ghastly**[46] turn. I fancy that, even as it is, Jonathan Small would give a good deal not to have employed him."

"But how came he to have so singular a companion?"

"Ah, that is more than I can tell. Since, however, we had already determined

们在这里查到了什么?

"安达曼群岛位于孟加拉湾,距苏门答腊北 340 英里。

哼!哼!这都是什么?气候潮湿、珊瑚暗礁、鲨鱼、布莱尔港、囚犯营、罗特兰德岛、三叶杨——啊,我们找到了!'

"安达曼群岛的原居民也许可称为这世界上最小的种族,尽管一些人类学者宁愿选择非洲的布须曼人、美洲的迪格尔印第安人和火地岛人。平均身高都在 4 英尺以下,许多成年人可能比这还要矮得多。他们凶猛、乖僻、倔强,一旦得到他们的信任,就可以结下最忠诚的友谊。

注意这一点,华生。好了,然后听听这个。

"他们天生丑恶,长有畸形的大头、凶猛的小眼和扭曲的容貌。不过,手和脚特别小。他们倔强凶猛,英国军官竭尽全力,也无法把他们争取过来。对失事船只的水手们来说,他们用镶着石头的木棒打碎水手们的脑袋,或者是用毒箭射击,永远让人毛骨悚然。这种残杀总是以人肉盛筵结束。

和蔼可亲的好人,华生!如果放任这个家伙使用自己的独立装置,这件事就可能会变得更加可怕。我想,即使真是这样,乔纳森·斯莫尔也会放弃许多,不会雇用他。"

"可他是怎么找到这样一个奇怪同伴的呢?"

四签名

that Small had come from the Andamans, it is not so very wonderful that this islander should be with him. No doubt we shall know all about it in time. Look here, Watson; you look regularly done. Lie down there on the sofa and see if I can put you to sleep."

He took up his violin from the corner, and as I stretched myself out he began to play some low, dreamy, **melodious**[47] air—his own, no doubt, for he had a remarkable gift for improvisation. I have a vague remembrance of his **gaunt**[48] limbs, his earnest face and the rise and fall of his bow. Then I seemed to be floated peacefully away upon a soft sea of sound until I found myself in dreamland, with the sweet face of Mary Morstan looking down upon me.

"啊，这我就无从得知了。不过，既然我们已经确定斯莫尔来自安达曼群岛，这个岛民和他在一起也就不那么令人惊奇了。毫无疑问，我们迟早会知道所有这一切。喂，华生，看来你是筋疲力尽了。在那张沙发上躺下来，看我是否能让你入睡。"

他从屋角拿起小提琴，我在沙发上伸展四肢，他开始奏起一支低沉如梦、旋律优美的曲子——毫无疑问是他自己的曲子，因为他有即兴演奏的非凡天赋。我还模糊记得他骨瘦如柴的四肢、郑重其事的脸庞和上下起伏的琴弓。随后，我仿佛在柔和的音乐之海上安详地漂浮而去，进入了梦乡，只见玛丽·摩斯坦楚楚动人的脸庞正在俯视着我。

Notes:
1. infallibility *n.* 绝无错误；绝对可靠性
2. wharf *n.* 码头；停泊处
3. landing-stage 栈桥
4. placard *n.* 宣传广告画；广告
5. inscription *n.* 题名；题字
6. launch *n.* 汽艇；游艇
7. ominous *adj.* 不吉的；不祥的
8. preconcerted *adj.* 预定的；事先计划的
9. stoutish *adj.* 略胖的
10. imp *n.* 小淘气；小鬼
11. ponder *vi.* （仔细）考虑；深思；默想
12. prodigy *n.* 奇才；天才（尤指神童）
13. outlandish *adj.* 古怪的；奇异的
14. winder *n.* (window 的变体) 窗户
15. streak *n.* （与周围有所不同的）条纹
16. wherry *n.* 摆渡船；一种小平底船
17. colossal *adj.* 巨大的
18. penitentiary *n.* 教养所；感化院；
19. on the cards *adv.* 可能
20. dispatch *vt.* 发送
21. fatigued *adj.* 疲乏的
22. antipathy *n.* 厌恶；反感；不相容（to）
23. ubiquitous *adj.* 无处不在的
24. foul play *n.* 不公平的比赛；不公平
25. detection *n.* 察觉；侦查
26. gratifying *adj.* 可喜的；令人满足的
27. minute *adj.* 极详细的；准确的
28. haphazard *adj.* 随意的；无计划的
29. gorgeous *adj.* 极好的
30. expostulation *n.* 劝告
31. tumultuous *adj.* 混乱的；嘈杂的

32. funnel *n.* （轮船；火车等的）烟囱
33. constitution *n.* 体格；体质
34. mace *n.* 钉头；权杖
35. agility *n.* 敏捷；活泼
36. peninsula *n.* 半岛
37. hazard *vt.* 尝试着做
38. gazetteer *n.* 地名索引；地名词典
39. aborigines *n.* 土著居民；原始的居民
40. anthropologist *n.* 人类学者；人类学家
41. hideous *adj.* 极其丑陋的
42. misshapen *adj.* 奇形怪状的
43. intractable *adj.* 难对付的；难管教的
44. invariably *adv.* 始终不变地；总是
45. amiable *adj.* 好脾气的；和蔼的
46. ghastly *adj.* 极坏的；可怕的
47. melodious *adj.* 音调悦耳的；旋律优美的
48. gaunt *adj.* 憔悴的；骨瘦如柴的

# Chapter 9

## A BREAK IN THE CHAIN

# 第九章

## 线索中断

It was late in the afternoon before I woke, strengthened and refreshed. Sherlock Holmes still sat exactly as I had left him, save that he had laid aside his violin and was deep in a book. He looked across at me as I stirred, and I noticed that his face was dark and troubled.

"You have slept soundly," he said. "I feared that our talk would wake you."

"I heard nothing," I answered. "Have you had fresh news, then?"

"Unfortunately, no. I confess that I am surprised and disappointed. I expected something definite by this time. Wiggins has just been up to report. He says that no trace can be found of the launch. It is a **provoking**[1] check, for every hour is of importance."

"Can I do anything? I am perfectly fresh now, and quite ready for another night's outing."

"No; we can do nothing. We can only wait. If we go ourselves the message might come in our absence and delay be caused. You can do what you will, but I must remain on guard."

"Then I shall run over to Camberwell and call upon Mrs. Cecil Forrester. She asked me to, yesterday."

"On Mrs. Cecil Forrester?" asked Holmes with the twinkle of a smile in his eyes.

"Well, of course on Miss Morstan, too. They were anxious to hear what happened."

"I would not tell them too much," said Holmes. "Women are never to be entirely trusted—not the best of them."

I did not pause to argue over this **atrocious**[2] sentiment.

"I shall be back in an hour or two," I remarked.

"All right! Good luck! But, I say, if you are crossing the river you may as well return Toby, for I don't think it is at all likely that we shall have any use for him now."

I took our **mongrel**[3] accordingly and left him, together with a half-sovereign, at the old naturalist's in Pinchin Lane. At Camberwell I found Miss Morstan a little weary after her night's adventures but very eager to hear the news. Mrs. Forrester, too, was full of curiosity. I told them all that we had

我醒来时已经是傍晚了，体力恢复，精神振作。夏洛克·福尔摩斯完全还像我入睡前那样端坐在那里，只是他已经把小提琴放在了一边，专心在看一本书。我醒来时，他看着我，我注意到他的脸色阴沉困惑。

"你睡得真香，"他说，"我还担心我们的谈话会吵醒你。"

"我什么也没有听到，"我回答说，"那你得到什么新消息了吗？"

"不幸的是，还没有。我承认，我非常吃惊和失望。我还料想这时会有确切消息。威金斯刚上来报告过。他说无法找到汽艇的任何踪迹。这一停滞真让人恼火，因为每时每刻都很重要。"

"我能做什么吗？我现在精神饱满，为下一晚外出完全作好了准备。"

"不，我们什么也不能做，只能等。如果我们自己离开，消息可能会在我们离开时过来，那就要耽搁。你愿意做什么就可以做什么，但我必须守在这里。"

"那我想跑到坎伯威尔拜访塞西尔·弗里斯特太太。昨天她就请我去。"

"是拜访塞西尔·弗里斯特太太吗？"福尔摩斯眼里闪着笑意问道。

"啊，当然也要拜访摩斯坦小姐。她们都渴望听到发生了什么事儿。"

"我可不会告诉她们太多，"福尔摩斯说，"绝不能完全相信女人——即便是最好的女人，也不能。"

我没有停下来，和他辩论这个恶劣观点。

"我一两个小时就回来，"我说。

"好吧！祝你好运！可是，我说，如果你要过河，不妨把托比送回去，因为我想我们现在根本不可能再用它了。"

于是，我把那条杂种狗带到了品钦巷，还给了老博物学家，并给了他半镑金币。到了坎伯威尔，我发现，经过一夜冒险之后，摩斯坦小姐有点儿疲惫，但非常渴望听到消息。弗里斯特太太也充满了好奇。我向她们讲了我们

done, suppressing, however, the more dreadful parts of the tragedy. Thus, although I spoke of Mr. Sholto's death, I said nothing of the exact manner and method of it. With all my omissions, however, there was enough to startle and amaze them.

"It is a romance!" cried Mrs. Forrester. "An injured lady, half a million in treasure, a black cannibal, and a wooden-legged ruffian. They take the place of the conventional dragon or wicked earl."

"And two knight-errants to the rescue," added Miss Morstan with a bright glance at me.

"Why, Mary, your fortune depends upon the issue of this search. I don't think that you are nearly excited enough. Just imagine what it must be to be so rich and to have the world at your feet!"

It sent a little thrill of joy to my heart to notice that she showed no sign of elation at the prospect. On the contrary, she gave a toss of her proud head, as though the matter were one in which she took small interest.

"It is for Mr. Thaddeus Sholto that I am anxious," she said. "Nothing else is of any **consequence**[4]; but I think that he has behaved most kindly and honourably throughout. It is our duty to clear him of this dreadful and unfounded charge."

It was evening before I left Camberwell, and quite dark by the time I reached home. My companion's book and pipe lay by his chair, but he had disappeared. I looked about in the hope of seeing a note, but there was none.

"I suppose that Mr. Sherlock Holmes has gone out," I said to Mrs. Hudson as she came up to lower the blinds.

"No, sir. He has gone to his room, sir. Do you know, sir," sinking her voice into an impressive whisper, "I am afraid for his health."

"Why so, Mrs. Hudson?"

"Well, he's that strange, sir. After you was gone he walked and he walked, up and down, and up and down, until I was weary of the sound of his footstep. Then I heard him talking to himself and muttering, and every time the bell rang out he came on the stairhead, with 'What is that, Mrs. Hudson?' And now

做的一切,但隐瞒了那个惨案更可怕的地方。因此,我说到了肖尔托先生之死,但对确切的方式和方法什么也没有说。然而,尽管我进行了种种省略,还是够让她们震惊不已。

"这是一部传奇故事!"弗里斯特太太说,"一位受到伤害的女士、50万英镑的财宝、一个黑种食人生番,还有一个木腿恶棍,取代了传统的龙或邪恶的伯爵。"

"还有两位侠客的援救,"摩斯坦小姐神情欢快地望着我补充说。

"啊,玛丽,你的财富要靠这次搜寻的结果。我看你并不怎么兴奋。请想一下,这样富起来,全世界都在你的脚下,该是什么样子!"

我注意到她对这情景没有露出任何兴高采烈的迹象,这使我心里高兴得有点儿发抖。相反,她骄傲地扬了扬头,好像她对这件事不大关心。

"我是为撒迪厄斯·肖尔托先生担忧,"她说,"其他所有的一切都不重要,但我认为他始终表现得非常亲切体面。我们的责任就是为他洗清这可怕的无稽之罪。"

我离开坎伯威尔之前,天已黄昏,回到家时天完全黑了。同伴的书和烟斗还在他的椅边,但他已经不见了。我环顾四周,希望看到一张字条,但什么也没有。

"我想夏洛克·福尔摩斯先生已经出去了吧,"哈得逊太太上来放下窗帘时,我对她说。

"不,先生。他到自己的房间去了,先生。先生,你知道吧,"她放低声音,令人难忘地耳语道,"我怕是他的健康问题。"

"为什么会是这样,哈得逊太太?"

"啊,先生,他是那样奇怪。你走后,他走来走去,走来走去,直到我听烦了他的脚步声。后来,我听到他自言自语咕咕哝哝,每次门铃响,他都会走到楼梯口问:'怎么了,哈得逊太太?'现在,他把自己关在屋里,但

四签名

he has slammed off to his room, but I can hear him walking away the same as ever. I hope he's not going to be ill, sir. I ventured to say something to him about cooling medicine, but he turned on me, sir, with such a look that I don't know how ever I got out of the room."

"I don't think that you have any cause to be uneasy, Mrs. Hudson," I answered. "I have seen him like this before. He has some small matter upon his mind which makes him restless."

I tried to speak lightly to our worthy landlady, but I was myself somewhat uneasy when through the long night I still from time to time heard the dull sound of his tread, and knew how his keen spirit was chafing **against**[5] this **involuntary**[6] inaction.

At breakfast-time he looked worn and haggard, with a little fleck of feverish colour upon either cheek.

"You are knocking yourself up, old man," I remarked. "I heard you marching about in the night."

"No, I could not sleep," he answered. "This infernal problem is consuming me. It is too much to be **balked**[7] by so petty an obstacle, when all else had been overcome. I know the men, the launch, everything; and yet I can get no news. I have set other agencies at work and used every means at my **disposal**[8]. The whole river has been searched on either side, but there is no news, nor has Mrs. Smith heard of her husband. I shall come to the conclusion soon that they have **scuttled**[9] the craft. But there are objections to that."

"Or that Mrs. Smith has put us on a wrong scent."

"No, I think that may be dismissed. I had inquiries made, and there is a launch of that description."

"Could it have gone up the river?"

"I have considered that possibility, too, and there is a search-party who will work up as far as Richmond. If no news comes to-day I shall start off myself to-morrow and go for the men rather than the boat. But surely, surely, we shall hear something."

We did not, however. Not a word came to us either from Wiggins or from the other agencies. There were articles in most of the papers upon the Norwood

我仍然可以听到他在不停地走动。先生,我希望他不会生病。先生,我刚才冒昧地对他说吃些镇静药,但他转向我这样看着我,所以我都不知道自己是如何走出了那个房间。"

"我想你没有任何理由不安,哈得逊太太,"我回答说,"我以前也见过他这样。他心里有一点小事,就会坐立不安。"

我尽力轻松地对我们可敬的女房东说话,但当我在漫漫长夜仍然不时听到他沉闷的脚步声,知道他的敏锐精神对这种本能迟钝而恼火时,我自己也有点儿不安。

第二天早饭时,他看上去疲惫憔悴,脸颊有一点发烧的颜色。

"老兄,你要让自己筋疲力尽,"我说,"我听到你夜里在走来走去。"

"不,我睡不着,"他回答说,"这个可恨的问题让我心神疲惫。所有其他障碍都已经克服了,这个微不足道的障碍却挡住了去路,真让人受不了。我知道那些人、汽艇和所有的一切,但我就是无法得到任何消息。我已经让其他机构行动起来,动用我能支配的一切手段。整条河的两岸都已经搜寻了一遍,但没有任何消息,史密斯太太也没有听到丈夫的消息。我马上就要得出结论,认为他们已经凿洞把船沉到了河底。可是,有一些情况却使这种结论不成立。"

"要么是史密斯太太让我们迷失了方向。"

"不,我想这可以不予考虑。我已经让人打听过,确实有这样一艘汽艇。"

"它可能顺河而上吗?"

"我也想到了那种可能性,而且有一支搜寻队要逐步搜寻到里士满。如果今天还没有消息,我明天就要亲自出发去找那些人,而不是那艘船。但是,我们肯定、肯定会听到一些消息。"

然而,我们没有听到消息,威金斯和其他机构都没有给我们送来消息。

四签名

tragedy. They all appeared to be rather hostile to the unfortunate Thaddeus Sholto. No fresh details were to be found, however, in any of them, save that an inquest was to be held upon the following day. I walked over to Camberwell in the evening to report our ill-success to the ladies, and on my return I found Holmes **dejected**[10] and somewhat **morose**[11]. He would hardly reply to my questions and busied himself all the evening in an **abstruse**[12] chemical analysis which involved much heating of retorts and distilling of vapours, ending at last in a smell which fairly drove me out of the apartment. Up to the small hours of the morning I could hear the clinking of his test-tubes which told me that he was still engaged in his **malodorous**[13] experiment.

In the early dawn I woke with a start and was surprised to find him standing by my bedside, clad in a rude sailor dress with a pea-jacket and a coarse red scarf round his neck.

"I am off down the river, Watson," said he. "I have been turning it over in my mind, and I can see only one way out of it. It is worth trying, at all events."

"Surely I can come with you, then?" said I.

"No; you can be much more useful if you will remain here as my representative. I am loath to go, for it is quite on the cards that some message may come during the day, though Wiggins was despondent about it last night. I want you to open all notes and telegrams, and to act on your own judgment if any news should come. Can I rely upon you?"

"Most certainly."

"I am afraid that you will not be able to wire to me, for I can hardly tell yet where I may find myself. If I am in luck, however, I may not be gone so very long. I shall have news of some sort or other before I get back."

I had heard nothing of him by breakfast time. On opening the Standard, however, I found that there was a fresh **allusion**[14] to the business.

> With reference to the Upper Norwood tragedy [it remarked] *we have reason to believe that the matter promises to be even more complex and mysterious than was originally supposed. Fresh evidence has shown that it is quite impossible that Mr. Thaddeus Sholto could have been in any way concerned*

大多数报纸都刊登了诺伍德惨案的文章。他们都对不幸的撒迪厄斯·肖尔托相当有敌意。然而,除了官方要在第二天验尸,没有发现任何新的细节。我傍晚步行去坎伯威尔,向两位女士报告我们的失利情况。我回来时发现福尔摩斯垂头丧气,有点儿闷闷不乐。他几乎没有回答我的问题,整个晚上都在那里忙着一项深奥的化学实验。这项实验多次加热曲颈瓶和蒸汽蒸馏,最后产生的气味迫使我离开了房间。直到第二天凌晨,我还能听见试管的丁当声。这告诉我,他还在那里进行这臭烘烘的实验。

黎明时分,我猛地惊醒,惊讶地发现他站在我的床边,身穿粗陋的水手服装,外面套着厚呢短大衣,脖子上围着一条粗织的红围巾。

"华生,我要顺河而下,"他说,"我一直在脑海里反复考虑这个问题,看到只能这样做了。无论如何,这值得一试。"

"那我肯定能和你一起去吧?"我说。

"不,如果你留在这里作我的代表,可能要有用得多。我不愿意去,因为今天很有可能会送来消息,尽管昨晚威金斯垂头丧气。我想让你打开所有来信和电报,如果有什么消息,可以按照你自己的判断行动。我能依靠你吗?"

"当然能。"

"我怕你无法给我发电报,因为我绝不可能晓得自己可能在哪里。可是,如果运气好的话,我不会去很久。我回来前,一定会有这样或那样的消息。"

早饭时,我还没有听到他的任何消息。然而,打开《旗帜报》,我发现上面最新提到了这个案子。

关于上诺伍德惨案,我们有理由相信,案情要比原来推测的复杂和神秘。新的证据已经表明,撒迪厄斯·肖尔托先生完全不可能与本案有任何关系。

四签名

in the matter. He and the housekeeper, Mrs. Bernstone, were both released yesterday evening. It is believed, however, that the police have a clue as to the real **culprits**[15], and that it is being prosecuted by Mr. Athelney Jones, of Scotland Yard, with all his well-known energy and **sagacity**[16]. Further arrests may be expected at any moment.

"That is satisfactory so far as it goes," thought I. "Friend Sholto is safe, at any rate. I wonder what the fresh clue may be, though it seems to be a **stereotyped**[17] form whenever the police have made a **blunder**[18]."

I tossed the paper down upon the table, but at that moment my eye caught an advertisement in the agony **column**[19]. It ran in this way:

LOST—Whereas Mordecai Smith, boatman, and his son Jim, left Smith's Wharf at or about three o'clock last Tuesday morning in the steam launch Aurora, black with two red stripes, funnel black with a white band, the sum of five pounds will be paid to anyone who can give information to Mrs. Smith, at Smith's Wharf, or at 221B, Baker Street, as to the whereabouts of the said Mordecai Smith and the launch Aurora.

This was clearly Holmes's doing. The Baker Street address was enough to prove that. It struck me as rather **ingenious**[20] because it might be read by the fugitives without their seeing in it more than the natural anxiety of a wife for her missing husband.

It was a long day. Every time that a knock came to the door or a sharp step passed in the street, I imagined that it was either Holmes returning or an answer to his advertisement. I tried to read, but my thoughts would wander off to our strange quest and to the ill-assorted and **villainous**[21] pair whom we were pursuing. Could there be, I wondered, some radical flaw in my companion's reasoning? Might he not be suffering from some huge self-deception? Was it not possible that his nimble and speculative mind had built up this wild theory upon faulty premises? I had never known him to be wrong, and yet the keenest reasoner may occasionally be deceived. He was likely, I thought, to fall into

昨晚，他和女管家伯恩斯通太太已被释放。至于真正的罪犯，人们认为警方有了线索。此案将由伦敦警察厅以干练睿智著称的阿塞尔尼·琼斯先生提起公诉。随时都有可能逮捕更多的罪犯。

"就目前情况来说，这还算令人满意，"我想，"至少朋友肖尔托是安全的。我不知道新的线索可能是什么，无论什么时候警方出大错，好像总是这老一套。

我把报纸扔在桌子上，但这时，我的目光看到了私人广告栏里的一则启事。启事是这样写的：

**失踪**——船主莫迪凯·史密斯和他的儿子吉姆上周二凌晨3点左右乘'曙光女神号'汽艇离开史密斯码头。'曙光女神号'黑色船身带两道红色条纹，黑色烟囱带一道白边。凡是能向史密斯码头或贝克街221号B座史密斯太太提供信息者，将获得5英镑酬金。

这显然是福尔摩斯干的。贝克街的住址就足以证明这一点。我之所以认为这个启事颇为巧妙，是因为即使那些逃亡者看到，也会认为那不过是妻子寻找失踪丈夫自然产生的焦虑之情。

这是漫长的一天。每次传来敲门声或街上突然经过脚步声，我都以为是福尔摩斯回来或有人前来回应启事。我努力想看书，但思想常常跑到我们对那个案件的奇异调查上，跑到我们正在追踪的那两个不相匹配的歹徒身上。我怀疑，会不会是同伴的推理出现了根本错误呢？他会不会在犯自欺欺人的极大错误呢？会不会是他机敏善思的头脑在错误前提上建立了这种轻率理论呢？我从来没有见过他出现错误，但最敏锐的推理者偶尔也可能受骗。我想，他很可能是逻辑过

error through the over-refinement of his logic—his preference for a subtle and bizarre explanation when a plainer and more commonplace one lay ready to his hand. Yet, on the other hand, I had myself seen the evidence, and I had heard the reasons for his deductions. When I looked back on the long chain of curious circumstances, many of them trivial in themselves but all tending in the same direction, I could not disguise from myself that even if Holmes's explanation were incorrect the true theory must be equally **outre**[22] and startling.

At three o'clock on the afternoon there was a loud peal at the bell, an **authoritative**[23] voice in the hall, and, to my surprise, no less a person than Mr. Athelney Jones was shown up to me. Very different was he, however, from the brusque and masterful professor of common sense who had taken over the case so confidently at Upper Norwood. His expression was downcast, and his bearing meek and even apologetic.

"Good-day, sir; good-day," said he. "Mr. Sherlock Holmes is out, I understand."

"Yes, and I cannot be sure when he will be back. But perhaps you would care to wait. Take that chair and try one of these cigars."

"Thank you; I don't mind if I do," said he, mopping his face with a red **bandanna**[24] handkerchief.

"And a whisky and soda?"

"Well, half a glass. It is very hot for the time of year, and I have had a good deal to worry and try me. You know my theory about this Norwood case?"

"I remember that you expressed one."

"Well, I have been obliged to reconsider it. I had my net drawn tightly round Mr. Sholto, sir, when pop he went through a hole in the middle of it. He was able to prove an alibi which could not be shaken. From the time that he left his brother's room he was never out of sight of someone or other. So it could not be he who climbed over roofs and through trapdoors. It's a very dark case, and my professional credit is at stake. I should be very glad of a little assistance."

"We all need help sometimes," said I.

"Your friend, Mr. Sherlock Holmes, is a wonderful man, sir," said he in

于精细而出错——当他手里有比较清楚和普通的解释时，他宁愿喜欢微妙奇异的解释。然而，另一方面，我亲眼见过证据，也听过他推断的理由。我回想这一长串奇怪情况，其中许多微不足道，但全都指明同一方向，就毫不掩饰地承认，即使福尔摩斯的解释不正确，真正的理论肯定也同样越出常轨令人吃惊。

下午3点，门铃声轰然响起，门厅传来一个权威的声音，让我吃惊的是，给我领来的不是别人，正是阿塞尔尼·琼斯先生。然而，他和曾经在上诺伍德那样自信地接手本案的粗暴专横的常识专家大相径庭。只见他的表情沮丧，举止温顺，甚至充满歉意。

"你好，先生，你好，"他说，"我听说，福尔摩斯先生出去了。"

"是的，我拿不准他什么时候回来。不过，也许你愿意等。坐在那张椅子上，抽一根雪茄。"

"谢谢你，我会抽的话肯定就抽了，"说着，他用印花大红手帕擦了擦脸。

"一杯威士忌酒加苏打好吗？"

"好吧，要半杯。今年这个时候还很热，让我烦恼的事儿有好多，也是对我的考验。你知道我对这个诺伍德案的推测吗？"

"我记得你说过一次。"

"啊，我不得不重新考虑这个案子。先生，我本来已经紧紧地网住了肖尔托先生，他突然中途噗地钻了出去。他能提出无法动摇的自己不在犯罪现场的证明。他从离开哥哥的房间时起，他从来没有离开过别人的视线。所以，爬过房顶从暗门进入房间的人不可能是他。这是一个非常难破的案子，所以我的职业声望濒临危险。如果能得到你们帮助的话我会非常高兴的。"

"我们有时都需要帮助，"我说。

"先生，你的朋友夏洛克·福尔摩斯先生是一个了不起的人，"他用沙哑

a husky and **confidential**[25] voice. "He's a man who is not to be beat. I have known that young man go into a good many cases, but I never saw the case yet that he could not throw a light upon. He is irregular in his methods and a little quick perhaps in jumping at theories, but, on the whole, I think he would have made a most promising officer, and I don't care who knows it. I have had a wire from him this morning, by which I understand that he has got some clue to this Sholto business. Here is his message."

He took the telegram out of his pocket and handed it to me. It was dated from Poplar at twelve o'clock.

*Go to Baker Street at once* [it said]. *If I have not returned, wait for me. I am close on the track of the Sholto gang. You can come with us to-night if you want to be in at the finish.*

"This sounds well. He has evidently picked up the scent again," said I.

"Ah, then he has been at fault too," exclaimed Jones with evident satisfaction. "Even the best of us are thrown off sometimes. Of course this may prove to be a false alarm but it is my duty as an officer of the law to allow no chance to slip. But there is someone at the door. Perhaps this is he."

A heavy step was heard ascending the stair, with a great **wheezing**[26] and rattling as from a man who was sorely put to it for breath. Once or twice he stopped, as though the climb were too much for him, but at last he made his way to our door and entered. His appearance corresponded to the sounds which we had heard. He was an aged man, clad in seafaring **garb**[27], with an old pea-jacket buttoned up to his throat. His back was bowed, his knees were shaky, and his breathing was painfully **asthmatic**[28]. As he leaned upon a thick oaken cudgel his shoulders heaved in the effort to draw the air into his lungs. He had a coloured scarf round his chin, and I could see little of his face save a pair of keen dark eyes, overhung by bushy white brows and long gray side-whiskers. Altogether he gave me the impression of a respectable **master mariner**[29] who had fallen into years and poverty.

"What is it, my man?" I asked.

的声音推心置腹地说,"他是一个打不败的人。我知道这个年轻人研究过好多案子,但我从来没有见过他无法弄清的案子。他的方法不合常规,也许在推测时有点儿快,但总的来说,我认为他本来会成为一名极有前途的警官,而且我不介意有谁知道这一点。今天早上我收到了他的一封电报,由此知道,他已经对肖尔托这个案子有了一些线索。这就是他那封电报。"

他从口袋里掏出电报,递给了我。这封电报是12点钟发自白杨镇。

[电报] 马上到贝克街。如果我还没有回来,就等我。我快接近了肖尔托案一伙的行踪。如果你想参与了结本案,今晚可以和我们同去。

"这听上去不错。他显然又已经找到了线索,"我说。

"啊,这么说,他也出过错,"琼斯显然带着一种满意的口吻说,"就连我们当中最出色的人有时也会失手。当然,这也可能是一场虚惊,但作为警官,我的职责就是不让任何机会错过。可是,门口有人。说不定是他。"

这时传来了上楼的沉重脚步声,还有一个人呼哧呼哧的痛苦喘息声。他停了一两次,好像上楼对他太吃力了,但最后他终于来到门口,走了进来。他的外貌和我们听到的声音相互一致。他是一个老年人,穿着水手服,外面套着厚呢短大衣,纽扣一直扣到了颈部。他背部佝偻,膝盖颤抖,气喘吁吁,非常痛苦。他拄着一根粗橡木棍,肩膀不停地起伏,努力向肺里吸着气,下巴四周围着一条彩色围巾,除了一双敏锐的黑眼睛,我几乎看不到他的脸,悬垂的是浓密的白眉毛和长长的灰色连鬓胡。总之,他给我的印象是一位上了年纪、穷困潦倒、令人尊敬的船长。

"老兄,出了什么事儿?"我问道。

四签名

He looked about him in the slow methodical fashion of old age.

"Is Mr. Sherlock Holmes here?" said he.

"No; but I am acting for him. You can tell me any message you have for him."

"It was to him himself I was to tell it," said he.

"But I tell you that I am acting for him. Was it about Mordecai Smith's boat?"

"Yes. I know well where it is. An' I know where the men he is after are. An' I know where the treasure is. I know all about it."

"Then tell me, and I shall let him know."

"It was to him I was to tell it," he repeated with the **petulant**[30] obstinacy of a very old man.

"Well, you must wait for him."

"No, no; I ain't goin' to lose a whole day to please no one. If Mr. Holmes ain't here, then Mr. Holmes must find it all out for himself. I don't care about the look of either of you, and I won't tell a word."

He shuffled towards the door, but Athelney Jones got in front of him.

"Wait a bit, my friend," said he. "You have important information, and you must not walk off. We shall keep you, whether you like or not, until our friend returns."

The old man made a little run towards the door, but, as Athelney Jones put his broad back up against it, he recognized the uselessness of resistance.

"Pretty sort o' treatment this!" he cried, stamping his stick. "I come here to see a gentleman, and you two, who I never saw in my life, seize me and treat me in this fashion!"

"You will be none the worse," I said. "We shall **recompense**[31] you for the loss of your time. Sit over here on the sofa, and you will not have long to wait."

He came across sullenly enough and seated himself with his face resting on his hands. Jones and I resumed our cigars and our talk. Suddenly, however, Holmes's voice broke in upon us.

"I think that you might offer me a cigar too," he said.

他用老年人的方式慢条斯理地环顾四周。

"夏洛克·福尔摩斯先生在这里吗?"他问道。

"没有,但我是在代他行事。你找有什么事儿,都可以告诉我。"

"我要对他本人说,"他说。

"可是,我告诉你,我是在代他行事。是有关莫迪凯·史密斯船的事儿吗?"

"是的。我完全知道它在哪里,知道他追踪的人在哪里,也知道财宝在哪里。我一切都知道。"

"那就告诉我,我会转告他的。"

"我要告诉的是他,"他以倔老头的态度重复说。

"啊,那你必须等他。"

"不,不,我不会为讨谁喜欢而浪费整整一天。如果福尔摩斯先生不在这里,那福尔摩斯先生必然会亲自查明所有这一切。我可不在乎你们的感受,所以我一个字也不会说。"

他慢腾腾地向门口走去,但阿塞尔尼·琼斯抢在了他前面。

"等一下,我的朋友,"他说,"你有重要消息,你一定不能离开。无论你是否乐意,我们都要留你,直到我们的朋友回来。"

老人小跑向门口,但当阿塞尔尼·琼斯把宽阔的后背靠在门上时,老人认识到反抗也无济于事。

"岂有此理!"他捣着手杖大声说道,"我来这里见一位先生,你们俩我素不相识,却抓住我,这样对待我!"

"你丝毫不会受影响,"我说,"我们会偿还你损失的时间。过来坐在沙发上,你不会等太久。"

他闷闷不乐地走过来,两手托着脸坐下。我和琼斯又继续抽烟谈话。然而,福尔摩斯的声音突然打断了我们。

"我想你们也可以给我一支雪茄,"他说。

四签名

We both started in our chairs. There was Holmes sitting close to us with an air of quiet amusement.

"Holmes!" I exclaimed. "You here! But where is the old man?"

"Here is the old man," said he, holding out a heap of white hair. "Here he is—**wig**[32], whiskers, eyebrows, and all. I thought my disguise was pretty good, but I hardly expected that it would stand that test."

"Ah, you **rogue**[33]!" cried Jones, highly delighted. "You would have made an actor and a rare one. You had the proper workhouse cough, and those weak legs of yours are worth ten pound a week. I thought I knew the glint of your eye, though. You didn't get away from us so easily, you see."

"I have been working in that get-up all day," said he, lighting his cigar. "You see, a good many of the criminal classes begin to know me—especially since our friend here took to publishing some of my cases: so I can only go on the war-path under some simple disguise like this. You got my wire?"

"Yes; that was what brought me here."

"How has your case prospered?"

"It has all come to nothing. I have had to release two of my prisoners, and there is no evidence against the other two."

"Never mind. We shall give you two others in the place of them. But you must put yourself under my orders. You are welcome to all the official credit, but you must act on the lines that I point out. Is that agreed?"

"Entirely, if you will help me to the men."

"Well, then, in the first place I shall want a fast police-boat—a steam launch—to be at the Westminster Stairs at seven o'clock."

"That is easily managed. There is always one about there, but I can step across the road and telephone to make sure."

"Then I shall want two staunch men in case of resistance."

"There will be two or three in the boat. What else?"

"When we secure the men we shall get the treasure. I think that it would be a pleasure to my friend here to take the box round to the young lady to whom half of it rightfully belongs. Let her be the first to open it. Eh, Watson?"

我们俩都从椅子上惊跳起来。只见福尔摩斯正坐在我们身边，一副笑容可掬的神态。

"福尔摩斯！"我惊叫道，"是你在这里！可那个老头在哪里？"

"老人就在这里，"他拿出一把白发说。"他就在这里——假发、腮须、眉毛，都在这里。尽管我想我的伪装相当不错，但我简直没想到它会经受住这种考验。"

"啊，你这坏蛋！"琼斯兴高采烈地喊道，"你真可以当演员了，而且会一名是杰出的演员。你具有贫民院那样标准的咳嗽声，你那双弱不禁风的腿价值每周10英镑。不过，我想我认出了你的眼神。你明白，你从我们身边逃脱还没有那么容易。"

"我一整天都打扮成这个样子在工作，"他点起雪茄说，"你明白，好多好多犯罪分子都渐渐认识了我——尤其是我们这位朋友把我的一些侦探事迹发表以来，所以我只能这样简单化装走上战场。你收到我的电报了吗？"

"收到了，所以我才来这里。"

"你的案子进展得怎么样了？"

"一切都毫无结果。我不得不释放了两个人犯，而且对另外两个也没有任何证据。"

"不用担心。我们会给你另外两个人来代替他们。但是，你必须听我的吩咐。所有官方的荣誉都归你享用，但你必须按章行事。这你同意吗？"

"只要你帮助我找到他们，完全同意。"

"那好吧，首先我想要一艘警用快艇——一艘汽艇——7点在威斯敏斯特码头待命。"

"这个容易做到。那附近总会停一艘，但我可以到路对面打电话确定一下。"

"那我还想要两名坚定可靠的人员，以防对方反抗。"

"船里都会有两三个人。还要别的什么吗？"

"我们抓住那些人，就会得到财宝。我想我这位朋友一定会高兴把财宝箱带

四签名

"It would be a great pleasure to me."

"Rather an irregular proceeding," said Jones, shaking his head. "However, the whole thing is irregular, and I suppose we must wink at it. The treasure must afterwards be handed over to the authorities until after the official investigation."

"Certainly. That is easily managed. One other point. I should much like to have a few details about this matter from the lips of Jonathan Small himself. You know I like to work the details of my cases out. There is no objection to my having an unofficial interview with him, either here in my rooms or elsewhere, as long as he is efficiently guarded?"

"Well, you are master of the situation. I have had no proof yet of the existence of this Jonathan Small. However, if you can catch him, I don't see how I can refuse you an interview with him."

"That is understood, then?"

"Perfectly. Is there anything else?"

"Only that I insist upon your dining with us. It will be ready in half an hour. I have **oysters**[34] and **a brace of**[35] **grouse**[36], with something a little choice in white wines. —Watson, you have never yet recognized my merits as a housekeeper."

给那位小姐,因为财宝其中一半属于她合法所有。让她第一个打开。华生,好吗?"

"这对我将是莫大的荣幸。"

"做法相当不正规,"琼斯摇摇头说,"然而,整个事情都不正规,我想我们必须睁一只眼闭一只眼。随后,财宝必须交给当局,直至经过正式调查。"

"当然可以。这个容易做到。还有一点。我非常想从乔纳森·斯莫尔本人嘴里听到这桩案子的几个细节。你知道,我喜欢解决自己经手案子的那些细节。只要有效看住他,你不会反对我和他在这房间或其他地方进行一次非正式会谈吧?"

"好吧,你是掌握案情的人。我还没有证据能证明乔纳森·斯莫尔这个人的存在。不过,如果你能抓住他,我看我无法拒绝你和他会谈。"

"这么说,明白了?"

"完全明白。还有别的什么吗?"

"只有我坚持留你和我们一起吃晚饭了。半小时就准备好。我有牡蛎和两只松鸡,还有一点上等白葡萄酒。——华生,你还从来没有表扬过我管家的功绩呢。"

Notes:
1. provoking *adj.* 惹人恼火的；气人的
2. atrocious *adj.* 凶暴的；残忍的；恶劣的
3. mongrel *n.* 杂种狗
4. consequence *n.* 重要（性）
5. chafe against 发怒；焦躁
6. involuntary *adj.* 无意识做出的；非故意的
7. balk *vt.* 阻碍；阻止
8. at one's disposal 供任意使用；可自行支配
9. scuttle *vt.* 使船沉没
10. dejected *adj.* 沮丧的；垂头丧气的
11. morose *adj.* 闷闷不乐的；阴郁的
12. abstruse *adj.* 难解的；深奥的
13. malodorous *adj.* 难闻的；有恶臭的
14. allusion *n.* 暗示；暗指；提及
15. culprit *n.* 罪犯；嫌疑犯
16. sagacity *n.* 精明；精确的判断；洞察力
17. stereotyped *adj.* 套用老调的
18. blunder *n.* （因无知、粗心等造成）的错误
19. agony column *n.* （报刊上登载的寻人、寻物、离婚等启事的）私事广告栏
20. ingenious *adj.* 巧妙的
21. villainous *adj.* 邪恶的；凶恶的；可憎的
22. outre *adj.* 越出常轨的
23. authoritative *adj.* 有权力的；有权威的
24. bandanna *n.* 印花大手帕
25. confidential *adj.* 秘密的；表示信任或亲密的
26. wheeze *vi.* 喘息；发出呼哧呼哧的喘息声
27. garb *n.* 装束；打扮；外衣
28. asthmatic *adj.* 哮喘的；患哮喘症
29. master mariner 船长
30. petulant *adj.* 暴躁的；脾气坏的
31. recompense *vt.* 赔偿；补偿

32. wig *n.* 假发
33. rogue *n.* 骗子；家伙
34. oyster *n.* 牡蛎；蚝
35. a brace of 一对
36. grouse *n.* 松鸡

四签名

# Chapter 10

## THE END OF THE ISLANDER

# 第十章

## 岛民的结局

Our meal was a merry one. Holmes could talk exceedingly well when he chose, and that night he did choose. He appeared to be in a state of nervous **exaltation**[1]. I have never known him so brilliant. He spoke on a quick succession of subjects—on **miracle plays**[2], on **mediaeval**[3] pottery, on **Stradivarius**[4] violins, on the Buddhism of Ceylon, and on the warships of the future—handling each as though he had made a special study of it. His bright humour marked the reaction from his black depression of the **preceding**[5] days. Athelney Jones proved to be a sociable soul in his hours of relaxation and faced his dinner with the air of a bon vivant. For myself, I felt **elated**[6] at the thought that we were nearing the end of our task, and I caught something of Holmes's gaiety. None of us **alluded**[7] during dinner to the cause which had brought us together.

When the cloth was cleared Holmes glanced at his watch and filled up three glasses with port.

"One bumper," said he, "to the success of our little expedition. And now it is high time we were off. Have you a pistol, Watson?"

"I have my old service-revolver in my desk."

"You had best take it, then. It is well to be prepared. I see that the cab is at the door. I ordered it for half-past six."

It was a little past seven before we reached the Westminster wharf and found our launch awaiting us. Holmes eyed it critically.

"Is there anything to mark it as a police-boat?"

"Yes, that green lamp at the side."

"Then take it off."

The small change was made, we stepped on board, and the ropes were cast off. Jones, Holmes, and I sat in the stern. There was one man at the rudder, one to tend the engines, and two burly police-inspectors forward.

"Where to?" asked Jones.

"To the Tower. Tell them to stop opposite to Jacobson's Yard."

这顿饭我们吃得非常愉快。只要愿意，福尔摩斯可以侃侃而谈。那天晚上他的确愿意谈。他仿佛处在一种神经兴奋的状态。我还从来不知道他这样才华横溢。他飞快地说起了一连串的话题——奇迹剧啦，中世纪陶器啦，斯特拉迪瓦里小提琴啦，锡兰佛教啦，未来的军舰啦——谈论每个主题，他都像曾经专门研究过似的。前几天的忧郁沮丧顿时化作了欢快情绪。阿塞尔尼·琼斯在放松时刻是一个爱好交际的人，面对这顿晚餐，他带着锦衣玉食者的架子。对我自己来说，我一想到我们的任务快要结束，就兴高采烈，而且也感染了一些福尔摩斯的快乐情绪。吃饭期间，我们谁也没有提到让我们聚到一起的原因。

桌布收拾干净后，福尔摩斯瞥了一眼手表，斟满了三杯波尔多红葡萄酒。

"干一杯，"他说，"为我们小小远征的成功干杯。现在我们该走了。华生，你有手枪吗？"

"我的书桌里有一支军用旧左轮手枪。"

"那你最好带上，作好准备。我看到马车在门口。我吩咐马车6点半来。"

我们到达威斯敏斯特码头时，刚过7点，发现汽艇正在等候我们。福尔摩斯挑剔地注视着汽艇。

"有什么表明是警用船吗？"

"有，船边有绿灯。"

"那就取下来。"

作了小小变化后，我们登上船，解开船缆。我和琼斯、福尔摩斯坐在船尾。一人掌舵，一人管发动机，两名体格魁梧的警官坐在前面。

"开到哪里？"琼斯问道。

"开到伦敦塔，告诉他们停在雅各布森船坞对面。"

四签名

Our craft was evidently a very fast one. We shot past the long lines of loaded barges as though they were **stationary**[8]. Holmes smiled with satisfaction as we overhauled a river steamer and left her behind us.

"We ought to be able to catch anything on the river," he said.

"Well, hardly that. But there are not many launches to beat us."

"We shall have to catch the Aurora, and she has a name for being a **clipper**[9]. I will tell you how the land lies, Watson. You recollect how annoyed I was at being baulked by so small a thing?"

"Yes."

"Well, I gave my mind a thorough rest by plunging into a chemical analysis. One of our greatest statesmen has said that a change of work is the best rest. So it is. When I had succeeded in dissolving the **hydrocarbon**[10] which I was at work at, I came back to our problem of the Sholtos, and thought the whole matter out again. My boys had been up the river and down the river without result. The launch was not at any landing-stage or wharf, nor had it returned. Yet it could hardly have been scuttled to hide their traces, though that always remained as a possible hypothesis if all else failed. I knew that this man Small had a certain degree of low cunning, but I did not think him capable of anything in the nature of delicate **finesse**[11]. That is usually a product of higher education. I then reflected that since he had certainly been in London some time—as we had evidence that he maintained a continual watch over Pondicherry Lodge—he could hardly leave at **a moment's notice**[12], but would need some little time, if it were only a day, to arrange his affairs. That was the balance of probability, at any rate."

"It seems to me to be a little weak," said I; "it is more probable that he had arranged his affairs before ever he set out upon his expedition."

"No, I hardly think so. This lair of his would be too valuable a retreat in case of need for him to give it up until he was sure that he could do without it. But a second consideration struck me. Jonathan Small must have felt that the peculiar appearance of his companion, however much he may have top-coated him, would give rise to gossip, and possibly be associated with this Norwood tragedy. He was quite sharp enough to see that. They had started from their

显然,我们的船速度很快,飞快地驶过长长一溜满载货物的平底船,仿佛这些船静止不动。当我们追上一艘河里的汽船并把它抛在身后时,福尔摩斯满意地微笑着。

"我们应该能追上河上的任何东西,"他说。

"啊,差不多。不过,没有多少汽艇能赶上我们。"

"我们必须追上'曙光女神号',它是一艘有名的快艇。华生,我要把情况告诉你。你还记得我为一件小事受阻有多么恼火吗?"

"记得。"

"啊,我通过化学分析实验,让自己的思想得到了彻底休息。我们的一位最伟大的政治家曾经说过,改变工作是最好的休息。的确如此。我成功地溶解从事的碳氢化合物时,又回到了肖尔托的问题上,把整个事情又想了一遍。我派的那些男孩在河上下游都找了一遍,没有结果。这只汽艇既没有在任何栈桥或码头,也没有回来。然而,绝不可能是沉船来隐藏其踪迹,如果其他的一切都失败,总还有一种可能的假设。我知道斯莫尔这个人有一定程度的粗俗狡猾,但我认为他不可能有任何周密的手段。这样做,通常要受过高等教育。于是,我想到,既然他肯定已经在伦敦呆了一段时间——因为我们有证据表明他不断监视樱塘别墅——他绝不可能马上离开,而是需要一点时间来安排自己的事务,即使只有一天。无论如何,这有可能。"

"在我看来,这似乎有点儿不充分,"我说,"更可能的是,他开始远行之前,就已经安排好了自己的事务。"

"不,我几乎不这样想。这个老巢对他非常重要,万一需要,就可以潜伏,除非他确信无用,否则不会放弃。但是,我又想到了第二点。乔纳森·斯莫尔一定会感到,同伙的奇怪模样,无论穿得多么严实,都会引起别人议论,并可

headquarters under cover of darkness, and he would wish to get back before it was broad light. Now, it was past three o'clock, according to Mrs. Smith, when they got the boat. It would be quite bright, and people would be about in an hour or so. Therefore, I argued, they did not go very far. They paid Smith well to hold his **tongue**[13], **reserved**[14] his launch for the final escape, and hurried to their lodgings with the treasure-box. In a couple of nights, when they had time to see what view the papers took, and whether there was any suspicion, they would make their way under cover of darkness to some ship at Gravesend or in the Downs, where no doubt they had already arranged for passages to America or the Colonies."

"But the launch? They could not have taken that to their lodgings."

"Quite so. I argued that the launch must be no great way off, in spite of its **invisibility**[15]. I then put myself in the place of Small and looked at it as a man of his capacity would. He would probably consider that to send back the launch or to keep it at a wharf would make pursuit easy if the police did happen to get on his track. How, then, could he conceal the launch and yet have her at hand when wanted? I wondered what I should do myself if I were in his shoes. I could only think of one way of doing it. I might hand the launch over to some boat-builder or repairer, with directions to make a trifling change in her. She would then be removed to his shed or yard, and so be **effectually**[16] concealed, while at the same time I could have her at a few hours' notice."

"That seems simple enough."

"It is just these very simple things which are extremely **liable**[17] to be overlooked. However, I determined to act on the idea. I started at once in this harmless seaman's rig and inquired at all the yards down the river. I drew blank at fifteen, but at the sixteenth—Jacobson's—I learned that the *Aurora* had been handed over to them two days ago by a wooden-legged man, with some trivial directions as to her rudder. 'There ain't naught amiss with her rudder,' said the foreman. 'There she lies, with the red streaks.' At that moment who should come down but Mordecai Smith, the missing owner. He was rather the worse for liquor. I should not, of course, have known him, but he **bellowed out**[18] his name and the name of his launch. 'I want her to-night at eight o'clock,' said

能联想到这个诺伍德惨案。斯莫尔目光敏锐,足以看到这一点。他们在夜幕掩护下,已经从老巢出发,而且他希望天亮前赶回来。那么,据史密斯太太说,他们上船时过了3点。天就要大亮,再过大约一小时四处就会有人。所以,我认为他们不会走很远。他们付给史密斯的钱不少,让他守口如瓶,预定下他的汽艇,以备最后逃跑,然后带着财宝箱匆匆赶回住处。两夜后,当他们有时间看报纸上持什么观点,有没有引起什么怀疑后,会在夜幕的掩护下逃到格雷夫森德或唐斯码头的轮船上。毫无疑问,他们已经安排好逃往美洲或殖民地。"

"可汽艇呢?他们不可能把它带到住处。"

"的确如此。我认为,尽管看不到这艘汽艇,但肯定不会离多远。于是,我把自己放在斯莫尔的位置,以他这个人的能力来看这件事。他可能会想到,如果警察碰巧真的跟踪他,那把船送回或停在码头就会使追踪变得易如反掌。那么,他怎么才能把汽艇隐藏起来,需要时又能触手可及呢?我不知道,如果处在他的位置,我自己会怎么做。我只能想到一种做法。我可以把汽艇交给造船商或修理工,吩咐对汽艇作一点小小变动。汽艇就会因此被移到工棚或船坞,这样就可以有效隐藏,同时我提前几小时通知就可以使用。"

"这好像够简单的。"

"正是这些非常简单的事儿,才特别容易忽略。不过,我决定按照这种想法采取行动。我立刻穿上有益无害的水手服,到下游所有船坞去打听。我问了15个船坞,都没有成功,但问到第16个——雅克布森船坞——时,得知两天前一个木腿人把'曙光女神号'交给船坞,轻描淡写地吩咐说让修理一下船舵。'船舵没有任何毛病,'工头说。'就是那艘带有红色条纹的船。'正在这时,过来了一个人,正是失踪的船主莫迪凯·史密斯。他喝得一塌糊涂。我当然不会认识他,而是他大声吼出了自己的名字和汽艇的名字。'我今晚8

he—'eight o'clock sharp, mind, for I have two gentlemen who won't be kept waiting.' They had evidently paid him well, for he was very **flush**[19] of money, chucking shillings about to the men. I followed him some distance, but he subsided into an **alehouse**[20]; so I went back to the yard, and, happening to pick up one of my boys on the way, I stationed him as a **sentry**[21] over the launch. He is to stand at the water's edge and wave his handkerchief to us when they start. We shall be lying off in the stream, and it will be a strange thing if we do not take men, treasure, and all."

"You have planned it all very neatly, whether they are the right men or not," said Jones; "but if the affair were in my hands I should have had a body of police in Jacobson's Yard and arrested them when they came down."

"Which would have been never. This man Small is a pretty shrewd fellow. He would send a scout on ahead, and if anything made him suspicious he would lie **snug**[22] for another week."

"But you might have stuck to Mordecai Smith, and so been led to their hiding-place," said I.

"In that case I should have wasted my day. I think that it is a hundred to one against Smith knowing where they live. As long as he has liquor and good pay, why should he ask questions? They send him messages what to do. No, I thought over every possible course, and this is the best."

While this conversation had been proceeding, we had been shooting the long series of bridges which **span**[23] the Thames. As we passed the City the last rays of the sun were gilding the cross upon the summit of St. Paul's. It was twilight before we reached the Tower.

"That is Jacobson's Yard," said Holmes, pointing to a **bristle**[24] of masts and **rigging**[25] on the Surrey side. "Cruise gently up and down here under cover of this string of lighters." He took a pair of night-glasses from his pocket and gazed some time at the shore. "I see my sentry at his post," he remarked, "but no sign of a handkerchief."

"Suppose we go downstream a short way and lie in wait for them," said Jones eagerly.

We were all eager by this time, even the policemen and stokers, who had a

点想要这艘船,"他说——"记住,8点整,因为我有两位先生,他们是不愿等的。'他们显然付给他不少钱,因为他很有钱,对那些人抛掷着先令。我跟踪了他一段距离,但他躲进了一家酒馆。于是,我又回到船坞,碰巧途中遇到了我的一个小帮手,就派他在那里守着汽艇。当他们起航时,他要站在水边,向我们挥动手帕。我们在河上要保持一段距离,如果我们不能人赃俱获,那将是咄咄怪事。"

"无论他们是不是真凶,你都安排得非常巧妙,"琼斯说,"但如果这件事让我着手处理,我会在雅克布森船坞派一群警察,等他们一下来,就逮捕他们。"

"这绝对不行。斯莫尔这个人相当狡猾。他会先派人侦察。如果什么事儿让他产生怀疑,他会再隐藏一周。"

"但是,你要盯紧莫迪凯·史密斯,也可以找到他们的藏身地,"我说。

"如果是那样,我就会浪费自己的一天。我想,史密斯极有可能不知道他们住在哪里。只要他有酒喝、报酬高,他为什么要问问题呢?要做什么,他们会给他送信。不,各种可能的方法,我都想过了,这是最好的方法。"

这样说着,我们已经飞快地穿过了跨越泰晤士河一系列长长的桥梁。当我们经过城市时,太阳的余晖正金光闪闪地照在圣保罗教堂房顶的十字架上。我们还没有到达伦敦塔,就已黄昏。

"那就是雅克布森船坞,"福尔摩斯指着萨里那边林立的桅杆和帆缆说。"在这一连串驳船的掩护下,悄悄地来回巡航。"他从口袋里掏出夜用望远镜,盯着河岸看了一段时间。"我看到我的哨兵在岗位上,"他说,"但没有手帕的任何迹象。"

"让我们到下游等他们怎么样,"琼斯急切地说。

此时,我们都迫不及待,就连那些对要发生什么事儿都模糊不清的警察

very vague idea of what was going forward.

"We have no right to take anything for granted," Holmes answered. "It is certainly ten to one that they go downstream, but we cannot be certain. From this point we can see the entrance of the yard, and they can hardly see us. It will be a clear night and plenty of light. We must stay where we are. See how the folk swarm over yonder in the gaslight."

"They are coming from work in the yard."

"Dirty-looking rascals, but I suppose every one has some little immortal spark concealed about him. You would not think it, to look at them. There is no a *priori* probability about it. A strange **enigma**[26] is man!"

"Someone calls him a soul concealed in an animal," I suggested.

"Winwood Reade is good upon the subject," said Holmes. "He remarks that, while the individual man is an insoluble puzzle, in the **aggregate**[27] he becomes a mathematical certainty. You can, for example, never foretell what any one man will do, but you can say with precision what an average number will be up to. Individuals vary, but percentages remain constant. So says the **statistician**[28]. But do I see a handkerchief? Surely there is a white flutter over yonder."

"Yes, it is your boy," I cried. "I can see him plainly."

"And there is the *Aurora*," exclaimed Holmes, "and going **like the devil**[29]! Full speed ahead, engineer. Make after that launch with the yellow light. By heaven, I shall never forgive myself if she proves to have the heels of us!"

She had slipped unseen through the yard-entrance and passed between two or three small craft, so that she had fairly got her speed up before we saw her. Now she was flying down the stream, near in to the shore, going at a **tremendous**[30] rate. Jones looked gravely at her and shook his head.

"She is very fast," he said. "I doubt if we shall catch her."

"We *must* catch her!" cried Holmes between his teeth. "Heap it on, **stokers**[31]! Make her do all she can! If we burn the boat we must have them!"

和火夫也迫不及待。

"我们无权认为什么事儿都理所当然,"福尔摩斯回答说,"他们当然十有八九要去下游,但我们无法确定。从这个地点,我们可以看到船坞的入口,而他们绝不可能看到我们。这将是一个晴朗的夜晚,光照很多。我们必须呆在所在的地方。看那些人往煤气灯那边涌得多么厉害。"

"他们正从船坞下班。"

"尽管这些人外表肮脏,但我想每个人内心都藏有一些不灭的火花。你看他们的外表,是想不到的。绝对没有从原因推出结果的可能性。人类就是奇怪的谜!"

"有人把他称为隐藏在动物中的灵魂,"我建议说。

"温伍德·里德对这个问题说得好,"福尔摩斯说,"他说,尽管每个人都是一个不解之谜,但综合起来,他会成为数学的必然。比如,你绝不可能预测任何一个人会做什么,但你可以精确地说出普通人会做什么。人人各不相同,但百分比保持不变。统计学家们也是这样说的。可是,我看到手帕了吗?那边肯定有一个白色东西飘动。"

"对,那是你的小帮手,"我大声说道,"我可以清楚地看到他。"

"那就是'曙光女神号',"福尔摩斯大声叫道,"行驶得飞快!全速前进,机械师。追上那艘带有黄灯的汽艇。老天在上,如果它超过我们,我就永远无法原谅自己!"

"'曙光女神号'已经神不知鬼不觉地悄悄溜过船坞入口,在两三条小船之间穿行,所以还没等我们看到它,它已经完全加速。现在,它靠近河岸,速度惊人,正飞流而下。琼斯神情严峻地看着'曙光女神号',摇了摇头。

"它很快,"他说,"我怀疑我们是否能追上它。"

"我们必须追上它!"福尔摩斯咬牙叫道,"火夫,加煤!让它全速前进!

四签名

We were fairly after her now. The furnaces roared, and the powerful engines whizzed and clanked like a great metallic heart. Her sharp, steep **prow**[32] cut through the still river-water and sent two rolling waves to right and to left of us. With every throb of the engines we sprang and quivered like a living thing. One great yellow lantern in our bows threw a long, flickering funnel of light in front of us. Right ahead a dark blur upon the water showed where the Aurora lay, and the swirl of white foam behind her spoke of the pace at which she was going. We flashed past barges, steamers, merchant-vessels, in and out, behind this one and round the other. Voices hailed us out of the darkness, but still the Aurora thundered on, and still we followed close upon her track.

"Pile it on, men, pile it on!" cried Holmes, looking down into the engine-room, while the fierce glow from below beat upon his eager, **aquiline**[33] face. "Get every pound of steam you can."

"I think we gain a little," said Jones with his eyes on the *Aurora*.

"I am sure of it," said I. "We shall be up with her in a very few minutes."

At that moment, however, as our evil fate would have it, a tug with three barges in tow **blundered**[34] in between us. It was only by putting our helm hard down that we avoided a collision, and before we could round them and recover our way the *Aurora* had gained a good two hundred yards. She was still, however, well in view, and the murky, uncertain twilight was settling into a clear, starlit night. Our boilers were strained to their utmost, and the frail shell **vibrated**[35] and creaked with the fierce energy which was driving us along. We had shot through the pool, past the West India Docks, down the long Deptford Reach, and up again after rounding the Isle of Dogs. The dull blur in front of us resolved itself now clearly into the dainty *Aurora*. Jones turned our searchlight upon her, so that we could plainly see the figures upon her deck. One man sat by the stern, with something black between his knees, over which he stooped. Beside him lay a dark mass, which looked like a Newfoundland dog. The boy held the tiller, while against the red glare of the furnace I could see old Smith, stripped to the waist, and shovelling coals for dear life. They may have had some doubt at first as to whether we were really pursuing them, but now as we followed every winding and turning which they took there

我们就是把船烧了,也必须抓住他们!"

我们眼下紧追其后。锅炉熊熊燃烧。功率强大的发动机像巨大的金属心脏一样发出了呼啸声和铿锵声。又尖又陡的船头划破平静的河水,向我们左右冲起两股滚滚的浪花。船身像是有生命的东西一样,随着发动机的每次抽动,跳跃颤抖。船头的一盏大黄灯笼在我们前方射出了一道长长的摇曳的光束。正前方水面上一个模糊的黑点表明,那是"曙光女神号"所在的位置,它后面旋起的白色浪花说明了它航行的速度。我们掠过驳船、汽船和商船,弯弯曲曲,迂回穿梭。黑暗中有人向我们呼喊,但"曙光女神号"仍然轰鸣前进,所以我们也紧追不放。

"快加煤,伙计们,快加煤!"福尔摩斯冲轮机舱喊道,"尽可能加大蒸汽。"下面熊熊的火光照在他急切的鹰一样的脸上。

"我想我们逼近了一点,"琼斯眼睛望着"曙光女神号"说。

"我确信这一点,"我说,"我们再有几分钟就追上它了。"

然而,正在这时,就像我们该有厄运似的,三艘连在一起的货船闯入了我们和"曙光女神号"之间。只有努力转舵,我们才避免和它相撞,而还没等我们能绕过它们,恢复航线,"曙光女神号"已经超过了足有200码。然而,仍能完全看得见那艘船。阴沉不定的薄暮渐渐变成了繁星闪耀的晴朗夜空。我们的锅炉烧到了极限,脆弱的船壳因驱使我们前进的强大能量而簌簌颤动、吱嘎作响。我们已经飞速穿过了静止深水区,经过了西印度码头,顺着长长的德特福德河段一路下去,绕过多格斯小岛后,又逆流而上。我们前面阴暗模糊的黑点现在清楚地变成了精致的"曙光女神号"。琼斯把我们的探照灯转向它,因此我们可以清晰地看到甲板上的那些人影。一个人坐在船尾,膝盖之间有一个黑色东西,他弯腰看着那个东西。他旁边还躺着一团黑东西,好像是一只纽芬兰狗。

四签名

could no longer be any question about it. At Greenwich we were about three hundred paces behind them. At Blackwall we could not have been more than two hundred and fifty. I have coursed many creatures in many countries during my **checkered**[36] career, but never did sport give me such a wild thrill as this mad, flying man-hunt down the Thames. Steadily we drew in upon them, yard by yard. In the silence of the night we could hear the panting and clanking of their machinery. The man in the stern still crouched upon the deck, and his arms were moving as though he were busy, while every now and then he would look up and measure with a glance the distance which still separated us. Nearer we came and nearer. Jones yelled to them to stop. We were not more than four boat's-lengths behind them, both boats flying at a tremendous pace. It was a clear reach of the river, with Barking Level upon one side and the **melancholy**[37] Plumstead Marshes upon the other. At our hail the man in the stern sprang up from the deck and shook his two clenched fists at us, cursing the while in a high, cracked voice. He was a good-sized, powerful man, and as he stood poising himself with legs astride I could see that from the thigh downward there was but a wooden stump upon the right side. At the sound of his **strident**[38], angry cries, there was movement in the huddled bundle upon the deck. It straightened itself into a little black man—the smallest I have ever seen—with a great, **misshapen**[39] head and a shock of **tangled**[40], dishevelled hair. Holmes had already drawn his revolver, and I whipped out mine at the sight of this savage, distorted creature. He was wrapped in some sort of dark **ulster**[41] or blanket, which left only his face exposed, but that face was enough to give a man a sleepless night. Never have I seen features so deeply marked with all bestiality and cruelty. His small eyes glowed and burned with a sombre light, and his thick lips were writhed back from his teeth, which grinned and chattered at us with half animal fury.

"Fire if he raises his hand," said Holmes quietly.

We were within a boat's-length by this time, and almost within touch of our **quarry**[42]. I can see the two of them now as they stood, the white man with his legs far apart, shrieking out curses, and the **unhallowed**[43] dwarf with his hideous face, and his strong yellow teeth gnashing at us in the light of our

那个男孩把舵,在锅炉红光的映衬下,我可以看到老史密斯光着上身在拼命铲煤。起初,他们也许还有些怀疑我们是否真的是在追赶他们,但现在,无论他们如何转弯抹角,我们都跟在后面时,他们对此不再有任何疑问了。到了格林威治,我们在他们身后大约300步。到了布莱克沃尔,我们相距不可能多于250步。在变化多端的一生中,我曾经在许多国家追赶过许多野兽,但从来没有运动像顺泰晤士河而下飞一般疯狂追人这样惊心动魄。我们一码一码稳步接近他们。在寂静的夜里,我们可以听到他们机器的喷气声和铿锵声。船尾那个人仍然蹲在甲板上,两臂挥动,似乎很忙,他不时抬起头,目测我们还相距多远。我们越来越近了。琼斯呼喊让他们停下。我们在他们身后至多有4只船的长度了,两只船都在飞速前进。这是河流的开阔地段,一边是巴尔金平地,另一边是荒凉的普拉姆斯泰德沼泽地。船尾那个人听到我们的呼喊,从甲板上一跃而起,冲我们挥动拳头,破口大骂。他身材高大,强壮有力,两腿叉开站在那里,保持平衡。我从他的右大腿下面可以看到只有一根木桩。听到他刺耳愤怒的叫声,甲板上蜷缩的那团东西动了起来。那团东西挺直后,变成了一个小黑人——这是我见过的最小的人——大脑袋奇形怪状,上面是一堆乱蓬蓬的头发。福尔摩斯已经拔出了手枪。我看到这个扭曲的野人,也突然掏出了手枪。他裹着深色宽松粗呢长外套或毯子,只露出了脸,但那张脸足以让人一夜难眠。我从来没有见过如此鲜明带着一切兽性和残忍的面容。他的小眼睛闪闪发亮,燃烧着阴沉的光,厚嘴唇从牙齿向外翻起,他龇牙咧嘴,带着半是兽性的愤怒,冲我们喋喋不休。

"如果他抬手,就开枪,"福尔摩斯平静地说。

此时,我们不到一船远了,快要摸到我们的猎物了。我可以看到其中两个人现在站了起来。那个白人两腿叉开,尖声大骂。那个邪恶的侏儒面貌丑陋,

lantern.

It was well that we had so clear a view of him. Even as we looked he plucked out from under his covering a short, round piece of wood, like a school-ruler, and clapped it to his lips. Our pistols rang out together. He whirled round, threw up his arms, and, with a kind of choking cough, fell sideways into the stream. I caught one glimpse of his **venomous**[44], menacing eyes amid the white swirl of the waters. At the same moment the wooden-legged man threw himself upon the rudder and put it hard down, so that his boat made straight in for the southern bank, while we shot past her stern, only clearing her by a few feet. We were round after her in an instant, but she was already nearly at the bank. It was a wild and desolate place, where the moon glimmered upon a wide expanse of marsh-land, with pools of **stagnant**[45] water and beds of decaying vegetation. The launch, with a dull thud, ran up upon the mud-bank, with her bow in the air and her stern flush with the water. The fugitive sprang out, but his stump instantly sank its whole length into the **sodden**[46] soil. In vain he struggled and **writhed**[47]. Not one step could he possibly take either forward or backward. He yelled in impotent rage and kicked frantically into the mud with his other foot, but his struggles only bored his wooden pin the deeper into the sticky bank. When we brought our launch alongside he was so firmly anchored that it was only by throwing the end of a rope over his shoulders that we were able to haul him out and to drag him, like some evil fish, over our side. The two Smiths, father and son, sat sullenly in their launch but came aboard meekly enough when commanded. The *Aurora* herself we hauled off and made fast to our stern. A solid iron chest of Indian workmanship stood upon the deck. This, there could be no question, was the same that had contained the ill-omened treasure of the Sholtos. There was no key, but it was of considerable weight, so we transferred it carefully to our own little cabin. As we steamed slowly upstream again, we flashed our searchlight in every direction, but there was no sign of the Islander. Somewhere in the dark ooze at the bottom of the Thames lie the bones of that strange visitor to our shores.

"See here," said Holmes, pointing to the wooden hatchway. "We were hardly quick enough with our pistols." There, sure enough, just behind where we had

在灯笼的光照中，露出坚固的黄牙，对我们咬牙切齿。

正好我们可以非常清楚地看到他。甚至在我们看着时，他就从遮盖物下面掏出一个又短又圆、像学校直尺一般的木头，然后用力把它放在唇边。我们的手枪同时响起。他飞快地转过身，举起双臂，然后发出憋闷的咳嗽声，侧身跌进了河里。我瞥见了河水白色漩涡中他那双咄咄逼人的恶毒眼睛。与此同时，木腿人扑向船舱，用劲扳下，他的船径直向南岸冲去，我们只相差几英尺躲开它，从它的船尾飞速掠过。我们立即转弯，朝它追去，但它已经接近岸边。这是一个荒无人烟的地方，月光照耀在广阔的沼泽地上。沼泽地是一潭潭死水和一堆堆腐烂植物。汽艇发出一声钝响，冲上泥岸，船头翘向空中，船尾沉入水里。逃亡者跳出来，但他那只木腿完全陷入了浸透的泥里。他徒然挣扎，扭动身体。连一步也不可能进退。他无可奈何地高声怒叫着，用另一只脚拼命踢泥，但他的挣扎只会让木腿越来越深地陷入泥岸。我们把汽艇靠岸时，他被牢牢地锚在那里，所以我们只有把绳子的一端抛过去，套住他的肩膀，才能把他像恶鱼一样用力拖出来，拽到我们这边。史密斯父子俩闷闷不乐地坐在船里，但听到我们的命令后，顺从地上了船。我们把"曙光女神号"拖走，紧紧地拴在我们的船尾。一只印度精制的坚固铁箱立在甲板上。毫无疑问，这就是曾经装有肖尔托家不祥财宝的箱子。没有任何钥匙，但箱子相当沉重。于是，我们小心翼翼地把它转移到我们自己的小船舱，又慢慢地逆流而上，将探照灯照向四方，但没有那个岛民的任何迹象。泰晤士河底黑色淤泥里的某个地方躺着那个访问我们河岸的陌生客人的遗骨。

"看这里，"福尔摩斯指着木舱口说，"我们的手枪还是不够快。"果然，就在我们一直站的地方后面插着一支我们非常熟悉的杀人镖。那一定是在

been standing, stuck one of those murderous darts which we knew so well. It must have whizzed between us at the instant we fired. Holmes smiled at it and shrugged his shoulders in his easy **fashion**[48], but I confess that it turned me sick to think of the horrible death which had passed so close to us that night.

我们开枪时射到了我们之间。福尔摩斯对此微微一笑,以轻松的方式耸了耸肩,但我承认,一想到那天夜里可怕的死亡曾经离我们如此之近,就让我感到不快。

四签名

Notes:
1. exaltation *n.* 兴奋；得意
2. miracle play（中世纪表演《圣经》故事的）奇迹剧
3. mediaeval *adj.* 中古的；中世纪的
4. Stradivarius *n.* 弦乐器（尤指斯特拉迪瓦里或其家族制作的小提琴）
5. preceding *adj.* 前面的
6. elated *adj.* 兴高采烈的
7. allude *vi.*（婉转）提到或顺便提到（to）
8. stationary *adj.* 不动的；静止的
9. clipper *n.*（旧时的）快速帆船；出色的东西
10. hydrocarbon *n.* 碳氢化合物；烃
11. finesse *n.* 手腕；手段；技巧
12. at a moment's notice 立即；已经召唤（或通知）就
13. hold one's tongue 保持沉默；肃静
14. reserve *vt.* 预订
15. invisibility *n.* 看不清；难看见
16. effectually *adj.* 有效地；全然
17. liable *adj.* 易于……的；有……倾向的（to）
18. bellow out 大声喊叫
19. flush *adj.*（尤指钱）充裕的；富裕的
20. alehouse *n.* 啤酒店；酒馆
21. sentry *n.* 哨兵；看守
22. snug *adj.* 隐密的
23. span *vt.* 横跨
24. bristle *n.* 短而硬的毛发；刷子毛
25. rigging *n.* 船上的全部帆缆；索具
26. enigma *n.* 谜；不可思议的事物
27. aggregate *n.* 总计
28. statistician *n.* 统计学家
29. like the devil 猛烈地
30. tremendous *adj.* 极大的；巨大的
31. stoker *n.* 司炉；烧炉工人

32. prow *n.* 船首

33. aquiline *adj.* 鹰的；似鹰的

34. blunder *vi.* 跌跌撞撞；慌乱地走

35. vibrate *vi.* 振动；颤动

36. checkered *adj.* 多变的

37. melancholy *adj.* 忧郁的；悲伤的

38. strident *adj.* 尖锐的；刺耳的

39. misshapen *adj.* 奇形怪状的；畸形的

40. tangled *adj.* 缠结的；紊乱的

41. ulster *n.* 阿尔斯特宽大衣；一种长而宽松的男女兼用的外套

42. quarry *n.* 猎取的目标；猎物

43. unhallowed *adj.* 不圣洁的；污渎的

44. venomous *adj.* 恶毒的；充满仇恨的

45. stagnant *adj.* 不流动的；污浊的

46. sodden *adj.* 湿润的；浸透了的

47. writhe *vi.* （因极度痛苦而）扭动或翻滚

48. fashion *n.* 样子；方式；风格

四签名

# Chapter 11

## THE GREAT AGRA TREASURE

# 第十一章
## 大笔阿格拉财宝

Our captive sat in the cabin opposite to the iron box which he had done so much and waited so long to gain. He was a sunburned **reckless**[1]-eyed fellow, with a network of lines and wrinkles all over his **mahogany**[2] features, which told of a hard, open-air life. There was a singular **prominence**[3] about his bearded chin which marked a man who was not to be easily turned from his purpose. His age may have been fifty or thereabouts, for his black, curly hair was thickly shot with gray. His face in repose was not an unpleasing one, though his heavy brows and aggressive chin gave him, as I had lately seen, a terrible expression when moved to anger. He sat now with his handcuffed hands upon his lap, and his head sunk upon his breast, while he looked with his keen, twinkling eyes at the box which had been the cause of his ill-doings. It seemed to me that there was more sorrow than anger in his rigid and contained **countenance**[4]. Once he looked up at me with a gleam of something like humour in his eyes.

"Well, Jonathan Small," said Holmes, lighting a cigar, "I am sorry that it has come to this."

"And so am I, sir," he answered frankly. "I don't believe that I can swing over the job. I give you my word on the Book that I never raised hand against Mr. Sholto. It was that little hell-hound, Tonga, who shot one of his cursed darts into him. I had no part in it, sir. I was as grieved as if it had been my blood-relation. I **welted**[5] the little devil with the slack end of the rope for it, but it was done, and I could not undo it again."

"Have a cigar," said Holmes; "and you had best take a pull out of my flask, for you are very wet. How could you expect so small and weak a man as this black fellow to overpower Mr. Sholto and hold him while you were climbing the rope?"

"You seem to know as much about it as if you were there, sir. The truth is that I hoped to find the room clear. I knew the habits of the house pretty well, and it was the time when Mr. Sholto usually went down to his supper. I shall make no secret of the business. The best defence that I can make is just the simple truth. Now, if it had been the old major I would have swung for him with a light heart. I would have thought no more of knifing him than

我们的俘虏坐在船舱里，对面是他历尽艰险、等了很久才得到的铁箱。看上去他是一个晒得黝黑、不顾一切的家伙，红褐色的脸上纵横交错布满了皱纹，这表明他是在野外过着一种艰苦生活。他胡子拉碴的下巴格外突出，表明他是一个不会轻易转移目标的人。他的年龄可能有50岁左右，因为他鬈曲的黑发搀杂有不少灰白的头发。他的脸平静时并不令人讨厌，尽管我最近曾经见到，他愤怒时浓密的眉毛和挑衅的下巴使他的表情非常可怕。他现在坐在那里，戴铐的双手放在膝盖上，头垂在胸前，用那双敏锐闪烁的眼睛望着箱子。这曾经是他作恶的原因。在我看来，他的严厉平静的面容悲痛多于愤怒。有一次，他抬头望着我，眼里闪着一丝幽默。

"啊，乔纳森·斯莫尔，"福尔摩斯点起一支雪茄说，"我很抱歉事情弄到了这步田地。"

"先生，我也很抱歉，"他坦率地回答说，"我相信我无法跳过这件事。我凭《圣经》向你发誓，我从来没有对肖尔托先生下手。是那个小恶鬼汤加把一支该死的飞镖射向了他。先生，我根本没有插手这件事。我非常伤心，就像那是我的血亲一样。我为此用绳子鞭打了那个小鬼，但事已定局，我无法再挽回。"

"抽一支雪茄，"福尔摩斯说，"你最好喝一口瓶子里的酒，因为你浑身都湿了。你在爬绳时，怎么能指望这个弱小的黑家伙制服肖尔托先生并控制他呢？"

"先生，你知道这么多，好像你就在现场一样。事实上，我是希望发现房间里空无一人的。我相当清楚那座房子的生活习惯，肖尔托先生常常就是那个时候下楼吃晚饭。我对这件事要毫不隐瞒。我能作的最好辩护就是实话实说。那么，如果是那个老少校，我会轻松地掐死他。我杀死他就不会再想这件事，就像我抽过这支雪茄不再想它一样。可是，该死的是，我却要为这

四签名

of smoking this cigar. But it's cursed hard that I should be **lagged**[6] over this young Sholto, with whom I had no quarrel whatever."

"You are under the charge of Mr. Athelney Jones, of Scotland Yard. He is going to bring you up to my rooms, and I shall ask you for a true account of the matter. You must **make a clean breast of**[7] it, for if you do I hope that I may be of use to you. I think I can prove that the poison acts so quickly that the man was dead before ever you reached the room."

"That he was, sir. I never got such a turn in my life as when I saw him grinning at me with his head on his shoulder as I climbed through the window. It fairly shook me, sir. I'd have half killed Tonga for it if he had not scrambled off. That was how he came to leave his club, and some of his darts too, as he tells me, which I dare say helped to put you on our track; though how you kept on it is more than I can tell. I don't feel no **malice**[8] against you for it. But it does seem a queer thing," he added with a bitter smile, "that I, who have a fair claim to half a million of money, should spend the first half of my life building a breakwater in the Andamans, and am like to spend the other half digging drains at Dartmoor. It was an evil day for me when first I clapped eyes upon the merchant Achmet and had to do with the Agra treasure, which never brought anything but a curse yet upon the man who owned it. To him it brought murder, to Major Sholto it brought fear and guilt, to me it has meant slavery for life."

At this moment Athelney Jones thrust his broad face and heavy shoulders into the tiny cabin.

"Quite a family party," he remarked. "I think I shall have a pull at that flask, Holmes. Well, I think we may all congratulate each other. Pity we didn't take the other alive, but there was no choice. I say, Holmes, you must confess that you **cut it**[9] rather fine. It was all we could do to **overhaul**[10] her."

"All is well that ends well," said Holmes. "But I certainly did not know that the Aurora was such a **clipper**[11]."

"Smith says she is one of the fastest launches on the river, and that if he had had another man to help him with the engines we should never have caught her. He swears he knew nothing of this Norwood business."

个年轻的肖尔托而被送进监狱,因为我和他没有任何争执。"

"你是在伦敦警察厅阿塞尔尼·琼斯先生的看管之下。他准备把你带到我的房间,我要求你对这件事实话实说。你必须全盘托出,因为如果你全盘托出,我说不定还能帮你的忙。我想我能证明那种毒药发作很快,你还没有到达房间,那个人就死了。"

"先生,他正是这样。当我爬过窗户看到他脑袋歪在肩膀上朝我咧嘴笑时,我一生从来没有受到过这种惊吓。这完全让我心烦意乱。如果汤加没有爬走,我就会差点儿杀了他。这就是后来他告诉我,他是如何遗忘那根木棒和一些毒镖的。我想,这有助于你追寻到我们,尽管我无法说出你是怎么一直追踪的。我对你没有任何恶意。不过,这好像的确是一件怪事。"他苦笑着补充说,"我有权拥有50万英镑,前半生却在安达曼群岛修筑防波堤,后半生好像要在达特穆尔挖排水沟。当我第一天看到商人阿奇麦特,并和阿格拉财宝发生关系后,那就成了我倒霉的一天。对拥有这财宝的人只是带来了诅咒,对他带来了谋杀,对肖尔托少校因财宝带来了恐惧和罪恶,对我则意味着终身奴役。"

这时,阿塞尔尼·琼斯把宽阔的脸庞和粗壮的肩膀伸进小小的舱里。

"真像是家庭聚会,"他说,"福尔摩斯,我想我要从那个瓶子里喝一口。啊,我想我们大家可以互相祝贺。可惜我们没有活捉那一个,但别无选择。我说,福尔摩斯,你必须承认,你这件事干得相当出色。我们所能做的就是追上它。"

"结果好是好,"福尔摩斯说,"但我确实不知道'曙光女神号'是这样一艘快船。"

"史密斯说,'曙光女神号'是泰晤士河上最快的汽艇之一。如果还有一个人帮他照管发动机,我们就永远追不上它了。他发誓说,他对这个诺伍德惨案一无所知。"

四签名

"Neither he did," cried our prisoner—"not a word. I chose his launch because I heard that she was a flier. We told him nothing; but we paid him well, and he was to get something handsome if we reached our vessel, the Esmeralda, at Gravesend, outward bound for the Brazils."

"Well, if he has done no wrong we shall see that no wrong comes to him. If we are pretty quick in catching our men, we are not so quick in condemning them." It was amusing to notice how the **consequential**[12] Jones was already beginning to give himself airs on the strength of the capture. From the slight smile which played over Sherlock Holmes's face, I could see that the speech had not been lost upon him.

"We will be at Vauxhall Bridge presently," said Jones, "and shall land you, Dr. Watson, with the treasure-box. I need hardly tell you that I am taking a very grave responsibility upon myself in doing this. It is most irregular, but of course an agreement is an agreement. I must, however, as a matter of duty, send an inspector with you, since you have so valuable a charge. You will drive, no doubt?"

"Yes, I shall drive."

"It is a pity there is no key, that we may make an **inventory**[13] first. You will have to break it open. Where is the key, my man?"

"At the bottom of the river," said Small shortly.

"Hum! There was no use your giving this unnecessary trouble. We have had work enough already through you. However, Doctor, I need not warn you to be careful. Bring the box back with you to the Baker Street rooms. You will find us there, on our way to the station."

They landed me at Vauxhall, with my heavy iron box, and with a **bluff**[14], **genial**[15] inspector as my companion. A quarter of an hour's drive brought us to Mrs. Cecil Forrester's. The servant seemed surprised at so late a visitor. Mrs. Cecil Forrester was out for the evening, she explained, and likely to be very late. Miss Morstan, however, was in the drawing-room; so to the drawing-room I went, box in hand, leaving the **obliging**[16] inspector in the cab.

She was seated by the open window, dressed in some sort of white **diaphanous**[17] material, with a little touch of scarlet at the neck and waist. The

"他也不知道,"我们的囚犯喊道——"一个字也不知道。我之所以选择这艘汽艇,是因为我听说它是一艘特快船。我们什么也没有告诉他,但我们付给他不少钱。如果他把我们送到格雷夫森德开往巴西的'埃斯梅拉达号'轮船,他就会得到一大笔钱。"

"啊,如果他没有罪,我们不会冤枉他。如果说我们抓人相当快的话,那对他们判刑并不是那么快。"傲慢的琼斯已经开始露出了因抓住罪犯而摆架子的神气,注意到这一点非常有趣。从夏洛克·福尔摩斯脸上掠过的微微一笑,我可以看出,这句话没有逃过他的注意。

"我们马上就要到沃克斯豪尔桥了,"琼斯说,"华生医生,你带着宝箱上岸。我几乎不用告诉你,这样做,我自己要承担非常重大的责任。尽管这样做极不正规,但当然,协议就是协议。不过,我一定义不容辞派一名警官和你一起去,因为你有非常重要的责任。你肯定愿意坐车吗?"

"是的,我愿意坐车。"

"可惜没有钥匙,否则我们可以先列一张清单。你不得不砸开箱子。钥匙在哪里,我的伙计?"

"在河底,"斯莫尔简短地说。

"哼!你给这个不必要的麻烦毫无用处。为了你,我们已经够忙活了。不过,医生,我不必警告你,要小心。把箱子带回贝克街的房间。在去警察局的路上,你会找到我们。"

他们让我带着沉重的铁箱在沃克斯豪尔上岸,有一位坦率温和的警官陪伴。一刻钟后,马车把我们送到了塞西尔·弗里斯特太太家。仆人好像对我这么晚来访感到吃惊。她解释说,弗里斯特太太晚上出去了,可能很晚才回来。不过,摩斯坦小姐在客厅里,于是我提着宝箱走进了客厅,把那位彬彬有礼的警官留在了马车上。

她坐在打开的窗边,身穿某种透明的白色衣服,脖子上和腰间都带一点

soft light of a shaded lamp fell upon her as she leaned back in the basket chair, playing over her sweet grave face, and **tinting**[18] with a dull, metallic sparkle the rich coils of her **luxuriant**[19] hair. One white arm and hand drooped over the side of the chair, and her whole pose and figure spoke of an absorbing **melancholy**[20]. At the sound of my footfall she sprang to her feet, however, and a bright flush of surprise and of pleasure coloured her pale cheeks.

"I heard a cab drive up," she said. "I thought that Mrs. Forrester had come back very early, but I never dreamed that it might be you. What news have you brought me?"

"I have brought something better than news," said I, putting down the box upon the table and speaking jovially and **boisterously**[21], though my heart was heavy within me. "I have brought you something which is worth all the news in the world. I have brought you a fortune."

She glanced at the iron box.

"Is that the treasure then?" she asked, coolly enough.

"Yes, this is the great Agra treasure. Half of it is yours and half is Thaddeus Sholto's. You will have a couple of hundred thousand each. Think of that! An annuity of ten thousand pounds. There will be few richer young ladies in England. Is it not glorious?"

I think I must have been rather over-acting my delight, and that she detected a hollow ring in my congratulations, for I saw her eyebrows rise a little, and she glanced at me curiously.

"If I have it," said she, "I owe it to you."

"No, no," I answered, "not to me but to my friend Sherlock Holmes. With all the will in the world, I could never have followed up a clue which has taxed even his analytical genius. As it was, we very nearly lost it at the last moment."

"Pray sit down and tell me all about it, Dr. Watson," said she.

I narrated briefly what had occurred since I had seen her last. Holmes's new method of search, the discovery of the *Aurora*, the appearance of Athelney Jones, our expedition in the evening, and the wild chase down the Thames. She listened with parted lips and shining eyes to my recital of our adventures. When I spoke of the dart which had so narrowly missed us, she turned so white

猩红色。她倚靠在藤椅上，罩灯柔和的光落在她身上，照在她可爱端庄的脸上，将她富丽浓密的鬈发染成了暗淡的金属色。一只洁白的手臂搭在椅子一侧，整个姿态和身段流露出一种迷人的忧郁。然而，听到我的脚步声，她一跃而起，一道惊喜的红晕染上了她苍白的脸颊。

"我听到马车开过来，"她说，"我以为是弗里斯特太太早早回来了，但我做梦也没有想到会是你。你给我带来了什么消息？"

"我带来了比消息还要好的东西，"我说着，把箱子放在桌子上，尽管心情沉重，但露出了欢天喜地的样子。"我带来的东西抵得上世界上所有的消息。我给你带来了一大笔财富。"

她瞥了一眼铁箱。

"就是那笔财宝吧？"她冷冷地问道。

"是的，这就是那一大笔阿格拉财宝。一半是你的，一半是撒迪厄斯·肖尔托先生的。你们将各得 20 万英镑。想一下吧！年金一万英镑。英国年轻女士这样富有的寥寥无几。难道这不值得称道吗？"

我想我一定高兴得有些过火，她察觉到我的祝贺缺乏诚意，因为我看到她微微抬了一下眉毛，好奇地瞥了我一眼。

"如果我拥有它，"她说，"我就归功于你。"

"不，不，"我回答说，"不要归功于我，而是归功于我的朋友夏洛克·福尔摩斯。我就是有世界上所有的意志，也不可能追踪到一条线索，因为这曾经耗尽了他的分析天才。事实上，我们到最后差点儿失去这条线索。"

"请坐下来，把所有情况告诉我，华生医生，"她说。

我简短叙述了上次见她以来发生过的事儿。福尔摩斯新的搜寻法、'曙光女神号'的发现、阿塞尔尼·琼斯的出现、我们晚上的探险，以及泰晤士

that I feared that she was about to faint.

"It is nothing," she said as I hastened to pour her out some water. "I am all right again. It was a shock to me to hear that I had placed my friends in such horrible peril."

"That is all over," I answered. "It was nothing. I will tell you no more gloomy details. Let us turn to something brighter. There is the treasure. What could be brighter than that? I got leave to bring it with me, thinking that it would interest you to be the first to see it."

"It would be of the greatest interest to me," she said. There was no eagerness in her voice, however. It had struck her, doubtless, that it might seem **ungracious**[22] upon her part to be indifferent to a prize which had cost so much to win.

"What a pretty box!" she said, stooping over it. "This is Indian work, I suppose?"

"Yes; it is Benares metal-work."

"And so heavy!" she exclaimed, trying to raise it. "The box alone must be of some value. Where is the key?"

"Small threw it into the Thames," I answered. "I must borrow Mrs. Forrester's poker."

There was in the front a thick and broad **hasp**[23], **wrought**[24] in the image of a sitting Buddha. Under this I thrust the end of the poker and twisted it outward as a lever. The hasp sprang open with a loud **snap**[25]. With trembling fingers I flung back the lid. We both stood gazing in astonishment. The box was empty!

No wonder that it was heavy. The ironwork was two-thirds of an inch thick all round. It was massive, well made, and solid, like a chest constructed to carry things of great price, but not one shred or crumb of metal or jewellery lay within it. It was absolutely and completely empty.

"The treasure is lost," said Miss Morstan calmly.

As I listened to the words and realized what they meant, a great shadow seemed to pass from my soul. I did not know how this Agra treasure had weighed me down until now that it was finally removed. It was selfish, no

河上的疯狂追击。她嘴唇分开，两眼发光，倾听我叙述我们的历险。当我说到飞镖差点儿射中我们时，她脸色变得煞白，我担心她就要晕倒。

"这没什么，"我赶忙给她倒了一些水，她说，"我又好了。听到我让朋友们曾经遭到这样可怕的危险，我非常震惊。"

"都过去了，"我回答说，"这没什么。我不再给你讲令人沮丧的细节了。让我们转向比较欢快的事儿吧。比这更欢快的可能是什么呢？我得到许可，随身带来，想着这会让你感兴趣，先睹为快。"

"这对我将是最大的兴趣，"她说。然而，她的声音没有流露出任何急切之情。毫无疑问，这已经使她想到，她对费了很大劲儿才得到手的财宝无动于衷，似乎不尽人情。

"多么漂亮的箱子！"她弯腰看着箱子说，"我想这是印度产品吧？"

"是的，这是贝拿勒斯金属制品。"

"这么沉啊！"她试着抬了抬箱子说，"光这箱子一定就值一些钱。钥匙在哪里？"

"斯莫尔把它扔进了泰晤士河，"我回答说，"我必须借用一下弗里斯特太太的火钳。"

箱子前面有一个又粗又宽的搭扣，搭扣做成了打坐的佛像。我把火钳顶端插在搭扣下面作为杠杆，向外扭转。搭扣嘭的一声弹开。我用颤抖的手指掀起箱盖。我们俩站在那里，惊讶地注视着。箱子是空的！

难怪箱子沉。铁制品四周有三分之二英寸厚，宽大结实，制作精良，就像专门用来藏无价之宝的箱子，但里面连一丝一片金属或珠宝也没有，完全是空无一物。

"财宝丢了，"摩斯坦小姐平静地说。

听着这句话，我明白了话意，一个巨大的阴影仿佛从我心里消失。我不

四签名

doubt, disloyal, wrong, but I could realize nothing save that the golden barrier was gone from between us.

"Thank God!" I ejaculated from my very heart.

She looked at me with a quick, questioning smile.

"Why do you say that?" she asked.

"Because you are within my reach again," I said, taking her hand. She did not withdraw it. "Because I love you, Mary, as truly as ever a man loved a woman. Because this treasure, these riches, sealed my lips. Now that they are gone I can tell you how I love you. That is why I said, 'Thank God.'"

"Then I say 'Thank God,' too," she whispered as I drew her to my side.

Whoever had lost a treasure, I knew that night that I had gained one.

知道这笔阿格拉财宝是多么沉重地压在我心头,直到它被最后移开。毫无疑问,这非常自私、不忠和错误,但我只能意识到我们之间的金色障碍已经消失。

"感谢上帝!"我从内心脱口喊道。

她带着疑问的微笑飞快地看了我一眼。

"你为什么这样说?"她问道。

"因为我又能够到你了,"我握住她的手说。她没有抽回。"玛丽,因为我爱你,就像任何男人爱女人那样真实。因为这种财宝、这些财富封住了我的嘴。既然它们消失了,我就可以告诉你,我是多么爱你。这就是我说'感谢上帝'的原因。"

"那我也会说'感谢上帝,'"我把她拉到身边时,她轻声说道。

无论是谁丢失了财宝,我知道我那天夜里都得到了一份。

四签名

Notes:
1. reckless *adj.* 鲁莽的；不顾一切的
2. mahogany *adj.* 红褐色的
3. prominence *n.* 突出；重要
4. countenance *n.* 面容；表情；镇静
5. welt *vt.* 装饰，鞭打
6. lag *vt.* 把（犯人）关进监狱
7. make a clean breast of 坦白讲出……
8. malice *n.* 恶意
9. cut it 停止；快走
10. overhaul *vt.* 赶上；追上
11. clipper *n.* 快速帆船（19世纪中期一种尖船头的海船，船桅高、流线型，为高速行驶而建造）
12. consequential *adj.* 自尊自大的；傲慢的
13. inventory *n.* 详细目录；存货清单
14. bluff *adj.* 直率的；爽快的
15. genial *adj.* 和蔼的；亲切的；友好
16. obliging *adj.* 乐于助人的；(言行等）谦和的；有礼貌的
17. diaphanous *adj.*（织物等）半透明的；透明的
18. tint *vt.* 给……染色；给……着色
19. luxuriant *adj.* 茂盛的；华丽的
20. melancholy *n.* 忧郁；悲哀
21. boisterously *adv.* 兴高采烈地；吵闹地
22. ungracious *adj.* 讨厌的；使人不快的
23. hasp *n.*（门、窗、盖子等的）搭扣
24. wrought *adj.*（work 的过去式及过去分词）制造的；锻成的
25. snap *n.* 劈啪声

# Chapter 12

## DR. JENS VON STORCH
## JOCHEM MAROTZKE

# Chapter 12

## THE STRANGE STORY OF JONATHAN SMALL

## 第十二章

## 乔纳森·斯莫尔的奇异故事

A very patient man was that inspector in the cab, for it was a weary time before I rejoined him. His face clouded over when I showed him the empty box.

"There goes the reward!" said he gloomily. "Where there is no money there is no pay. This night's work would have been worth a **tenner**[1] each to Sam Brown and me if the treasure had been there."

"Mr. Thaddeus Sholto is a rich man," I said; "he will see that you are rewarded, treasure or no."

The inspector shook his head **despondently**[2], however.

"It's a bad job," he repeated; "and so Mr. Athelney Jones will think."

His forecast proved to be correct, for the detective looked blank enough when I got to Baker Street and showed him the empty box. They had only just arrived, Holmes, the prisoner, and he, for they had changed their plans so far as to report themselves at a station upon the way. My companion lounged in his armchair with his usual **listless**[3] expression, while Small sat stolidly opposite to him with his wooden leg **cocked**[4] over his sound one. As I exhibited the empty box he leaned back in his chair and laughed aloud.

"This is your doing, Small," said Athelney Jones angrily.

"Yes, I have put it away where you shall never lay hand upon it," he cried **exultantly**[5]. "It is my treasure, and if I can't have the loot I'll take darned good care that no one else does. I tell you that no living man has any right to it, unless it is three men who are in the Andaman convict-barracks and myself. I know now that I cannot have the use of it, and I know that they cannot. I have acted all through for them as much as for myself. It's been the sign of four with us always. Well, I know that they would have had me do just what I have done, and throw the treasure into the Thames rather than let it go to **kith**[6] or **kin**[7] of Sholto or Morstan. It was not to make them rich that we did for Achmet. You'll find the treasure where the key is and where little Tonga is. When I saw that your launch must catch us, I put the loot away in a safe place. There are no rupees for you this journey."

THE SIGN OF FOUR

坐在马车里的那名警官很有耐心，因为我回到车上之前这段时间令人厌烦。我给他看空箱子时，他的脸上阴云密布。

"奖金也没了！"他闷闷不乐地说，"没有财宝，就没有奖金。如果财宝在那里的话，今晚这工作对我和同伴萨姆·布朗来说每人就可以得到10英镑。"

"撒迪厄斯·肖尔托先生是一个富人，"我说，"无论有没有财宝，他都会给你们酬劳。"

然而，警官沮丧地摇了摇头。

"这事儿干得很糟，"他反复说，"阿塞尔尼·琼斯先生也会这样认为。"

侦探的预见果然没错，因为当我回到贝克街，让他看空箱子时，他一脸困惑。他们——福尔摩斯、琼斯和囚犯——刚刚到达贝克街，因为他们已经改变了计划，途中到警察局报告。我的同伴像往常一样无精打采地坐在椅子上。斯莫尔不动声色地坐在他对面，那条木腿翘在好腿上。当我展示那只空箱子时，他靠在椅子上朗声大笑。

"斯莫尔，这是你干的好事，"阿塞尔尼·琼斯发怒说。

"是的，我已经把它放在你们永远找不到的地方了，"他狂喜地叫道，"这是我的财宝，如果我不能拥有这笔钱，就要好好关照不让任何人拥有。我告诉你，除非是安达曼岛囚犯营的三个人和我自己，否则任何活着的人都对它没有权利。我现在知道，我没有机会使用它，我也知道他们同样没有机会使用它。我自己就代表他们全权处理。这永远是我们的四签名。啊，我知道他们会同意我这样做，宁愿把财宝扔进泰晤士河，也不愿让它落入肖尔托或摩斯坦的亲友之手。我们干掉阿奇麦特，并不是为了让他们发财。你会在钥匙所在的地方和小汤加所在的地方找到财宝。当我看到你们的汽艇一定会追上我们时，我就把这笔钱放到了一个安全的地方。你们此行连一个卢比都不会得到。"

"You are deceiving us, Small," said Athelney Jones sternly; "if you had wished to throw the treasure into the Thames, it would have been easier for you to have thrown box and all."

"Easier for me to throw and easier for you to recover," he answered with a shrewd, side-long look. "The man that was clever enough to hunt me down is clever enough to pick an iron box from the bottom of a river. Now that they are scattered over five miles or so, it may be a harder job. It **went to my heart**[8] to do it though. I was half mad when you came up with us. However, there's no good grieving over it. I've had ups in my life, and I've had downs, but I've learned not to cry over spilled milk."

"This is a very serious matter, Small," said the detective. "If you had helped justice, instead of **thwarting**[9] it in this way, you would have had a better chance at your trial."

"Justice!" snarled the ex-convict. "A pretty justice! Whose loot is this, if it is not ours? Where is the justice that I should give it up to those who have never earned it? Look how I have earned it! Twenty long years in that fever-ridden swamp, all day at work under the **mangrove**[10]-tree, all night chained up in the filthy convict-huts, bitten by mosquitoes, racked with **ague**[11], bullied by every cursed black-faced policeman who loved to take it out of a white man. That was how I earned the Agra treasure, and you talk to me of justice because I cannot bear to feel that I have paid this price only that another may enjoy it! I would rather swing a score of times, or have one of Tonga's darts in my hide, than live in a convict's cell and feel that another man is at his ease in a palace with the money that should be mine."

Small had dropped his mask of **stoicism**[12], and all this came out in a wild whirl of words, while his eyes blazed, and the handcuffs clanked together with the impassioned movement of his hands. I could understand, as I saw the fury and the passion of the man, that it was no groundless or unnatural terror which had possessed Major Sholto when he first learned that the injured convict was upon his track.

"You forget that we know nothing of all this," said Holmes quietly. "We have not heard your story, and we cannot tell how far justice may originally

"斯莫尔，你是在骗我们，"阿塞尔尼·琼斯厉声说道，"如果你希望把财宝扔进泰晤士河，连箱子一块扔会更容易。"

"我扔比较容易，你们重新找到也比较容易，"斯莫尔狡猾地斜了一眼，回答说，"足够聪明把我找到的那个人，也会足够聪明从河底捞起铁箱。既然它们散落达5英里左右，捞起来可能就比较难。不过，这样做也让我伤心。当你们追上我们时，我都快发疯了。然而，伤心没有任何用处。尽管我这一生有起有落，但我已经学会不为无益的事儿后悔。"

"斯莫尔，这是一件非常严重的事儿，"侦探说，"如果你协助司法当局，而不是这样阻挠，你受审时就会有更好的机会。"

"司法当局！"这个有前科的罪犯咆哮着说，"漂亮的司法当局！如果这笔钱不是我们的，又是谁的？如果我把财宝让给那些不劳而获的人，正义又在哪里？看我是怎么得到的！长达20年住在那个热病困扰的湿地，整天在红树下做工，整夜被锁在肮脏的囚棚里，蚊子叮咬，疟疾折磨，受到每个爱拿白人出气的该死的黑脸警察的欺侮。我就是这样得到阿格拉财宝的，而你却对我说什么正义，因为我曾经付出了这种代价，无法忍受另一个人坐享其成！我宁愿上20次绞架或中汤加一次飞镖，也不愿住在囚牢里，让另一个人用应该属于我的钱在豪宅里逍遥自在！"

斯莫尔已经放下了淡泊的面具，所有这一切都狂泻而出。他两眼冒火，手铐随着双手的激烈动作丁当作响。看到这个人狂怒冲动，我就能理解，肖尔托少校听到这个受委屈的罪犯正在追踪他时，惊恐万分绝不是空穴来风、违背自然。

"你忘了我们对所有这一切都一无所知，"福尔摩斯平静地说，"我们根本没有听说过你的经历，所以无法断定司法公正原来可能在多大程度上站在

have been on your side."

"Well, sir, you have been very fair-spoken to me, though I can see that I have you to thank that I have these bracelets upon my wrists. Still, I bear no **grudge**[13] for that. It is all fair and above-board. If you want to hear my story, I have no wish to hold it back. What I say to you is God's truth, every word of it. Thank you, you can put the glass beside me here, and I'll put my lips to it if I am dry.

I am a Worcestershire man myself, born near Pershore. I dare say you would find a heap of Smalls living there now if you were to look. I have often thought of taking a look round there, but the truth is that I was never much of a credit to the family, and I doubt if they would be so very glad to see me. They were all steady, chapel-going folk, small farmers, well known and respected over the countryside, while I was always a bit of a rover. At last, however, when I was about eighteen, I gave them no more trouble, for I got into a mess over a girl and could only get out of it again by taking the Queen's shilling and joining the Third Buffs, which was just starting for India.

I wasn't destined to do much soldiering, however. I had just got past the goose-step and learned to handle my musket, when I was fool enough to go swimming in the Ganges. Luckily for me, my company sergeant, John Holder, was in the water at the same time, and he was one of the finest swimmers in the service. A crocodile took me just as I was halfway across and nipped off my right leg as clean as a surgeon could have done it, just above the knee. **What with**[14] the shock and the loss of blood, I fainted, and should have been drowned if Holder had not caught hold of me and paddled for the bank. I was five months in hospital over it, and when at last I was able to limp out of it with this timber toe strapped to my stump, I found myself invalided out of the Army and unfitted for any active occupation.

I was, as you can imagine, pretty **down on my luck**[15] at this time, for I was a useless cripple, though not yet in my twentieth year. However, my misfortune soon proved to be **a blessing in disguise**[16]. A man named Abel White, who had come out there as an indigo-planter, wanted an overseer to look after his coolies and keep them up to their work. He happened to be a friend of our

你这边。"

"啊,先生,尽管我可以看出多亏你我才戴上了手镯,但还是你说话温文儒雅。不过,我毫不怨恨。这一切都公正平等、光明正大。如果你想听我的故事,我绝不愿隐瞒。我对你说的句句都是实话。谢谢你,你可以把杯子放在我身边。要是我口渴,就会把嘴唇凑到杯子上。

我自己是伍斯特郡人,出生在珀肖尔附近。我敢说,如果你要看的话,就会发现一大堆斯莫尔人现在住在那里。我经常想到哪里去看看,但事实上,我从来没有给家族带来过多大的荣誉,所以我怀疑他们是否会非常高兴见到我。他们都是经常上教堂的人和小农场主,赫赫有名,受人尊敬,而我始终有点儿像流浪汉。然而,我18岁时终于不再给他们添麻烦,因为我为一个女孩遇到了麻烦,只能通过当兵吃军饷,加入就要调往印度的第三团,才能脱身。

然而,我注定当不了几天兵。我刚学会正步,学会使用步枪,这时竟然傻到了去恒河里游泳。我幸运的是,连队的约翰·霍尔德军士同时也在河里,他是部队最出色的游泳健将之一。正当我游到半路时,一条鳄鱼抓住了我,把我的右腿咬了下来,正好咬在膝盖以上,就像外科医生做手术那样干净利落。由于震惊和失血,我晕了过去。要不是霍尔德抓住我游向岸边,我就会被淹死。我在医院住了5个月,最后在我的残腿上装上了这个木腿,才一瘸一拐出了院。我因残废而退伍,不适合从事任何消耗体力的职业。

你们可以想象,我此时穷困潦倒,因为我是一个无用的瘸子,尽管我还不到20岁。然而,我不久便因祸得福。一个名叫艾贝尔·怀特、到印度来种植靛青的人,想要一个工头监督苦力们干活。这个人碰巧是我们上校的朋友。我出事以来上校就关心我。长话短说,上校大力推荐我担任这个职位,因为这个工作大多数是骑在马上,我的腿不会有大障碍,因为我剩下的大腿

四签名

colonel's, who had taken an interest in me since the accident. To make a long story short, the colonel recommended me strongly for the post, and, as the work was mostly to be done on horseback, my leg was no great obstacle, for I had enough thigh left to keep a good grip on the saddle. What I had to do was to ride over the plantation, to keep an eye on the men as they worked, and to report the idlers. The pay was **fair**[17], I had comfortable quarters, and altogether I was content to spend the remainder of my life in indigo-planting. Mr. Abel White was a kind man, and he would often drop into my little **shanty**[18] and smoke a pipe with me, for white folk out there feel their hearts warm to each other as they never do here at home.

Well, I was never in luck's way long. Suddenly, without a note of warning, the great **mutiny**[19] broke upon us. One month India lay as still and peaceful, to all appearance, as Surrey or Kent; the next there were two hundred thousand black devils let loose, and the country was a perfect hell. Of course you know all about it, gentlemen—a deal more than I do, very like, since reading is not **in my line**[20]. I only know what I saw with my own eyes. Our plantation was at a place called Muttra, near the border of the Northwest Provinces. Night after night the whole sky was alight with the burning **bungalows**[21], and day after day we had small companies of Europeans passing through our estate with their wives and children, on their way to Agra, where were the nearest troops. Mr. Abel White was an **obstinate**[22] man. He had it in his head that the affair had been exaggerated, and that it would blow over as suddenly as it had sprung up. There he sat on his veranda, drinking whisky-pegs and smoking **cheroots**[23], while the country was in a blaze about him. Of course we stuck by him, I and Dawson, who, with his wife, used to do the book-work and the managing. Well, **one fine day**[24] the crash came. I had been away on a distant plantation and was riding slowly home in the evening, when my eye fell upon something all huddled together at the bottom of a steep **nullah**[25]. I rode down to see what it was, and the cold struck through my heart when I found it was Dawson's wife, all cut into ribbons, and half eaten by jackals and native dogs. A little further up the road Dawson himself was lying on his face, quite dead, with an empty revolver in his hand, and four **sepoys**[26] lying across each other

还够牢牢夹住马鞍。我要做的工作就是骑马巡视种植园，密切注视那些工人干活，然后举报那些偷懒的工人。工资比较令人满意，我有舒适的住处，总之可以心满意足在靛青种植园度过余生。艾贝尔·怀特先生是一个善良的人，常常到我的小屋，和我一起抽烟，因为那里的白人彼此都很热心，根本不像在这里一样。

唉，我的好运从来不会长久。突然，没有任何警告，一场针对我们的大叛乱爆发了。前一个月印度表面上像英国萨里郡或肯特郡一样风平浪静，后一个月20万黑鬼发泄怒火，整个国家完全成了地狱。当然，先生们，你们知道这一切——比我知道的要多得多，因为我不擅长看报纸。我只知道我亲眼看到的事儿。我们的种植园位于一个名叫穆特拉的地方，靠近西北几省边界。夜复一夜，燃烧的平房都火光冲天。日复一日都有一小队一小队的欧洲人带着妻子儿女，经过我们的靛青园，前往距离最近、驻有军队的阿格拉城。艾贝尔·怀特先生是一位固执的人。他认为这件事言过其实，一定会像当初风起云涌那样偃旗息鼓。他坐在阳台上一边喝威士忌苏打水，一边抽方头雪茄，而他周围则是一片火海。当然，我和道森夫妇都忠于职守，因为道森夫妇过去始终做文书和管理。唉，有一天，大难临头。那天我去远处的一个种植园，傍晚时分骑着马慢慢回家，这时我的目光落在了一个陡峭峡谷谷底蜷缩一团的东西上。我骑马下去看那是什么东西。当我发现那是道森的妻子时，顿时感到不寒而栗，只见她被人割成了一条一条，已经被豺狼和当地狗吃了一半。再向上走一点，道森趴在路上，完全死了，手里握着一把没有子弹的左轮手枪，4个印度兵相互交叉着趴在他前面。我勒住马缰，不知道该走哪一条路，但这时，我看到艾贝尔·怀特的平房冒起滚滚浓烟，火焰渐渐蹿过了房顶。此时，我知道，我对主人不可能有任何好处，如果我管这件

四签名

in front of him. I reined up my horse, wondering which way I should turn; but at that moment I saw thick smoke curling up from Abel White's bungalow and the flames beginning to burst through the roof. I knew then that I could do my employer no good, but would only throw my own life away if I meddled in the matter. From where I stood I could see hundreds of the black fiends, with their red coats still on their backs, dancing and howling round the burning house. Some of them pointed at me, and a couple of bullets sang past my head: so I broke away across the paddy-fields, and found myself late at night safe within the walls at Agra.

As it proved, however, there was no great safety there, either. The whole country was up like a swarm of bees. Wherever the English could collect in little bands they held just the ground that their guns commanded. Everywhere else they were helpless fugitives. It was a fight of the millions against the hundreds; and the cruellest part of it was that these men that we fought against, foot, horse, and gunners, were our own picked troops, whom we had taught and trained, handling our own weapons and blowing our own bugle-calls. At Agra there were the Third Bengal **Fusiliers**[27], some **Sikhs**[28], two troops of horse, and a battery of artillery. A volunteer corps of clerks and merchants had been formed, and this I joined, wooden leg and all. We went out to meet the rebels at Shahgunge early in July, and we beat them back for a time, but our powder gave out, and we had to fall back upon the city.

Nothing but the worst news came to us from every side—which is not to be wondered at, for if you look at the map you will see that we were right in the heart of it. **Lucknow**[29] is rather better than a hundred miles to the east, and Cawnpore about as far to the south. From every point on the compass there was nothing but torture and murder and outrage.

The city of Agra is a great place, swarming with fanatics and fierce devil-worshippers of all sorts. Our handful of men were lost among the narrow, winding streets. Our leader moved across the river, therefore, and took up his position in the old fort of Agra. I don't know if any of you gentlemen have ever read or heard anything of that old fort. It is a very queer place—the queerest that ever I was in, and I have been in some **rum**[30] corners, too. First of all it

事，只会丢掉自己的生命。我从自己站立的地方可以看到几百个黑鬼，仍然穿着红色外套，围着燃烧的房子手舞足蹈大声嚎叫。其中一些人对准我，两颗子弹飕地从我头边掠过。于是，我突然策马越过稻田，深夜才安全到达阿格拉城。

然而，事实证明，那里也根本不保险。整个国家就像一窝蜂似的。凡是英国人能聚集一小群人的地方，他们只能坚守自己枪炮控制的地盘。其他各处的英国人都成了无依无靠的逃亡者。这是几百万人对几百人的一场战斗。其中最残酷的是，我们要决战的那些人，无论是步兵、骑兵还是炮兵，都是我们曾经教导训练过的精兵，他们拿的是我们的武器，吹的是我们的军号。阿格拉驻有孟加拉第三燧发枪团、一些印度锡克教兵、两个马队和一个炮兵连。职员和商人还组成了一支志愿军团。我装着木腿，也参加了这个团。7月初，我们出城去沙根吉对付叛军，把他们打退了一段时间，但我们的弹药用完，所以我们不得不又退守城里。

四面八方传到我们这里来的只是最坏的消息——这不足为奇，因为如果你看一下地图，就会明白，我们正处在叛乱的中心。勒克瑙在东方，距离一百多英里。坎普尔在南方，距离差不多一样远。四面八方到处都是酷刑、凶杀和暴行。

阿格拉城是一个很大的地方，聚集着各种各样的狂热分子和可怕凶猛的魔鬼信徒。我们这一群人散布在狭窄弯曲的街道。所以，我们的首领就穿过河，在阿格拉古堡建起了阵地。我不知道你们几位先生是否读到过或听说过那个古堡的事儿。这是一个非常奇怪的地方——这是我到过的最奇怪的地方，我也去过了一些奇特的角落。首先，它面积巨大。我想围墙内一定有好多英亩。还有一处现代建筑，那里容纳了我们所有的驻军、妇女、

四签名

is enormous in size. I should think that the enclosure must be acres and acres. There is a modern part, which took all our **garrison**[31], women, children, stores, and everything else, with plenty of room over. But the modern part is nothing like the size of the old quarter, where nobody goes, and which is given over to the **scorpions**[32] and the **centipedes**[33]. It is all full of great deserted halls, and winding passages, and long corridors twisting in and out, so that it is easy enough for folk to get lost in it. For this reason it was seldom that anyone went into it, though now and again a party with torches might go exploring.

The river washes along the front of the old fort, and so protects it, but on the sides and behind there are many doors, and these had to be guarded, of course, in the old quarter as well as in that which was actually held by our troops. We were short-handed, with hardly men enough to man the angles of the building and to serve the guns. It was impossible for us, therefore, to station a strong guard at every one of the innumerable gates. What we did was to organize a central guard-house in the middle of the fort, and to leave each gate under the charge of one white man and two or three natives. I was selected to take charge during certain hours of the night of a small isolated door upon the south-west side of the building. Two Sikh **troopers**[34] were placed under my command, and I was instructed if anything went wrong to fire my musket, when I might rely upon help coming at once from the central guard. As the guard was a good two hundred paces away, however, and as the space between was cut up into a **labyrinth**[35] of passages and corridors, I had great doubts as to whether they could arrive in time to be of any use in case of an actual attack.

Well, I was pretty proud at having this small command given me, since I was a raw **recruit**[36], and a **game**[37]-legged one at that. For two nights I kept the watch with my **Punjabees**[38]. They were tall, fierce-looking chaps, Mahomet Singh and Abdullah Khan by name, both old fighting men, who had **borne arms against**[39] us at Chilian Wallah. They could talk English pretty well, but I could get little out of them. They preferred to stand together, and **jabber**[40] all night in their queer Sikh **lingo**[41]. For myself, I used to stand outside the gateway, looking down on the broad, winding river and on the twinkling lights of the great city. The beating of drums, the rattle of **tom-toms**[42], and the yells and howls of the

儿童、物资储备,以及其他所有的一切,地方多得是。但现代部分说什么也没法和古代部分相比。因为没有人去那里,所以那里就成了蝎子和蜈蚣的天下。古代部分到处都是为人所弃的大厅、弯弯曲曲的通道和蜿蜒迂回的长廊,人走进去,很容易迷路。因此,很少有人走进古堡,尽管也可能有一群人拿着火把去探险。

河水从古堡前面流过,这样就保护了古堡,但古堡两侧和后面有许多门。当然,古堡这些门和我们部队实际占据的地方都必须把守。我们人手不足,几乎不够在古堡各个角落和炮位配备人手。因此,大门无计其数,我们在每个门口都派重兵是不可能的。我们做的是在堡垒中央建立一个中心警卫室,每个门由一个白人和两三个当地人负责把守。我被选中每天夜里固定时段守卫堡垒西南一个孤立的小门。我手下有两个锡克教骑兵。我得到的指示就是,如果出事,就开枪,这时我就有可能依靠马上从中心警卫室赶来的援兵。然而,警卫相距足有200步,而且中间隔有迷宫似的通道和走廊。我非常怀疑,万一真的受到攻击,他们是否能及时赶到派上用场。

啊,我对自己享有这样小小的指挥权颇为自豪,因为我是一个没有经验的新兵,而且还是一个瘸子。我和两个旁遮普兵守了两夜。他们身材高大,模样凶猛,一个名叫穆罕默德·辛格,另一个名叫阿卜杜拉·汗,两人都是老兵,曾经在齐连瓦拉拿起武器反对我们。他们可以说一口相当不错的英语,但我从他们那里听不到多少东西。他们喜欢站在一起,整夜用古怪的锡克方言叽哩咕噜说个不停。我自己则常常站在门外,低头望着宽阔弯曲的河流和大城里闪烁的灯光。咚咚的鼓声、印度的铜锣声,以及因鸦片和快感而陶醉的叛军们的大喊大叫,整夜都足以提醒我们,河对面就是我们危险的邻居。每隔两小时,值夜军官都常常巡查一次所有岗哨,务必做到一切平安。

四签名

rebels, drunk with opium and with **bang**[43], were enough to remind us all night of our dangerous neighbours across the stream. Every two hours the officer of the night used to come round to all the posts to make sure that all was well.

The third night of my watch was dark and dirty, with a small driving rain. It was dreary work standing in the gateway hour after hour in such weather. I tried again and again to make my Sikhs talk, but without much success. At two in the morning the rounds passed and broke for a moment the weariness of the night. Finding that my companions would not be led into conversation, I took out my pipe and laid down my musket to strike the match. In an instant the two Sikhs were upon me. One of them snatched my firelock up and levelled it at my head, while the other held a great knife to my throat and swore between his teeth that he would plunge it into me if I moved a step.

My first thought was that these fellows were in league with the rebels, and that this was the beginning of an assault. If our door were in the hands of the sepoys the place must fall, and the women and children be treated as they were in Cawnpore. Maybe you gentlemen think that I am just making out a case for myself, but I give you my word that when I thought of that, though I felt the point of the knife at my throat, I opened my mouth with the intention of giving a scream, if it was my last one, which might alarm the main guard. The man who held me seemed to know my thoughts; for, even as I braced myself to it, he whispered: 'Don't make a noise. The fort is safe enough. There are no rebel dogs on this side of the river.' There was the ring of truth in what he said, and I knew that if I raised my voice I was a dead man. I could read it in the fellow's brown eyes. I waited, therefore, in silence, to see what it was that they wanted from me."

"'Listen to me, **sahib**[44],' said the taller and fiercer of the pair, the one whom they called Abdullah Khan. 'You must either be with us now, or you must be silenced forever. The thing is too great a one for us to hesitate. Either you are heart and soul with us on your oath on the cross of the Christians, or your body this night shall be thrown into the ditch, and we shall pass over to our brothers in the rebel army. There is no middle way. Which is it to be—death or life? We can only give you three minutes to decide, for the time is passing, and all must be done before the rounds come again.'

我值班的第三夜,天昏地暗,狂风暴雨持续了一小会儿。在这种天气里一小时一小时站在门口,真是单调乏味。我一次又一次努力让那两个锡克教士兵说话,但没有取得多大成功。凌晨两点,巡查经过,才稍微打破了夜晚的疲倦。我发现两个同伴不愿交谈,就放下步枪,掏出烟斗,划燃火柴。两个锡克教士兵立即扑向我。一个人夺走了我的明火枪,瞄准我的脑袋;另一个人将一把大刀抵在我的脖子上,咬牙切齿地骂道,如果我动一步,他就把刀子捅进我的脖子。

我的第一个想法就是,这两个家伙和那些叛军是一伙的,而且这是一次攻击的开始。如果我们这个堡门落入印度兵的手里,这个地方就一定会失守,妇女儿童会受到和在坎普尔一样的遭遇。也许你们几位先生会认为,我只是在为自己辩护,但我保证,我想到这一点时,尽管感到刀尖抵住我的喉咙,我还是张开嘴想尖叫一声,即使那是我最后一声尖叫,也可以给中心警卫室发出警报。那个抓住我的人好像明白我的心思,因为我正要振作精神尖叫,他低声说道:'别出声。堡垒足够安全。河这边没有叛狗。'他说的话听上去真实,而且我知道,只要我抬高声音,就死定了。我从这个家伙的褐色眼睛中可以看得出来。所以,我默默等待,看他们想要我做什么。"

"'先生,听我说,'两个人中比较高大凶猛、他们叫作阿卜杜拉·汗的人说,'你要么现在跟我们合作,要么你永远也无法出声。事情重大,我们谁也不得犹豫。要么你向上帝发誓全心全意跟我们一起干,要么你的尸体今晚被扔进沟里,然后我们就到叛军弟兄那边。绝对没有第二个选择。要哪条路——生还是死?我们只能给你3分钟决定,因为时间短暂,必须在巡逻来之前把一切搞定。'

四签名

"'How can I decide?' said I. 'You have not told me what you want of me. But I tell you now that if it is anything against the safety of the fort I will **have no truck with**[45] it, so you can drive home your knife and welcome.'

"'It is nothing against the fort,' said he. 'We only ask you to do that which your countrymen come to this land for. We ask you to be rich. If you will be one of us this night, we will swear to you upon the naked knife, and by the threefold oath which no Sikh was ever known to break, that you shall have your fair share of the loot. A quarter of the treasure shall be yours. We can say no fairer.'

"'But what is the treasure then?' I asked. 'I am as ready to be rich as you can be if you will but show me how it can be done.'

"'You will swear, then,' said he, 'by the bones of your father, by the honour of your mother, by the cross of your faith, to raise no hand and speak no word against us, either now or afterwards?'

"'I will swear it,' I answered, '**provided**[46] that the fort is not endangered.'

"'Then my comrade and I will swear that you shall have a quarter of the treasure which shall be equally divided among the four of us.'

"'There are but three,' said I.

"'No; Dost Akbar must have his share. We can **tell the tale**[47] to you while we wait them. Do you stand at the gate, Mahomet Singh, and give notice of their coming. The thing stands thus, sahib, and I tell it to you because I know that an oath is binding upon a **Feringhee**[48], and that we may trust you. Had you been a lying Hindoo, though you had sworn by all the gods in their false temples, your blood would have been upon the knife and your body in the water. But the Sikh knows the Englishman, and the Englishman knows the Sikh. **Hearken**[49], then, to what I have to say.

"'There is a **rajah**[50] in the northern provinces who has much wealth, though his lands are small. Much has come to him from his father, and more still he has set by himself, for he is of a low nature and **hoards**[51] his gold rather than spend it. When the troubles broke out he would be friends both with the lion and the tiger—with the sepoy and with the Company's **raj**[52]. Soon, however, it seemed to him that the white men's day was come, for through

"'我怎么能决定呢?'我说,'你们还没有对我说你们想要我做什么。但是,我现在告诉你们,如果有任何危及堡垒安全的事儿,我绝不会参与,你们可以给我一刀,我愉快接受。'

"'这和堡垒没有任何关系,'他说,'我们只要求你做你们同胞到这个国家来做的那件事。我们是要你发财。如果你今晚愿意成为我们中的一员,我们就以这把刀对你发誓,而且要三次盟誓,你会平分到这笔钱。这种誓言从来没有一个锡克教徒违犯过。四分之一财宝归你。不能比这再公平了。'

"'可那是什么财宝?'我问道,'只要你们愿意给我说怎么才能做到,我就情愿和你们一样发财。'

"'那你愿意,'他说,'用你父亲的骨头、你母亲的荣誉和你的宗教信仰发誓,现在和今后绝不举手反对我们,也绝不说反对我们的话吗?'

"'如果堡垒不遭到危险,'我回答说。'我愿意这样发誓。'

"那我和伙伴愿意发誓,财宝我们四人平分,你将拥有四分之一。'

"'只有三个人啊,'我说。

"不,多斯特·阿克巴必须拥有一份。我们等他们时,可以告诉你这个故事。穆罕默德·辛格,请你站在门口,他们一来,你就通知我们。先生,事情是这样。我之所以告诉你,是因为我知道誓言对欧洲人有约束力,我们可以信任你。如果你是一个说谎的印度人,纵然你向虚伪神庙里的所有神灵发誓,你的血也会染上我的刀子,你的尸体会被扔进河里。但是,锡克教徒了解英国人,英国人也了解锡克教徒。那就听我来说。

"北方几省有一个王公,他土地虽少,财富却很多。许多财富是他父亲传给他的,还有更多是他自己贮备的。因为他天性卑劣,宁愿囤积金子,也舍不得花。动乱爆发后,他既愿意和狮子友好,又愿意和老虎友好——就是

四签名

all the land he could hear of nothing but of their death and their overthrow. Yet, being a careful man, he made such plans that, come what might, half at least of his treasure should be left to him. That which was in gold and silver he kept by him in the **vaults**[53] of his palace, but the most precious stones and the **choicest**[54] pearls that he had he put in an iron box and sent it by a trusty servant, who, under the guise of a merchant, should take it to the fort at Agra, there to lie until the land is at peace. Thus, if the rebels won he would have his money, but if the Company conquered, his jewels would be saved to him. Having thus divided his **hoard**[55], he threw himself into the cause of the sepoys, since they were strong upon his borders. By his doing this, mark you, sahib, his property becomes the due of those who have been true to their salt.

"'This pretended merchant, who travels under the name of Achmet, is now in the city of Agra and desires to gain his way into the fort. He has with him as travelling-companion my foster-brother Dost Akbar, who knows his secret. Dost Akbar has promised this night to lead him to a **side-postern**[56] of the fort, and has chosen this one for his purpose. Here he will come presently, and here he will find Mahomet Singh and myself awaiting him. The place is lonely, and none shall know of his coming. The world shall know the merchant Achmet no more, but the great treasure of the rajah shall be divided among us. What say you to it, sahib?'

"In Worcestershire the life of a man seems a great and a sacred thing; but it is very different when there is fire and blood all round you, and you have been used to meeting death **at every turn**[57]. Whether Achmet the merchant lived or died was a thing as light as air to me, but at the talk about the treasure my heart turned to it, and I thought of what I might do in the old country with it, and how my folk would stare when they saw their ne'er-do-well coming back with his pockets full of gold **moidores**[58]. I had, therefore, already made up my mind. Abdullah Khan, however, thinking that I hesitated, pressed the matter more closely.

"'Consider, sahib,' said he, 'that if this man is taken by the commandant he will be hung or shot, and his jewels taken by the government, so that no man will be a rupee the better for them. Now, since we do the taking

既和印度兵来往，又和东印度公司的统治者来往。然而，过了不久，在他看来，白人的末日已经来临，因为全国上下他只听到他们死亡和垮台的消息。不过，他是一个小心谨慎的人，于是就制定了这样的计划，无论可能会发生什么事儿，他都至少应该给自己留一半财宝。他把金银放在宫里的地下室，最贵重的宝石和最上等的珍珠放进一只铁箱，派一个扮作商人的亲信带到阿格拉的堡垒，藏在那里，直到全国太平。这样，如果叛军得胜，他就会拥有那些金银，但如果东印度公司获胜，他则会留住那些珠宝。他这样分开自己的积蓄后，就投身到了印度兵的叛乱之中，因为他们在他的边界上非常强大。先生，请注意，他这样做，财产就会归属忠于主人的那些人。

"'这个乔装商人旅行时化名阿奇麦特，如今在阿格拉城里，想要进入堡垒。和他同行的是我的同奶兄弟多斯特·阿克巴，阿克巴知道他的秘密。多斯特·阿克巴已经答应今晚领他从一个侧后门进入堡垒，并选择这个门达到自己的目的。他马上就要来了。他会发现穆罕默德·辛格和我本人在等着他。这个地方人迹罕至，谁也不会知道他来。世界上就再也不会有人知道阿奇麦特这个商人了，我们就会平分王公的巨额财富。先生，你对这有什么看法？'

"在伍斯特郡，人的生命看来好像重要而神圣，但当你周围血火连天时，情况就会截然不同，而且你已经习惯常常迎接死亡。无论阿奇麦特这个商人生还是死，在我看来，就像空气一样无足轻重，但说到那笔财宝，我动了心。我想到了回故乡后可能会用这笔财富做什么，想到了人们看到我这个从不干好事的人口袋里装满金币回来，一定会瞪大眼睛。因此，我已经下定了决心。然而，阿卜杜拉·汗以为我举棋不定，就对这件事步步紧逼。

"'先生，考虑一下，'他说，'如果这个人被指挥官抓住，就会被吊死或射杀，他的珠宝也会被充公，这样谁也得不到一个卢比。现在，既然我们拿到了手，

四签名

of him, why should we not do the rest as well? The jewels will be as well with us as in the Company's **coffers**[59]. There will be enough to make every one of us rich men and great chiefs. No one can know about the matter, for here we are cut off from all men. What could be better for the purpose? Say again, then, sahib, whether you are with us, or if we must look upon you as an enemy.'

"'I am with you heart and soul,' said I.

"'It is well,' he answered, handing me back my firelock. 'You see that we trust you, for your word, like ours, is not to be broken. We have now only to wait for my brother and the merchant.'

"'Does your brother know, then, of what you will do?' I asked.

"'The plan is his. He has devised it. We will go to the gate and share the watch with Mahomet Singh.'

"The rain was still falling steadily, for it was just the beginning of the wet season. Brown, heavy clouds were drifting across the sky, and it was hard to see more than a stonecast. A deep **moat**[60] lay in front of our door, but the water was in places nearly dried up, and it could easily be crossed. It was strange to me to be standing there with those two wild Punjabees waiting for the man who was coming to his death.

"Suddenly my eye caught the glint of a shaded lantern at the other side of the moat. It vanished among the mound-heaps, and then appeared again coming slowly in our direction.

"'Here they are!' I exclaimed.

"'You will **challenge**[61] him, sahib, as usual,' whispered Abdullah. 'Give him no cause for fear. Send us in with him, and we shall do the rest while you stay here on guard. Have the lantern ready to uncover, that we may be sure that it is indeed the man.'

"The light had flickered onward, now stopping and now advancing, until I could see two dark figures upon the other side of the moat. I let them scramble down the sloping bank, splash through the **mire**[62], and climb halfway up to the gate before I challenged them.

"'Who goes there?' said I in a subdued voice.

何不把剩下的事儿也做了呢？那些珠宝跟我们在一起，跟放在东印度公司的金库是一样的。这些珠宝足以使我们每个人都大富大贵。谁也不可能知道这件事，因为我们这里和所有人都切断了联系。还能有比这更好的打算吗？那么，先生，再说一下，你是和我们在一起，还是我们必须把你看成敌人。'

"'我全心全意和你们在一起，'我说。

"'这很好，'他把明火枪还给我说，'你明白我们信任你，因为你的话像我们的一样不会违背。我们现在只有等待我的弟弟和那个商人。'

"'那你的弟弟知道你要做什么吗？'我问道。

"'这是他的计划。是他想出来的。我们到门口去，和穆罕默德·辛格一起守护。'

"雨还在不停地下着，因为这正是雨季的开始。褐色阴沉的乌云飘过天空，超过一石之遥就难以看清。一条深深的护城河横在我们的门前，但几处的水快要干涸了，可以轻易穿过去。在我看来，跟那两个旁遮普人站在那里等待那个前来送死的人非常奇怪。

"突然，我看到护城河对岸有一盏灯笼的微光消失在护堤堆当中，随后重新出现，朝我们这个方向慢慢走来。

"'他们来了！'我大声叫道。

"'你要像往常一样盘问他，'阿卜杜拉轻声说道，'千万不要让他害怕。把他交给我们带进去，你守在这里，剩下的我们来做。准备揭开灯笼，这样我们可以确定到底是不是那个人。'

"灯光闪烁向前，时停时进，直至看到护城河对岸的两个黑影。我让他们爬下堤坡，涉过泥沼，爬到了离门口一半的岸上，我才盘问他们。

'谁在那里？'我压低声音问道。

四签名

"'Friends,' came the answer. I uncovered my lantern and threw a flood of light upon them. The first was an enormous Sikh with a black beard which swept nearly down to his **cummerbund**[63]. Outside of a show I have never seen so tall a man. The other was a little fat, round fellow with a great yellow **turban**[64] and a bundle in his hand, done up in a shawl. He seemed to be all in a quiver with fear, for his hands twitched as if he had the **ague**[65], and his head kept turning to left and right with two bright little twinkling eyes, like a mouse when he ventures out from his hole. It gave me the chills to think of killing him, but I thought of the treasure, and my heart set **as hard as a flint**[66] within me. When he saw my white face he gave a little **chirrup**[67] of joy and came running up towards me.

"'Your protection, sahib,' he panted, 'your protection for the unhappy merchant Achmet. I have travelled across Rajpootana, that I might seek the shelter of the fort at Agra. I have been robbed and beaten and abused because I have been the friend of the Company. It is a blessed night this when I am once more in safety—I and my poor possessions.'

"'What have you in the bundle?' I asked.

"'An iron box,' he answered, 'which contains one or two little family matters which are of no value to others but which I should be sorry to lose. Yet I am not a beggar; and I shall reward you, young sahib, and your governor also if he will give me the shelter I ask.'

"I could not trust myself to speak longer with the man. The more I looked at his fat, frightened face, the harder did it seem that we should slay him in cold blood. It was best to get it over.

"'Take him to the main guard,' said I. The two Sikhs closed in upon him on each side, and the giant walked behind, while they marched in through the dark gateway. Never was a man so **compassed**[68] round with death. I remained at the gateway with the lantern.

"I could hear the measured tramp of their footsteps sounding through the lonely corridors. Suddenly it ceased, and I heard voices and a **scuffle**[69], with the sound of blows. A moment later there came, to my horror, a rush of footsteps coming in my direction, with a loud breathing of a running man. I

"'是朋友,'来人回答说。我揭开灯笼,将一大片灯光照向他们。最前面的是一位人高马大的锡克教徒,黑胡子差不多垂到了腰带。除了在表演中,我从来没有见过这样高大的人。另一个是一位有点儿圆胖的家伙,头上缠着大黄巾,手里拿着一只用披肩捆扎的包裹。他似乎怕得微微发抖,因为他的两只手抽搐,就像他患了疟疾一样。他像一只冒险钻出洞的老鼠,两只闪闪发亮的小眼睛不停地左顾右盼。想到要杀死他,我不寒而栗,但一想到财宝,我就铁了心肠。他看到我的白脸,发出一声小小的欢呼,向我跑来。

"'先生,保护我,'他喘息着说,'你保护阿奇麦特这个可怜的商人吧。我穿过拉杰普塔纳,来到阿格拉的堡垒寻求避难。我之所以曾经遭到抢劫、抽打和侮辱,是因为我曾经是东印度公司的朋友。这是一个神圣的夜晚,我又一次安全了——我和我的财产。'

"'你的包裹里有什么?'我问道。

"'一只铁箱,'他回答说。'里边装有一两件祖传东西,对别人没有任何价值,但要丢失我会遗憾。不过,年轻的先生,我不是乞丐,如果你的长官愿意给我请求避难的地方,我会奖赏你和他。'

"我不能再和这个人说下去了。我越看他受惊的胖脸,我们似乎越难把他残忍地杀死。最好让这件事过去。

"'把他带到中央警卫室,'我说。两个锡克教兵分别从两边逼近他,大个子走在后面,他们穿过黑暗的门道向里前进。从来没有一个人这样被死亡包围。我提着灯笼留在门口。

"我可以听到他们穿过人迹罕至的走廊发出的富有节奏的脚步声。突然,脚步声停止。随后,我听到了说话声、混战声和殴打声。过了一会儿,令我惊恐的是,响起一阵急促的脚步声,只见一个人气喘吁吁朝我这个方向跑来。我

turned my lantern down the long straight passage, and there was the fat man, running like the wind, with a smear of blood across his face, and close at his heels, bounding like a tiger, the great black-bearded Sikh, with a knife flashing in his hand. I have never seen a man run so fast as that little merchant. He was gaining on the Sikh, and I could see that if he once passed me and got to the open air he would save himself yet. My heart softened to him, but again the thought of his treasure turned me hard and bitter. I cast my firelock between his legs as he raced past, and he rolled twice over like a shot rabbit. Ere he could stagger to his feet the Sikh was upon him and buried his knife twice in his side. The man never uttered moan nor moved muscle but lay where he had fallen. I think myself that he may have broken his neck with the fall. You see, gentlemen, that I am keeping my promise. I am telling you every word of the business just exactly as it happened, whether it is in my favour or not."

He stopped and held out his **manacled**[70] hands for the whisky and water which Holmes had brewed for him. For myself, I confess that I had now conceived the utmost horror of the man not only for this cold-blooded business in which he had been concerned but even more for the somewhat **flippant**[71] and careless way in which he narrated it. Whatever punishment was in store for him, I felt that he might expect no sympathy from me. Sherlock Holmes and Jones sat with their hands upon their knees, deeply interested in the story but with the same disgust written upon their faces. He may have observed it, for there was a touch of defiance in his voice and manner as he proceeded.

"It was all very bad, no doubt," said he. "I should like to know how many fellows in my shoes would have refused a share of this loot when they knew that they would have their throats cut for their pains. Besides, it was my life or his when once he was in the fort. If he had got out, the whole business would **come to light**[72], and I should have been court-martialled and shot as likely as not; for people were not very **lenient**[73] at a time like that."

"Go on with your story," said Holmes shortly.

"Well, we carried him in, Abdullah, Akbar, and I. A fine weight he was, too, for all that he was so short. Mahomet Singh was left to guard the door. We took him to a place which the Sikhs had already prepared. It was some distance off,

把灯笼转向又长又直的通道。原来是那个胖子,一脸血污飞跑过来,黑胡子大高个锡克教徒手里拎着寒光闪闪的刀子像老虎一样跳跃着紧追其后。我从来没有见过像那个小商人跑得那样快的人。他超过了那个锡克教徒,而且我可以看到,如果他一旦越过我,跑到露天,就可以自救。我对他放软了心肠,但一想到他的财宝,我又心狠手辣起来。当他飞跑而过时,我把明火枪抛到了他的两腿之间,他像中弹的兔子一样打了两个滚。还没等他能摇晃着爬起来,那个锡克教兵就扑上去,在他的肋部戳了两刀。他一声没吭,一动不动,就躺倒在地。我暗自想到,他可能在摔倒时脖子就断了。先生们,你们看,我说话算数。不管是不是对我有利,我都把这件事的来龙去脉一五一十地告诉了你们。"

他停住话头,伸出两只戴着手铐的手去接福尔摩斯为他兑的加水威士忌。对我自己来说,我承认我现在认为这个人极其可怕,不仅因为他参与了这一残忍事件,更是因为他叙述这件事时轻率无礼、满不在乎的样子。无论等待他的是什么惩罚,我觉得他都不可能会从我这里得到任何同情。夏洛克·福尔摩斯和琼斯手放在膝盖上,坐在那里,对这个故事深表关注,但脸上都露出了厌恶的神情。他可能已经观察到了这一点,因为他继续说下去时,声音和举止都带有一点挑衅的意味。

"毫无疑问,这都很糟,"他说,"我想知道,有多少家伙处在我的位置,明明知道要是不那样做的话,就会挨刀子,谁还会拒绝分赃。此外,一旦他进入堡垒,不是我死就是他亡。如果他走出堡垒,整个事情就会败露,我就会受到军事审判,很可能被枪决,因为在那样的时刻,人们不会非常宽大。"

"接着讲你的故事,"福尔摩斯简短地说。

"好的,我们——阿卜杜拉·汗、多斯特·阿克巴,还有我——把他抬进去。尽管他个子很矮,但非常重。穆罕默德·辛格留在那里守门。我们把他抬到

where a winding passage leads to a great empty hall, the brick walls of which were all crumbling to pieces. The earth floor had sunk in at one place, making a natural grave, so we left Achmet the merchant there, having first covered him over with loose bricks. This done, we all went back to the treasure.

"It lay where he had dropped it when he was first attacked. The box was the same which now lies open upon your table. A key was hung by a silken cord to that carved handle upon the top. We opened it, and the light of the lantern gleamed upon a collection of gems such as I have read of and thought about when I was a little lad at Pershore. It was blinding to look upon them. When we had feasted our eyes we took them all out and made a list of them. There were one hundred and forty-three **diamonds of the first water**[74], including one which has been called, I believe, 'the Great Mogul,' and is said to be the second largest stone in existence. Then there were ninety-seven very fine emeralds, and one hundred and seventy rubies, some of which, however, were small. There were forty **carbuncles**[75], two hundred and ten **sapphires**[76], sixty-one **agates**[77], and a great quantity of **beryls**[78], **onyxes**[79], cats'-eyes, **turquoises**[80], and other stones, the very names of which I did not know at the time, though I have become more familiar with them since. Besides this, there were nearly three hundred very fine pearls, twelve of which were set in a gold **coronet**[81]. By the way, these last had been taken out of the chest, and were not there when I recovered it.

"After we had counted our treasures we put them back into the chest and carried them to the gateway to show them to Mahomet Singh. Then we solemnly renewed our oath to stand by each other and be true to our secret. We agreed to conceal our loot in a safe place until the country should be at peace again, and then to divide it equally among ourselves. There was no use dividing it at present, for if gems of such value were found upon us it would cause suspicion, and there was no privacy in the fort nor any place where we could keep them. We carried the box, therefore, into the same hall where we had buried the body, and there, under certain bricks in the best-preserved wall, we made a hollow and put our treasure. We made careful note of the place, and next day I drew four **plans**[82], one for each of us, and put the sign of the four of

了两个锡克教兵已经准备好的一个地方。这里离堡门有一段路程,一条弯弯曲曲的走廊通向一个空荡荡的大厅,大厅的砖墙都支离破碎。地上有一处凹陷,成了天然的墓穴。于是,我们首先用松动的墙砖盖住商人阿奇麦特,然后就把他留在了那里。做完这件事后,我们都回到了财宝那里。

"财宝躺在他第一次受到袭击的地方。箱子就是现在放在你们桌子上的这只。一把钥匙用丝绳挂在箱盖上的雕花把手上。我们打开箱子,灯笼的光线照在一堆珠宝上闪闪发亮,就像我小时候在珀肖尔时读过和想过的一样。看着这些珠宝,令人眼花缭乱。我们大饱眼福后,就把它们统统拿出来,列了一张清单。里面有143颗一流钻石,其中包括一颗叫作'大莫卧儿'的钻石,据说是现存的第二颗最大的钻石。然后还有97块上好翡翠、170块红宝石——不过,其中有些很小。有40块红榴石、210块蓝宝石、61块玛瑙,以及大量绿玉、缟玛瑙、猫眼石、绿宝石和我当时不知道名字的其他宝石。后来,我对它们就越来越熟悉了。此外,还有将近300颗上好珍珠,其中12颗珍珠镶在一顶金王冠上。顺便说一下,这最后12颗珍珠拿出了箱子,我重新找到箱子时,它们已不在那里。

"我们清点过财宝后,又把它们放回箱子,带到门口让穆罕默德·辛格看了一下。随后,我们重又郑重盟誓,要相互支持,严守秘密,同意把宝箱藏在一个安全地方,等国家重新太平后,大家再平分。目前平分毫无使用价值,因为如果发现我们有如此贵重的宝石,就会引起别人怀疑,而且堡垒没有任何隐秘,任何地方都无法保存。于是,我们把箱子搬进掩埋尸体的那个大厅,在那里保存最好的一面墙上拆下几块砖,掏了一个洞,把财宝放了进去。我们仔细记住了这个地方。第二天,我画了四张平面图,每人各拿一张,在下面写上我们四个人的签名,因为我们曾经盟誓,我们各自都要代表四个人的

us at the bottom, for we had sworn that we should each always act for all, so that none might take advantage. That is an oath that I can put my hand to my heart and swear that I have never broken.

"Well, there's no use my telling you gentlemen what came of the Indian mutiny. After Wilson took Delhi and Sir Colin relieved Lucknow the back of the business was broken. Fresh troops came pouring in, and Nana Sahib **made himself scarce over**[83] the frontier. A **flying column**[84] under Colonel Greathed came round to Agra and cleared the **Pandies**[85] away from it. Peace seemed to be settling upon the country, and we four were beginning to hope that the time was at hand when we might safely go off with our shares of the **plunder**[86]. In a moment, however, our hopes were shattered by our being arrested as the murderers of Achmet.

"It **came about**[87] in this way. When the rajah put his jewels into the hands of Achmet he did it because he knew that he was a trusty man. They are suspicious folk in the East, however: so what does this rajah do but take a second even more trusty servant and set him to play the spy upon the first. This second man was ordered never to let Achmet out of his sight, and he followed him like his shadow. He went after him that night and saw him pass through the doorway. Of course he thought he had taken refuge in the fort and applied for admission there himself next day, but could find no trace of Achmet. This seemed to him so strange that he spoke about it to a sergeant of guides, who brought it to the ears of the commandant. A thorough search was quickly made, and the body was discovered. Thus at the very moment that we thought that all was safe we were all four seized and brought to trial on a charge of murder—three of us because we had held the gate that night, and the fourth because he was known to have been in the company of the murdered man. Not a word about the jewels came out at the trial, for the rajah had been **deposed**[88] and driven out of India: so no one had any particular interest in them. The murder, however, was clearly made out, and it was certain that we must all have been concerned in it. The three Sikhs got **penal servitude**[89] for life, and I was condemned to death, though my sentence was afterwards **commuted**[90] to the same as the others.

利益，谁也不能独吞。我可以把手放在心口发誓，这是我从来没有违背的一个誓言。

"好了，后来印度叛乱的结果是什么，我就不用告诉你们几位先生了。威尔逊占领德里，科林爵士援救勒克瑙之后，叛军瓦解。新的军队源源不断开进来。那那·萨希布悄悄越过了国境。格雷特里德上校率领的一支游击部队来到阿格拉，从中清除了潘迪兵。和平似乎又降临到了这个国家。所以，我们四人开始希望我们带着平分的赃物安全逃走的时刻即将来临。然而，我们的希望马上就被打得落花流水，因为我们都被抓了起来，罪名是杀害阿奇麦特。

"事情是这样发生的。那个王公把财宝交给阿奇麦特，他这样做，是因为他知道阿奇麦特是一个可靠的人。然而，东方人非常多疑。所以，这个王公只好又派了一个更可靠的仆人对第一个人进行盯梢，命令这个仆人千万不要让阿奇麦特离开他的视线，所以这个仆人就像影子一样尾随其后。那天夜里，他跟在后面，看到阿奇麦特穿门而过，肯定以为阿奇麦特已经在堡垒里避难，于是第二天就申请进入，但怎么也找不到阿奇麦特的任何踪迹。在他看来，这非常蹊跷，他就向守卫的一名军士说了这件事，军士又报告了指挥官。于是，马上进行彻底搜查，这样就发现了尸体。因此，就在我们以为一切平安时，我们四人都被抓获，并以谋杀罪受审——我们中的三个人受审是因为我们那天夜里把门，第四个人受审是因为有人知道他曾经和被害者同行。审讯时只字未提那些财宝，因为那个王公已被罢黜，并被赶出了印度，所以没有人对财宝特别关注。然而，谋杀案情明确，我们肯定都涉嫌此案。三个锡克教兵被终身劳役拘禁，我被判死刑，后来得到减刑，跟他们三个人一样。

四签名

"It was rather a queer position that we found ourselves in then. There we were all four tied by the leg and with **precious**[91] little chance of ever getting out again, while we each held a secret which might have put each of us in a palace if we could only have made use of it. It was enough to make a man **eat his heart out**[92] to have to stand the kick and the cuff of every petty **jack-in-office**[93], to have rice to eat and water to drink, when that **gorgeous**[94] fortune was ready for him outside, just waiting to be picked up. It might have driven me mad; but I was always a pretty stubborn one, so I just held on and **bided my time**[95].

"At last it seemed to me to have come. I was changed from Agra to Madras, and from there to Blair Island in the Andamans. There are very few white **convicts**[96] at this settlement, and, as I had behaved well from the first, I soon found myself a sort of **privileged**[97] person. I was given a hut in Hope Town, which is a small place on the slopes of Mount Harriet, and I was left pretty much to myself. It is a dreary, fever-stricken place, and all beyond our little clearings was infested with wild cannibal natives, who were ready enough to blow a poisoned dart at us if they saw a chance. There was digging and ditching and yam-planting, and a dozen other things to be done, so we were busy enough all day; though in the evening we had a little time to ourselves. Among other things, I learned to **dispense**[98] drugs for the surgeon, and picked up a **smattering**[99] of his knowledge. All the time I was on the lookout for a chance to escape; but it is hundreds of miles from any other land, and there is little or no wind in those seas: so it was a terribly difficult job to get away.

"The surgeon, Dr. Somerton, was a fast, sporting young chap, and the other young officers would meet in his rooms **of an evening**[100] and play cards. The surgery, where I used to make up my drugs, was next to his sitting-room, with a small window between us. Often, if I felt lonesome, I used to turn out the lamp in the surgery, and then, standing there, I could hear their talk and watch their play. I am fond of a hand at cards myself, and it was almost as good as having one to watch the others. There was Major Sholto, Captain Morstan, and Lieutenant Bromley Brown, who were in command of the native troops, and there was the surgeon himself, and two or three prison-officials, crafty old hands who played a nice sly safe game. A very **snug**[101] little party they used to make.

"当时，我们发现自己的处境相当奇特。我们四人都被判刑，再也不可能出去了，同时我们又各守一个秘密，只要我们能利用，就可以住进豪宅。当那一大笔财宝现成在外面等着让一个人去拿，却要不得不忍受每个微不足道、自命不凡的小官拳打脚踢、吃米喝水，这足以让他暗自伤神。尽管这可能让我发疯，但我总是非常固执，所以就坚持下去，等待时机。

"最后，在我看来，时机已经来临。我从阿格拉转押到了马德拉斯，又从那里转押到了安达曼群岛的布莱尔岛。这个地方白人囚犯寥寥无几，而且因为我一开始就表现良好，所以马上就受到了特殊优待。我在哈里特山坡上的霍普小镇得到了一间小屋，相当自由。那是一个热病肆虐的沉闷地方，而且我们小小的林中空地外面都是吃人的野人部落。如果他们看到机会，就会随时吹来毒镖。我们在那里挖地、开沟和种山药，还有十几件其他工作，所以我们整天真够忙的，尽管傍晚我们有一点属于自己的时间。在其他事情中，我还学会了替外科医生配药发药，对外科知识也略知一二。我始终都在寻找逃跑的机会，但这里离任何陆地都有几百英里，而且那些海面上风很小，或者根本没有风，因此要想逃跑十分困难。

"外科医生萨默顿大夫是一个行动迅速、喜爱运动的年轻人，其他年轻军官们每天晚上常常聚到他的房间打牌。我配药的外科手术室在他的客厅隔壁，我们之间有一扇小窗。如果我感到孤单寂寞，就常常关掉手术室的灯，然后站在那里，可以听到他们谈话，观看他们打牌。我自己也爱好打牌，看别人打牌几乎和自己打牌一样。那里有指挥土著部队的肖尔托少校、摩斯坦上尉和布朗利·布朗中尉，有这个医生本人，还有两三个监狱官。他们都是技高一筹的老手，打起牌来既漂亮狡猾又安全可靠，常常凑成一个温暖舒适的小团体。

四签名

"Well, there was one thing which very soon **struck**[102] me, and that was that the soldiers used always to lose and the civilians to win. Mind, I don't say there was anything unfair, but so it was. These prison-chaps had done little **else than**[103] play cards ever since they had been at the Andamans, and they knew each other's game to a point, while the others just played to pass the time and threw their cards down anyhow. Night after night the soldiers got up poorer men, and the poorer they got the more keen they were to play. Major Sholto was the **hardest hit**[104]. He used to pay in notes and gold at first, but soon it came to **notes of hand**[105] and for big sums. He sometimes would win for a few deals just to give him heart, and then the luck would set in against him worse than ever. All day he would wander about **as black as thunder**[106], and he took to drinking a deal more than was good for him.

"One night he lost even more heavily than usual. I was sitting in my hut when he and Captain Morstan came stumbling along on the way to their quarters. They were bosom friends, those two, and never far apart. The major was **raving**[107] about his losses.

"'It's **all up**[108], Morstan,' he was saying as they passed my hut. 'I shall have to send in my papers. I am a ruined man.'

"'Nonsense, old chap!' said the other, slapping him upon the shoulder. 'I've had a nasty **facer**[109] myself, but—' That was all I could hear, but it was enough to set me thinking.

"A couple of days later Major Sholto was strolling on the beach: so I took the chance of speaking to him.

"'I wish to have your advice, Major,' said I.

"'Well, Small, what is it?' he asked, taking his cheroot from his lips.

"'I wanted to ask you, sir,' said I, 'who is the proper person to whom hidden treasure should be handed over. I know where half a million worth lies, and, as I cannot use it myself, I thought perhaps the best thing that I could do would be to hand it over to the proper authorities, and then perhaps they would get my sentence shortened for me.'

"'Half a million, Small?' he gasped, looking hard at me to see if I was in earnest.

"那么，有一件事很快就给我留下了深刻印象，那就是军人总是输，文官总是赢。记住，我不是说有什么不公平，但情况就是这样。自从到达安达曼群岛以来，这些监狱官除了打牌，几乎什么事儿也不做。对方的牌技，他们都了如指掌。对方打牌，只是打发时间，总是输牌。夜复一夜，军人们越打越穷，越穷越想打。肖尔托少校输得最惨。起初，他常常用钞票和黄金支付，但很快就变成了用期票大额下注。他有时会赢几把，这只是给他提提劲，随后运气又会跟他作对，输得更惨。他整天面带怒容走来走去，开始借酒浇愁。

"有一天夜里，他输的比以往更多。我正坐在自己的小屋，这时他和摩斯坦上尉一路跌跌撞撞回到自己的住处。他们这两个人是知己，从不远离。少校正在对自己输钱的事儿大发雷霆。

"'摩斯坦，这彻底完了，'他们路过我的小屋时，他说，'我必须得递交辞呈。我破产了。'

"'老兄，胡说！'上尉拍着他的肩膀说，'我自己也曾经有过糟糕的意外打击，可——'这就是我所能听到的所有话，但这足以让我开始思考。

"两天后，肖尔托少校正在海滨溜达时，我就趁机和他说起了话。

"'少校，我希望听听你的意见，'我说。

"'啊，斯莫尔，什么事儿？'他拿开嘴唇上的方头雪茄问道。

"'先生，我想问你，'我说。'如果移交隐藏的财宝，应该交给谁合适。我知道价值 50 万英镑的财宝藏在哪里。因为我自己不能使用，我想，我所能做的最好事情也许是把它交给有关当局，说不定他们会给我减刑。'

"'斯莫尔，50 万英镑？'他喘着气说，同时死死地盯着我，看我是不是在当真。

四签名

"'Quite that, sir—in jewels and pearls. It lies there ready for anyone. And the queer thing about it is that the real owner is **outlawed**[110] and cannot hold property, so that it belongs to the first comer.'

"'To government, Small,' he stammered, 'to government.' But he said it in a halting fashion, and I knew in my heart that I had got him.

"'You think, then, sir, that I should give the information to the governor-general?' said I quietly.

"'Well, well, you must not do anything rash, or that you might **repent**[111]. Let me hear all about it, Small. Give me the facts.'

"I told him the whole story, with small changes, so that he could not identify the places. When I had finished he stood **stock still**[112] and full of thought. I could see by the twitch of his lip that there was a struggle going on within him.

"'This is a very important matter, Small,' he said at last. 'You must not say a word to anyone about it, and I shall see you again soon.'

"Two nights later he and his friend, Captain Morstan, came to my hut in the dead of the night with a lantern.

"'I want you just to let Captain Morstan hear that story from your own lips, Small,' said he.

"I repeated it as I had told it before.

"'It rings true, eh?' said he. 'It's good enough to act upon?'

"Captain Morstan nodded.

"'Look here, Small,' said the major. 'We have been talking it over, my friend here and I, and we have come to the conclusion that this secret of yours is hardly a government matter, after all, but is a private concern of your own, which of course you have the power of disposing of as you think best. Now the question is, What price would you ask for it? We might be inclined to take it up, and at least look into it, if we could agree as to terms.' He tried to speak in a cool, careless way, but his eyes were shining with excitement and greed.

"'Why, as to that, gentlemen,' I answered, trying also to be cool but feeling as excited as he did, 'there is only one bargain which a man in my position

"'先生,完全如此——是宝石和珍珠。放在那里,谁都可以随时去拿。奇怪的是,真正的主人被剥夺了公民权,无法拥有财产,所以先来先得。'

"'交给政府,斯莫尔,'他结结巴巴地说。'交给政府。'但是,他说这话时吞吞吐吐,我心里明白我已经搞定了他。

"'那么,先生,你认为我应该把这个情况报告总督吗?'我平静地说。

"'好了,好了,你不必操之过急,否则你可能会后悔。斯莫尔,让我听听所有这一切。把那些情况告诉我。'

"我把全部经过都告诉了他,同时作了一些小小的变化,以免他识别出那些地方。我说完后,他站在那里一动不动,浮想联翩。我从他嘴唇的抽搐可以看出,他的内心正在进行一场斗争。

"'斯莫尔,这是一件非常重要的事儿,'最后,他说,'你不要对任何人说一个字,我会马上再见你。'

"两夜后,他和他的朋友摩斯坦上尉深夜提着灯笼来到我的小屋。

"'斯莫尔,我要让摩斯坦上尉听听你亲口说的那个故事,'他说。

"我像以前讲的那样又讲了一遍。

"'这听上去不错吧?'他说,'值得去做吗?'

"摩斯坦上尉点了点头。

"'斯莫尔,听我说,'少校说,'我和我这位朋友,我们一直在讨论这件事,而且我们已经得出了结论,认为你这个秘密毕竟算不上是政府的事儿,而是你自己的私事,你当然有权按照你认为最好的方式处理。现在问题是,你要价多少呢?如果能就条款达成协议,我们也许倾向于接手这件事,至少调查一下。'他努力用冷静随便的方式说话,但他的眼睛因兴奋和贪婪而发亮。

"'啊,先生们,至于要价,'我也努力装作冷静地回答,但像他一样感到兴奋,

四签名

can make. I shall want you to help me to my freedom, and to help my three companions to theirs. We shall then take you into partnership and give you a fifth share to divide between you.'

"'Hum!' said he. 'A fifth share! That is not very tempting.'

"'It would come to fifty thousand apiece,' said I.

"'But how can we gain your freedom? You know very well that you ask an impossibility.'

"'**Nothing of the sort**[113],' I answered. 'I have thought it all out to the last detail. The only bar to our escape is that we can get no boat fit for the voyage, and no **provisions**[114] to last us for so long a time. There are plenty of little **yachts**[115] and **yawls**[116] at Calcutta or Madras which would **serve our turn**[117] well. Do you bring one over. We shall engage to get aboard her by night, and if you will drop us on any part of the Indian coast you will have done your part of the bargain.'

"'If there were only one,' he said.

"'None or all,' I answered. 'We have sworn it. The four of us must always act together.'

"'You see, Morstan,' said he, 'Small is a man of his word. He does not **flinch**[118] from his friends. I think we may very well trust him.'

"'It's a dirty business,' the other answered. 'Yet, as you say, the money will save our **commissions**[119] handsomely.'

"'Well, Small,' said the major, 'we must, I suppose, try and meet you. We must first, of course, test the truth of your story. Tell me where the box is hid, and I shall get **leave of absence**[120] and go back to India in the monthly **relief**[121]-boat to inquire into the affair.'

"'Not so fast,' said I, growing colder as he got hot. 'I must have the consent of my three comrades. I tell you that it is four or none with us.'

"'Nonsense!' he broke in. 'What have three black fellows to do with our agreement?'

"'Black or blue,' said I, 'they are in with me, and we all go together.'

"Well, the matter ended by a second meeting, at which Mahomet Singh, Abdullah Khan, and Dost Akbar were all present. We talked the matter over

'处在我这样位置的人只能提一个条件。我想要你们帮助我和三个伙伴得到自由。然后,我们会和你们合作,给你们五分之一的财宝,让你们平分。'

"'哼!'他说。'五分之一份额!这没有多大吸引力。'

"'每份会有 50 000 英镑,'我说。

"'可我们怎么才能让你们得到自由呢?你们非常清楚,你们的要求不可能做到。'

"'绝不是那样,'我回答说,'我已经想到了最后的细节。我们逃跑的唯一障碍就是,我们无法得到一只适合航行的船只和维持我们长久航行的粮食。加尔各答或马德拉斯有许多小游艇和快艇,它们对我们都非常适用。请你带过来一只。我们约定夜里上船。如果你们把我们送到印度海岸的任何一个地方,你们就完成了自己的协议。'

"'要是只有你一个人就好了,'他说。

"'要么都不走,要么都走,'我回答说,'我们曾经盟过誓。我们四人必须始终一起行动。'

"'摩斯坦,你看,'他说,'斯莫尔是一个说话算数的人。他不会为朋友而畏缩。我想,我们完全可以信任他。'

"'这是一个卑鄙的勾当,'摩斯坦回答说,'不过,像你说的那样,这笔钱会大大节省我们的佣金。'

"'啊,斯莫尔,'少校说,'我想,我们必须争取满足你。当然,我们必须首先试一下你的故事是否真实。告诉我箱子藏在哪里。我要请假坐每月的加班船返回印度去调查这件事。'

"'别那样快,'我说,他越激动,我越冷静,'我必须得到三个同伴的同意。我告诉你,要么我们四人一起行动,要么一个也不去。'

"'胡闹!'他打断说,'三个黑家伙和我们的协议有什么关系?'

"'黑也好,蓝也好,'我说,'他们和我都是一伙的,我们形影不离。'

"那么,第二次见面后,这件事才了结,穆罕默德·辛格,阿卜杜拉·汗

again, and at last we came to an arrangement. We were to provide both the officers with charts of the part of the Agra fort, and mark the place in the wall where the treasure was hid. Major Sholto was to go to India to test our story. If he found the box he was to leave it there, to send out a small yacht provisioned for a voyage, which was to lie off Rutland Island, and to which we were to make our way, and finally to return to his duties. Captain Morstan was then to apply for leave of absence, to meet us at Agra, and there we were to have a final division of the treasure, he taking the major's share as well as his own. All this we sealed by the most solemn oaths that the mind could think or the lips utter. I sat up all night with paper and ink, and by the morning I had the two charts all ready, signed with the sign of four—that is, of Abdullah, Akbar, Mahomet, and myself.

Well, gentlemen, I weary you with my long story, and I know that my friend Mr. Jones is impatient to get me safely stowed in **chokey**[122]. I'll make it as short as I can. The villain Sholto went off to India, but he never came back again. Captain Morstan showed me his name among a list of passengers in one of the mail-boats very shortly afterwards. His uncle had died, leaving him a fortune, and he had left the Army; yet he could stoop to treat five men as he had treated us. Morstan went over to Agra shortly afterwards and found, as we expected, that the treasure was indeed gone. The scoundrel had stolen it all without carrying out one of the conditions on which we had sold him the secret. From that I lived only for **vengeance**[123]. I thought of it by day and I nursed it by night. It became an overpowering, absorbing passion with me. I cared nothing for the law—nothing for the **gallows**[124]. To escape, to track down Sholto, to have my hand upon his throat—that was my one thought. Even the Agra treasure had come to be a smaller thing in my mind than the slaying of Sholto.

Well, I have set my mind on many things in this life, and never one which I did not carry out. But it was weary years before my time came. I have told you that I had picked up something of medicine. One day when Dr. Somerton **was down with**[125] a fever a little Andaman Islander was picked up by a convict-gang in the woods. He was sick to death and had gone to a lonely place to die.

和多斯特·阿克巴都在场。我们再次协商，最终才达成协议。我们要给两位军官提供阿格拉堡垒的藏宝图，标出那面墙上藏宝的地方。肖尔托少校要去印度检验一下我们说的是否属实。如果他找到宝箱，要把它留在那里，先派出一只备好航行给养的小快艇。这只小快艇要停在拉特兰岛附近。我们要向这只小快艇前进。最后，肖尔托少校回营履职。随后，摩斯坦上尉要请假去阿格拉迎接我们，我们在那里最后平分财宝，摩斯坦上尉带走少校和他自己那份。所有一切我们都通过所能想到和所能说出的最庄重的誓言盟誓。我拿着纸盒墨水坐了一个通宵，第二天早上准备好了两张藏宝图，签上四个名字——也就是穆罕默德·辛格、阿卜杜拉·汗、多斯特·阿克巴和我自己。

好了，先生们，我讲的长故事让你们听累了吧，我知道我的朋友琼斯先生迫不及待要把我安全送到拘留所。我尽可能长话短说。肖尔托这个坏蛋去了印度，但再也没有回来。不久之后，摩斯坦上尉给我看了一只邮船的旅客名单，其中就有肖尔托的名字。他的叔叔死后给他留下了一大笔遗产，所以他就离开了军队，但他居然能堕落到像他曾经对待我们那样对待5个人。不久以后，摩斯坦就到了阿格拉，像我们预料的那样，财宝果然不翼而飞。这个恶棍没有履行我们出卖给他秘密的一个条件，全部盗走了财宝。从此以后，我只为报仇而活着。我日思夜想，全神贯注，怒气冲冲，不可抗拒，不管什么法律，也不管什么绞刑架，唯一的想法就是逃走、追捕肖尔托、亲手锁住他的咽喉。在我心里，即使阿格拉财宝也没有杀死肖尔托来的重要。

那么，我这一生在许多事上下过决心，而且从来没有一件不成功。但是，在我的时机到来之前，这真是难熬的几年。我曾经告诉过你们，我已经获得了一些医学知识。有一天，当萨默顿医生发烧时，一帮罪犯在树林里偶然遇到了一个安达曼岛小岛民。他病得很重，就到一个人迹罕至的地方等死。尽

I took him **in hand**[126], though he was as **venomous**[127] as a young snake, and after a couple of months I got him all right and able to walk. He took a kind of fancy to me then, and would hardly go back to his woods, but was always hanging about my hut. I learned a little of his **lingo**[128] from him, and this made him all the fonder of me.

Tonga—for that was his name—was a fine boatman and owned a big, roomy canoe of his own. When I found that he was devoted to me and would do anything to serve me, I saw my chance of escape. I talked it over with him. He was to bring his boat round on a certain night to an old wharf which was never guarded, and there he was to pick me up. I gave him directions to have several gourds of water and a lot of yams, cocoanuts, and sweet potatoes.

He was **staunch**[129] and true, was little Tonga. No man ever had a more faithful mate. At the night **named**[130] he had his boat at the **wharf**[131]. As it chanced, however, there was one of the convict-guard down there—a vile **Pathan**[132] who had never missed a chance of insulting and injuring me. I had always vowed vengeance, and now I had my chance. It was as if fate had placed him in my way that I might pay my debt before I left the island. He stood on the bank with his back to me, and his carbine on his shoulder. I looked about for a stone to beat out his brains with, but none could I see.

Then a queer thought came into my head and showed me where I could lay my hand on a weapon. I sat down in the darkness and unstrapped my wooden leg. With three long hops I was on him. He put his carbine to his shoulder, but I struck him full, and knocked the whole front of his skull in. You can see the split in the wood now where I hit him. We both went down together, for I could not keep my balance; but when I got up I found him still lying quiet enough. I made for the boat, and in an hour we were well out at sea. Tonga had brought all his earthly possessions with him, his arms and his gods. Among other things, he had a long bamboo spear, and some Andaman cocoanut matting, with which I made a sort of a sail. For ten days we were **beating about**[133], trusting to luck, and on the eleventh we were picked up by a trader which was going from Singapore to Jiddah with a cargo of Malay pilgrims. They were a **rum**[134] crowd, and Tonga and I soon managed to settle down among them.

管他像小蛇一样恶毒，但我还是负责照顾他。两个月后，我让他恢复健康，又能走路了。他当时喜欢上了我，几乎不回树林，而是始终逗留在我的小屋附近。我从他那里学会了一点方言，这使他更喜欢我了。

汤加——这就是他的名字——是一名出色的船夫，拥有属于自己的一只宽敞的大独木舟。发现他对我忠心耿耿，愿意为我做任何事情后，我又看到了逃跑的机会。我和他讨论了这件事。他会在某天夜里把船划到一个从来无人看守的码头，接我上船。我还吩咐他准备几葫芦水、许多山药、可可豆和甘薯。

这个小汤加，他忠诚可靠。再没有比他更忠实的伙伴了。在那个指定的夜晚，他把船划到了码头。然而，凑巧的是，那里有一个看守囚犯的人——这是一个从来不放过任何机会侮辱和伤害我的恶毒的帕坦人。我总是发誓要报仇，现在我有了机会。仿佛是命运把他安排到了我路过的地方，说不定我离岛之前可以了结这笔债务。他肩上挎着卡宾枪，背对着我站在岸上。我环顾四周想找一块石头，砸出他的脑浆，但我一块也无法找到。

接着，一个奇怪的念头进入了我的脑海，指示我可以拿一件武器。我在黑暗中坐下来，解下木腿，大跳三步，扑向他。尽管他把卡宾枪背在肩上，但我还是完全打向了他，并把他的整个前脑骨砸了进去。你们现在还能看到我当时砸他时木头上留下的裂痕。因为我无法保持平衡，我们一起倒下，但当我站起来时，发现他仍然静静地躺在那里。我匆匆走向那只船，一小时后我们就完全出了海。汤加已经带上了他所有的尘世财产，还带上了他的武器和神像。另外，他还有一支长竹矛和几条安达曼可可席。我用这些席做成了一面帆。我们听天由命在海上漂浮了10天。第11天，一只从新加坡开往吉达、载着马来西亚朝圣者的商船救起了我们。他们是一群奇特的人，而我和汤加

四签名

They had one very good quality: they let you alone and asked no questions.

Well, if I were to tell you all the adventures that my little **chum**[135] and I went through, you would not thank me, for I would have you here until the sun was shining. Here and there we drifted about the world, something always turning up to keep us from London. All the time, however, I never lost sight of my purpose. I would dream of Sholto at night. A hundred times I have killed him in my sleep. At last, however, some three or four years ago, we found ourselves in England. I had no great difficulty in finding where Sholto lived, and I set to work to discover whether he had **realized on**[136] the treasure, or if he still had it. I made friends with someone who could help me—I name no names, for I don't want to get anyone else in a hole—and I soon found that he still had the jewels. Then I tried to get at him in many ways; but he was pretty sly and had always two prize-fighters, besides his sons and his *khitmutgar*, on guard over him.

One day, however, I got word that he was dying. I hurried at once to the garden, mad that he should slip out of my **clutches**[137] like that, and, looking through the window, I saw him lying in his bed, with his sons on each side of him. I'd have come through and taken my chance with the three of them, only even as I looked at him his jaw dropped, and I knew that he was gone. I got into his room that same night, though, and I searched his papers to see if there was any record of where he had hidden our jewels. There was not a line, however, so I came away, bitter and savage as a man could be. Before I left I bethought me that if I ever met my Sikh friends again it would be a satisfaction to know that I had left some mark of our hatred; so I scrawled down the sign of the four of us, as it had been on the chart, and I pinned it on his bosom. It was too much that he should be taken to the grave without some **token**[138] from the men whom he had robbed and befooled.

We earned a living at this time by my exhibiting poor Tonga at fairs and other such places as the black cannibal. He would eat raw meat and dance his war-dance: so we always had a hatful of pennies after a day's work. I still heard all the news from Pondicherry Lodge, and for some years there was no news to hear, except that they were hunting for the treasure. At last, however, came

很快就设法在他们当中安顿了下来。他们有一种非常好的品质：他们不打扰你，也不问任何问题。

好了，如果把我和小男孩航海时的全部历险过程都告诉你们，你们是不会感谢我的，因为我会让你们在这里呆到天光大亮。我们在世界上到处流浪，总有一些事儿阻止我们去伦敦。然而，我从来没有失去过自己的目标。我夜里总是梦见肖尔托，在睡梦中杀死了他上百次。然而，最后，在三、四年前，我们到了英国。我没费多大周折就找到了肖尔托住在哪里，着手调查他是变卖了财宝，还是仍然拥有财宝。我和能帮助我的人交上了朋友——我不提姓名，因为我不想牵连别人——我很快就发现他还拥有那些珠宝。于是，我想方设法接近他，但他相当狡猾，除了他的儿子和印度仆人，总有两个职业拳击手保护他。

然而，有一天，我得到消息说他奄奄一息。我马上赶到他的花园，对他要这样摆脱我的控制感到愤怒。随后，我通过窗户向里看，只见他躺在床上，两个儿子各站在一边。我本想冲进去对他们三个冒险下手，只是我在看他时，他的下巴垂了下来，就知道他死了。不过，那天夜里，我还是进入他的房间，搜查他的文件，想看看是不是记载有他把我们的珠宝藏在了什么地方。然而，一条信息也没有。于是，我就又恨又恼扬长而去。离开之前，我想到，如果我再遇到那些锡克教朋友，他们知道我留下了我们仇恨的痕迹，一定会皆大欢喜。于是，我草草写下了我们四个的签名，就像那张图上的签名那样，随后我把它别在他的胸口。如果他被送进坟墓而没有带上他曾经掠夺和欺骗的人的标志，那就太过分了。

此后，我们依靠在市集或其他类似地方把可怜的汤加当成食人生番展览谋生。他常常吃生肉，跳战阵舞，所以工作一天后，我们总会有一帽子的便士。我仍然听到樱塘别墅的所有消息。有几年，除了他们还在寻宝，没有听到任

what we had waited for so long. The treasure had been found. It was up at the top of the house in Mr. Bartholomew Sholto's chemical laboratory. I came at once and had a look at the place, but I could not see how, with my wooden leg, I was to make my way up to it. I learned, however, about a trapdoor in the roof, and also about Mr. Sholto's supper-hour. It seemed to me that I could manage the thing easily through Tonga. I brought him out with me with a long rope wound round his waist. He could climb like a cat, and he soon made his way through the roof, but, as ill luck would have it, Bartholomew Sholto was still in the room, to his cost. Tonga thought he had done something very clever in killing him, for when I came up by the rope I found him **strutting**[139] about as proud as a peacock. Very much surprised was he when I **made at**[140] him with the rope's end and cursed him for a little bloodthirsty **imp**[141]. I took the treasure box and let it down, and then slid down myself, having first left the sign of the four upon the table to show that the jewels had come back at last to those who had most right to them. Tonga then pulled up the rope, closed the window, and made off the way that he had come.

I don't know that I have anything else to tell you. I had heard a waterman speak of the speed of Smith's launch, the *Aurora*, so I thought she would be a handy craft for our escape. I **engaged with**[142] old Smith, and was to give him a big sum if he got us safe to our ship. He knew, no doubt, that there was some screw loose, but he was not in our secrets. All this is the truth, and if I tell it to you, gentlemen, it is not to amuse you—for you have not done me a very **good turn**[143]—but it is because I believe the best defence I can make is just to hold back nothing, but let all the world know how badly I have myself been served by Major Sholto, and how innocent I am of the death of his son."

"A very remarkable account," said Sherlock Holmes. "A fitting **windup**[144] to an extremely interesting case. There is nothing at all new to me in the latter part of your narrative except that you brought your own rope. That I did not know. By the way, I had hoped that Tonga had lost all his darts; yet he managed to shoot one at us in the boat."

"He had lost them all, sir, except the one which was in his blow-pipe at the time."

何消息。然而，我们等待很久的消息终于来了。财宝已经找到了。它在巴塞洛缪·肖尔托先生化学实验室的屋顶。我马上前去看那个地方，但因为我这个木腿，所以不明白怎样才能爬上去。然而，我听说屋顶有一个暗门，还听说肖尔托先生晚饭的时间。在我看来，我可以通过汤加轻松完成这件事。我把他带出去，在他的腰间缠上一条长绳。他可以像猫一样爬行，马上就通过屋顶爬了进去，但不幸的是，巴塞洛缪·肖尔托还在房间里，就付出了代价。汤加以为自己杀了他，是做了一件聪明事。因为我顺着绳子上去时，发现他正骄傲得像孔雀似的昂首阔步。我用绳子一端向他打去，骂他是小嗜血鬼时，他万分惊讶。我取出宝箱，把它放下来，然后自己顺着绳子滑下来，同时首先在桌子上留下四签名，表明财宝终于回到最有权拥有它的那些人。接着，汤加拉上绳子，关上窗户，然后从原路离开。

我知道我没有别的可告诉你们了。我曾经听一个船夫说过史密斯那只汽艇'曙光女神号'的速度，因此我认为它将是我们逃走的便利船只。我雇了老史密斯的船，如果他把我们安全送上轮船，就给他一大笔钱。毫无疑问，他知道有些不正常，但他没有参与我们的秘密。所有这一切都是事实。先生们，我把这告诉你们，并不会让你们高兴——因为你们没有给过我恩惠——但这正是我相信我能做的最好辩护就是毫不隐瞒，而是告诉世人肖尔托少校曾经多么恶劣地对待过我自己，我对他儿子的死是多么清白。"

"叙述非常出色，"夏洛克·福尔摩斯说，"极其有趣的案子有了适当的结局。除了你自己带的绳子，你叙述的后半部分对我毫无新意。我不知道你带了绳子。顺便说一下，我本指望汤加已经丢失了所有的飞镖，但他还是设法在船上向我们射出了一支。"

"先生，他是已经丢失了所有的飞镖，只是当时吹管里还有一支。"

四签名

"Ah, of course," said Holmes. "I had not thought of that."

"Is there any other point which you would like to ask about?" asked the convict **affably**[145].

"I think not, thank you," my companion answered.

"Well, Holmes," said Athelney Jones, "you are a man to be humoured, and we all know that you are a **connoisseur**[146] of crime; but duty is duty, and I have gone rather far in doing what you and your friend asked me. I shall feel more at ease when we have our story-teller here safe under lock and key. The cab still waits, and there are two inspectors downstairs. I am much obliged to you both for your assistance. Of course you will be wanted at the trial. Good-night to you."

"Good-night, gentlemen both," said Jonathan Small.

"You first, Small," remarked the wary Jones as they left the room. "I'll take particular care that you don't **club**[147] me with your wooden leg, whatever you may have done to the gentleman at the Andaman Isles."

"Well, and there is the end of our little drama," I remarked, after we had sat some time smoking in silence. "I fear that it may be the last investigation in which I shall have the chance of studying your methods. Miss Morstan has done me the honour to accept me as a husband in **prospective**[148]."

He gave a most **dismal**[149] groan.

"I feared as much," said he. "I really cannot congratulate you."

I was a little hurt.

"Have you any reason to be dissatisfied with my choice?" I asked.

"Not at all. I think she is one of the most charming young ladies I ever met and might have been most useful in such work as we have been doing. She had a decided genius that way; witness the way in which she preserved that Agra plan from all the other papers of her father. But love is an emotional thing, and whatever is emotional is opposed to that true cold reason which I place above all things. I should never marry myself, lest I **bias**[150] my judgment."

"I trust," said I, laughing, "that my judgment may survive the **ordeal**[151]. But

"啊，当然，"福尔摩斯说，"我没有想到这一点。"

"你还有别的要问的吗？"这个囚犯殷勤地问道。

"我想没有，谢谢你，"我的同伴回答说。

"啊，福尔摩斯，"阿塞尔尼·琼斯说，"我们会迁就你，我们都知道你是刑事分析行家，但职责就是职责，我在你和你的朋友要求我做的方面已经相当不错了。我们把这个讲故事的人妥善锁起来，我才会感到更放心。马车还在等着，楼下还有两名警官。我非常感谢你们两位的协助。当然，审判时需要你们出庭作证。祝你们晚安。"

"两位先生，晚安，"乔纳森·斯莫尔说。

"斯莫尔，你先请，"他们离开房间时，机警的琼斯说，"无论你对安达曼岛那位先生可能做了什么，我都要特别小心，不要让你用木腿打我。"

"好了，我们这出小小的戏剧结束了，"我们默默地坐了一段时间后，我说，"我怕这也许我有机会学习你的方法进行的最后一次调查了。摩斯坦小姐已经赏光接受我做她未来的丈夫了。"

他发出了一声极其沮丧的叹息。

"我也同样担心，"他说，"我真的无法恭喜你。"

我有点儿伤心。

"你对我的选择有什么不满的理由吗？"我问道。

"一点也没有。我认为她是我遇到过的最迷人的小姐之一，而且可能对我们一直从事的这种工作极其有用。她明显具有那方面的天才，从她把那张阿格拉平面图和她父亲其他所有文件分开保存这一点，就可以证明。但是，爱情是一种情感之物，无论是什么样的情感，它都和我放在首位的真实冷静的推理相互对立。我自己永远不会结婚，以免我的判断存在偏见。"

四签名

you look weary."

"Yes, the reaction is already upon me. I shall be as limp as a rag for a week."

"Strange," said I, "how terms of what in another man I should call laziness **alternate with**[152] your fits of splendid energy and vigour."

"Yes," he answered, "there are in me the **makings**[153] of a very fine **loafer**[154], and also of a pretty **spry**[155] sort of a fellow. I often think of those lines of old Goethe:

*Schade, dass die Natur nur einen Mensch aus dir schuf,*
*Denn zum wiirdigen Mann war und zum Schelmen der Stoff.*

"By the way, **apropos of**[156] this Norwood business, you see that they had, as I **surmised**[157], a **confederate**[158] in the house, who could be none other than Lal Rao, the butler: so Jones actually has the undivided honour of having caught one fish in his great haul."

"The division seems rather unfair," I remarked. "You have done all the work in this business. I get a wife out of it, Jones gets the credit, pray what remains for you?"

"For me," said Sherlock Holmes, "there still remains the cocaine-bottle." And he stretched his long white hand up for it.

"我相信,"我笑着说,"我的判断也许经得起严峻考验。不过,你看上去累了。"

"是的,已经对我有反应了。我一周都会像抹布一样疲软。"

"奇怪,"我说,"为什么在另一个人身上我应该称为懒惰的东西,却会在你身上不时迸发出值得赞扬的勃勃生机。"

"是的,"他回答说,"我身上具有非常出色的游手好闲者的素质,也具有充满生机的的素质。我常常想起老歌德的这两句话:

上帝仅仅赋予你一个人形,
原来是金玉其外败絮其中。

"顺便说一下,关于这个诺伍德案子,你明白,像我原来猜测的那样,在那座房子里有一个同伙,不是别人,正是在那个仆人拉尔·拉奥,所以琼斯在大捕捞中的确有抓住一条鱼的功劳。"

"分配似乎有点儿不公平,"我说,"在处理这个案子中,我做了所有的工作。我从中得到了妻子,琼斯得到了荣誉,请问留给你的是什么?"

"对我来说,"夏洛克·福尔摩斯说,"还留有可卡因瓶。"说着,他伸出白皙修长的手,去拿那个瓶子。

四签名

Notes:

1. tenner *n.* 〈多用于英国〉10英磅钞票；10英磅纸币
2. despondent *adj.* 垂头丧气的；沮丧
3. listless *adj.* 倦怠的；无精打采的
4. cocked *adj.* 翘起的
5. exultantly *adv.* 狂欢地；兴高采烈的地
6. kith *n.* 亲戚知己；邻居
7. kin *n.* 亲戚；家族
8. go to sb.'s heart 使某人伤心
9. thwart *vt.* 阻挠
10. mangrove *n.* 红树属植物；美洲红树
11. ague *n.* 疟疾
12. stoicism *n.* 禁欲主义；淡泊
13. grudge *n.* 不满；怨恨
14. what with 因为；由于
15. down on one's luck 遭不幸；倒霉
16. a blessing in disguise 祸中得福；塞翁失马；有益的痛苦经验
17. fair *adj.* 尚可的；不错的
18. shanty *n.* 简陋小屋；棚屋
19. mutiny *n.* 叛乱；兵变
20. in sb.'s line 是某人擅长的
21. bungalow *n.*（有凉台的）平房；别墅；小屋
22. obstinate *adj.* 固执的；倔强的
23. cheroot *n.* 方头雪茄烟
24. one fine day *n.* 有一天
25. nullah *n.* 干涸的河床；峡谷
26. sepoy *n.* 旧时英国军队中的印度兵
27. fusilier *n.*（旧指）燧发枪手；燧发枪手团
28. Sikh *n.*（印度的）锡克教徒
29. Lucknow *n.* 勒克瑙（印度北部城市）
30. rum *adj.* 奇怪的；危险的；可笑的
31. garrison *n.* 驻军；卫戍部队

32. scorpion *n.* 蝎子

33. centipede *n.* 蜈蚣

34. trooper *n.* 骑兵；骑警；军队；部队

35. labyrinth *n.* 迷宫

36. recruit *n.* 新兵；（机构中的）新成员

37. game *adj.* 残疾的；瘸的

38. Punjabi *n.* 旁遮普人

39. bear arms against 拿起武器反对（保卫）

40. jabber *v.* 快而含糊地说；闲聊

41. lingo *n.* 听不懂的话（指方言、术语等）；外国话

42. tom-tom *n.* 印度手鼓

43. bang *n.* 刺激；快感；麻醉品的服用

44. sahib *n.* 大人；老爷（旧时印度人对欧洲人的尊称）

45. have no truck with 不和（某人）来往；不能容忍

46. provided that 假如；倘若

47. tell the tale 编造虚假的故事

48. Feringhee *n.* 〈贬〉欧洲人（尤指在印度出生的葡萄牙人）

49. hearken *vi.* 倾听

50. rajah *n.* 〈印〉王侯；首长

51. hoard *vt.* 积蓄并储藏（某物）

52. raj *n.* 统治；主权；支配

53. vault *n.* 地下室

54. choice *adj.* 上等的；精选的

55. hoard *n.* （钱财、食物或其他珍贵物品的）储藏；积存

56. postern *n.* （城、教堂等的）后门

57. at every turn 常常；处处

58. moidore *n.* 从前的葡萄牙金币

59. coffer *n.* 金库

60. moat *n.* （古时城堡为了防御而在四周挖的）壕沟；护城河

61. challenge *vt.* 向……发出盘问口令

62. mire *n.* 泥潭

63. cummerbund *n.* （印度男人的）腹带；徽带

四签名

64. turban *n.* 长头巾

65. ague *n.* 疟疾

66. as hard as a flint 铁石心肠；冷酷无情

67. chirrup *n.* 啧啧声；吱喳声

68. compass *vt.* 围绕……而行；包围

69. scuffle *n.* 扭打；混战

70. manacle *vt.* 给……带上手铐

71. flippant *adj.* 轻率的；无礼的

72. come to light 显露；为大家所知

73. lenient *adj.* 宽大的；仁慈的

74. diamond of the first water 第一流的好人

75. carbuncle *n.* 红宝石

76. sapphire *n.* 蓝宝石

77. agate *n.* 玛瑙

78. beryl *n.* 绿柱石；绿玉

79. onyx *n.* 缟玛瑙；石华

80. turquoise *n.* 绿松石

81. coronet *n.* （贵族、王族的）宝冠

82. plan *n.* 平面图；示意图

83. make oneself scarce 〈口〉悄悄离开

84. flying column *n.* 游击部队

85. Pandy *n.* 潘迪（大兵变的首义印度兵，在受检阅时发动起义）

86. plunder *n.* 掠夺（物）；赃物

87. come about 发生

88. depose *vt.* 废黜；罢免

89. penal servitude 劳役拘禁

90. commute *vt.* 减刑

91. precious *adv.* 〈口〉很；非常

92. eat one's heart out 伤心（难过）到极点

93. jack in office *n.* 自命不凡的小官员

94. gorgeous *adj.* 极好的；称心的

95. bide one's time 等待时机

96. convict *n.* 罪犯；（长期服刑的）囚犯

97. privileged *adj.* 享有特权的

98. dispense *vt.* 配（药）；发（药）

99. smattering *n.* 略懂；浅知

100. of an evening  往往在晚上

101. snug *adj.* 温暖而舒适的；生活安乐的

102. strike *vt.* 给……以（深刻）印象

103. else than  只是；仅有

104. hard hit 〈美口〉经济上的破产

105. note of hand  期票；本票

106. as black as thunder  脸色阴森；面带怒容

107. rave *vi.* 愤怒地说；咆哮；怒喊

108. all up *adv.* 无望；彻底完了

109. facer *n.* 意外的打击

110. outlaw *vt.* 宣布……为不合法

111. repent *vi.* 后悔

112. stock still  完全静止地；不动地

113. nothing of the sort  根本没有那样的事情；决不是那样

114. provision *n.* 食物和饮料

115. yacht *n.* 快艇；帆船；游艇

116. yawl *n.* （前桅高后桅低的）小帆船；小渔船

117. serve one's turn  适用；管用

118. flinch *vi.* 退缩（from）

119. commission *n.* 佣金；回扣

120. leave of absence *n.* 休假

121. relief *n.* 加班（增开）的公共汽车、火车等

122. chokey *n.* 拘留所；监狱

123. vengeance *n.* 复仇；报仇

124. gallows *n.* 绞刑架

125. be down with  患……病；由于……病倒了

126. take in hand  接管……

127. venomous *adj.* 恶意的；恶毒的

四签名

128. lingo *n.* 听不懂的话（指方言、术语等）；外国话
129. staunch *adj.* 可信赖的；可靠的；忠诚的
130. named *adj.* 指定的
131. wharf *n.* 码头；停泊处
132. Pathan *n.* 帕坦人（印度西北边境的阿富汗族人）
133. beat about *v.* （船）在逆风前面辗转前进
134. rum *adj.* 奇怪的；难对付的；危险的
135. chum *n.* 好友
136. realize on 把……变卖
137. clutch *n.* 掌握；控制
138. token *n.* 标志；记号；纪念品
139. strut *vi.* 趾高气扬地走
140. make at 攻击
141. imp *n.* 小鬼
142. engage with 与……接洽
143. good turn *n.* 善意的或友谊的行为；恩惠
144. windup *n.* 终结；结局
145. affably *adv.* 殷勤地
146. connoisseur *n.* 鉴定家；行家；权威（in, of）
147. club *vt.* 用棍棒打；把……当棍棒打
148. prospective *adj.* 未来的
149. dismal *adj.* 忧郁的；凄凉的；可怕的
150. bias *vt.* 使有偏见；使有倾向性
151. ordeal *n.* 严峻的考验
152. alternate with 轮流；交换
153. making *n.* 素质
154. loafer *n.* 虚度光阴者；游手好闲者
155. spry *adj.* 充满生气的；活泼的；敏捷的
156. apropos of *adv.* 关于；至于
157. surmise *vt.* 推测；猜测
158. confederate *n.* 同伙；合谋者